To Heal a Fractured World

To Heal a Fractured World

The Ethics of Responsibility

Rabbi Jonathan Sacks

Schocken Books, New York

Copyright © 2005 by Jonathan Sacks

All rights reserved. Published in the United States
by Schocken Books, a division of Random House, Inc.,
New York. Originally published in Great Britain
by Continuum, London.

Schocken and colophon are registered trademarks of
Random House, Inc.

Library of Congress Cataloging-in-Publication Data
Sacks, Jonathan, Rabbi.
To heal a fractured world : the ethics of responsibility /
Jonathan Sacks.
p. cm.
Includes bibliographical references and index.
ISBN 0-8052-4241-4
1. Responsibility. 2. Jewish ethics. I. Title.

BJ1451.S23 2005
296.3'6—dc22
2005044054

www.schocken.com
Printed in the United States of America
First American Edition
9 8 7 6 5 4 3 2 1

To our daughter Dina
and son-in-law Oliver
on their wedding

May God rejoice in you
As you rejoice in one another

Contents

Acknowledgements

I owe a debt of thanks to my brother Alan and Rabbi J. David Bleich for suggesting, many years ago, that I write something on the concept of 'mending the world'. This is my belated response. My literary agent, Louise Greenberg, and publisher, Robin Baird-Smith, are two people with whom it is an honour to work. Rabbi Naftali Brawer, Dayan Ivan Binstock, Rabbi Mordechai Ginsbury, Peter Sheldon, Raymond Simonson, Professor Leslie Wagner, Michael Weiger and Dr Raphael Zarum read the first draft and made helpful suggestions, as did my editor Margaret Wallis. Dayan Yonoson Abraham went through the manuscript with gusto and fastidious care and saved me from several infelicities. The errors that remain are my own. I could not have undertaken the work without the support of my office team: Syma Weinberg, Zaki Cooper, Joanna Benarroch, Miriam Aussenberg, Alison Ma'ayan and Anna Sinclair. Aaron Prijs of the London School of Jewish Studies and Judith Greenberg helped in obtaining the books I needed. As always, I owe especial thanks to my wife Elaine whose patience and encouragement know no bounds. My deepest thanks on this occasion go to the thousands of volunteers in the Jewish community and beyond, whose work is a living embodiment of all I have written here. May the divine presence live in the work of their hands.

Part 1

The Call to Responsibility

Chapter 1

The Ethics of Responsibility

When I behold Your heavens, the work of Your fingers,
The moon and stars that You set in place,
What is man that You are mindful of him,
Mortal man that You take note of him?
Yet You have made him little less than the angels
And adorned him with glory and majesty.

(Psalm 8:3–5)

Being human means being conscious and being responsible.

(Viktor Frankl)[1]

One of Judaism's most distinctive and challenging ideas is its *ethics of responsibility*, the idea that God invites us to become, in the rabbinic phrase, his 'partners in the work of creation'. The God who created the world in love calls on us to create in love. The God who gave us the gift of freedom asks us to use it to honour and enhance the freedom of others. God, the ultimate Other, asks us to reach out to the human other. More than God is a strategic intervener, he is a teacher. More than he does our will, he teaches us how to do his. Life is God's call to responsibility. That is the theme of this book.

More than any previous generation in history, we have come to see the individual as the sole source of meaning. The gossamer filaments of connection between us and others, that once held together families, communities and societies, have become attenuated. We have become lonely selves in search of purely personal fulfilment. But that surely must be wrong. Life alone is only half a life. One spent pursuing the satisfaction of desire is less than satisfying and never all we desire. So it is worth reminding ourselves that there is such a thing as ethics, and it belongs to the life we live together and the goods we share – the goods that only exist in virtue of being shared.

3

That is one of Judaism's enduring insights. To give an example: in 1190 Moses Maimonides, the greatest rabbi of the Middle Ages, published *The Guide for the Perplexed*, the most challenging work of Jewish philosophy ever written. In it he addresses the most exalted themes of religious thought – the existence of God, the limits of human knowledge, the problem of evil and the reasons for the commands. It is a formidably difficult work. Yet in its closing chapter he summarizes his teachings with a quote from Jeremiah:

> This is what the Lord says:
> 'Let not the wise man boast of his wisdom
> or the strong man boast of his strength
> or the rich man boast of his riches,
> but let him who boasts boast about this:
> that he understands and knows Me,
> that I am the Lord, *who exercises kindness,*
> *justice and righteousness on earth,*
> for in these I delight',
> declares the Lord. (Jer. 9:23–4)

I find it moving that at the end of his journey through intellectual space, Maimonides is drawn back to this simple affirmation of kindness, righteousness and justice. We cannot know God, Maimonides implies ('If I could understand him', one Jewish writer said, 'I would be him'), but we can act like him. Within the limits of human intelligence, we can climb at least part of the way to heaven, but the purpose of the climb is the return to earth, knowing that here is where God wants us to be and where he has given us work to do. Judaism contains mysteries, but its ultimate purpose is not mysterious at all. It is to honour the image of God in other people, and thus turn the world into a home for the divine presence.

Maimonides lived what he taught. More than most, he valued solitude and meditation. He writes of it eloquently. Only when removed from the stresses and cares of the world, he says, can the soul soar in intellectual union with the Author of being. Yet he lived the latter years of his life as a physician (he was doctor to the Sultan in Cairo and had an extensive practice in his town, Fostat) and as a communal leader, consulted by Jews and non-Jews alike. The acknowledged head of Egyptian Jewry, he answered questions sent to him by communities throughout the world. When the Provençal scholar Samuel ibn Tibbon wanted to visit him to seek guidance on the translation of the *Guide* from Arabic to Hebrew, Maimonides wrote him back a letter describing his typical week, in which he rarely had time to take a meal, let alone discuss technicalities of translation. It is a moving glimpse of the life of the great philosopher, spending his time healing the sick, guiding the members of his community, studying and praying with them, concerned no less with their bodies than with their souls.

When the disciples of the greatest Talmudist of the late nineteenth century, R. Hayyim of Brisk (1853–1918), asked him to define the task of a rabbi, he replied: 'To redress the grievances of those who are abandoned and alone, to protect the dignity of the poor, and to save the oppressed from the hands of his oppressor'.[2] Constantly in debt, he gave most of his salary to the poor. In the winter he would leave his wood store unlocked so that the poor of the town could take the fuel they needed, without the embarrassment of having to ask. When the lay-leaders of the town complained that this was costing them money, he replied that he was saving them medical expenses, since otherwise he would be forced to sit in the cold and catch pneumonia. It was impossible, he said, for him to light a fire in his own home if he knew that, in other homes, the poor were freezing.

Judaism is a complex and subtle faith, yet it has rarely lost touch with its simple ethical imperatives. We are here to make a difference, to mend the fractures of the world, a day at a time, an act at a time, for as long as it takes to make it a place of justice and compassion where the lonely are not alone, the poor not without help; where the cry of the vulnerable is heeded and those who are wronged are heard. 'Someone else's physical needs are my spiritual obligation', a Jewish mystic taught. The truths of religion are exalted, but its duties are close at hand. We know God less by contemplation than by emulation. The choice is not between 'faith' and 'deeds', for it is by our deeds that we express our faith and make it real in the life of others and the world.

Jewish ethics is refreshingly down-to-earth. If someone is in need, give. If someone is lonely, invite them home. If someone you know has recently been bereaved, visit them and give them comfort. If you know of someone who has lost their job, do all you can to help them find another. The sages called this 'imitating God'. They went further: giving hospitality to a stranger, they said, is 'even greater than receiving the divine presence'. That is religion at its most humanizing and humane.

So too is its insistence that the ethical life is a form of celebration. Doing good is not painful, a matter of dour duty and a chastising conscience. There is a Hebrew word, a key term of the Bible, for which there is no precise English translation: *simhah*, usually translated as 'joy'. What it really means is *the happiness we share*, or better still, *the happiness we make by sharing*. One of the great statements of individual dignity and responsibility, Judaism is also an intensely communal faith, not simply a matter of the lonely soul in search of God, Plotinus' 'the flight of the alone to the Alone'. It is about sharing what we have, seeing possessions less as things we own than things we hold in trust, one of the conditions of which is that we use part of what we have to help others. That is not self-sacrifice. If there is one thing I have heard more often than any other from those who spend part of their time in service to others, it is that they gain more than they give. They do not want to be thanked; they want to thank. Lifting others, they find that they themselves have been lifted.

The ethic of responsibility is the best answer I know to the meaning and meaningfulness of a life. When I first became a rabbi, the most difficult duty I had to perform was a funeral service. New to the position and the people, I often hardly knew the deceased, while to everyone else present he or she had been a member of the family, or an old and close friend. There was nothing to do but to get help from others. I would ask them what the person who had died meant to them. It did not take long before I recognized a pattern in their replies.

Usually they would say that the deceased had been a supportive husband or wife, a loving parent, a loyal friend. They spoke about the good they had done to others, often quietly, discreetly, without ostentation. When you needed them, they were there. They shouldered their responsibilities to the community. They gave to charitable causes, and if they could not give money, they gave time. Those most mourned and missed were not the most successful, rich or famous. They were the people who enhanced the lives of others. These were the people who were loved.

This reinforced for me the crucial distinction between the *urgent* and the *important*. No one ever spoke, in praise of someone who had died, about the car they drove, the house they owned, the clothes they wore, the exotic holidays they took. No one's last thought was ever, 'I wish I had spent more time in the office'. The things we spend most of our time pursuing turn out to be curiously irrelevant when it comes to seeing the value of a life as a whole. They are urgent but not important, and in the crush and press of daily life, the urgent tends to win out over the important.

Happiness, as opposed to pleasure, is a matter of a life well lived, one that honours the important, not just the urgent. This has been confirmed by many recent research studies. One showed that life satisfaction increased 24 per cent with the level of altruistic activity.[3] Another discovered that those who had more opportunities to help others felt 11 per cent better about themselves.[4] Several studies have shown that the best predictor of happiness is the sense that you have a purpose in life.[5] Those who hold strong spiritual beliefs are typically satisfied with life, while those who have no spiritual beliefs are typically unsatisfied.[6] People who feel responsible for their lives express one-third more life satisfaction than those who feel they lack control.[7] When subjects were asked to choose any of twenty different factors contributing to happiness, there was only one no one chose: financial status.[8] People who own the most are only as happy as those who have the least, and *half* as happy as those who are content with what they have.[9] *The desire to give is stronger than the desire to have.* This alone is enough to defeat cynicism and fatalism about the human condition.

Happiness is the ability to say: I lived for certain values and acted on them. I was part of a family, embracing it and being embraced by it. I was part of a community, honouring its traditions, sharing its griefs and joys, ready to help others, knowing that they were ready to help me. I did not only ask what I could take; I asked what I could contribute. To know that you made a difference, that in this all-too-brief span of years you lifted someone's spirits, relieved someone's poverty or loneliness, or brought a moment of grace or justice to the world that would not have happened had it not been for you: these are as close as we get to the meaningfulness of a life, and they are matters of everyday rather than heroic virtue. Machiavelli famously said that it is better to be feared than to be loved. He was wrong.

*   *   *   **

Social responsibility needs reaffirmation because it has become problematic in recent times. What links me to children starving in Africa, or the victims of an earthquake in India? What, for that matter, implicates me in the fate of the unemployed, the homeless, the poor in my own society, my own neighbourhood? For one thing, the problems are too vast for my acts to make a difference. We have grown used to delegating such responsibilities to governments, in return for which we pay taxes – substituting politics for ethics, law for moral obligation, and impersonal agencies for personal involvement. As a result, ethics has tended to turn inward, becoming a matter of personal choice rather than collective responsibility. There was a time when people lived in close, ongoing contact with neighbours, creating networks of shared meaning and reciprocal duty. Nowadays we live anonymously among strangers whose religious, cultural and moral codes are different from ours. By what duty or right do we share a responsibility for their fate?

Some of the complexities of contemporary ethics were first signalled by Hans Jonas in his *The Imperative of Responsibility.*[10] In previous generations, he argued, people had a fairly clear sense of the connection between act and consequence, between what they *did* and what *happened.* Today's challenges are not like that. Global warming is not the result of one person using leaded petrol or an aerosol spray, but of billions of acts distributed throughout the world. The effects of environmental damage caused by the destruction of rain forests or over-exploitation of non-renewable energy sources may not be apparent during our lifetimes. Where then is my responsibility? My acts are less than a drop in the ocean of humanity. What I do or refrain from doing has an infinitesimal effect on the rest of the world. What duties do I have to something as amorphous as humanity in general, as inanimate as nature, or as intangible as generations not yet born? Any simple notion of responsibility is inadequate to such problems, which is why religious responsibility – responsibility to the infinite in terms of space, eternal in terms of time – can sometimes be more cogent than secular alternatives (not, I hasten to add, that religious individuals are more environmentally active than their secular counterparts: we all know the problem and we all try to help). James Lovelock was forced to have recourse to the pagan earth-goddess Gaia to construct a compelling environmental ethic.[11] I do not think we have to travel that far.

Another and deeply ironic turn has been the impact of the various social and natural sciences on our sense of human freedom. The entire thrust of modern thought, from Marx to Freud, from neuroscience to evolutionary psychology, has been to undermine the idea that we act because we choose, choose because we form intentions, form intentions because we are free, and because we are free, we have responsibility. The result is paradoxical. On the one hand our age holds out to human beings an unprecedented range of choices. Sociologists call modernity the move from status to contract, fate to choice. At the same time the very idea of choice has become opaque. We are what we are because of economic forces, irrational drives, genetic determinism, or the blind struggle of our genes to replicate themselves into the next generation, with or without our knowledge and consent. The attempt to have it both ways results in a combination of hedonism, cynicism and stoicism which (as their names recall) have their precedent in ancient Greece not long before its decline and fall. A conception of human life without responsibility fails to do justice to human dignity, and is no way to ensure our survival as a species.

More damaging still is the consumerization of society: the culture of artificially generated needs, met by overproduced, over-advertised goods (the 'must-haves'), which are then subverted by equally artificial sources of discontent. It is a wonderfully seductive god, the consumer society. None has been more gentle and reassuring ('because you're worth it'), or less demanding (recall Allan Bloom's contemporary paraphrase of the first commandment: 'I am the Lord your God who brought you out of the land of Egypt – Relax'). Yet if there is one thing I have learned from the people I have met, rich and poor, powerful and powerless, it is that the meaningfulness of a life lies not in what you take but in what you give. Wordsworth said it:

> The world is too much with us; late and soon,
> Getting and spending, we lay waste our powers.[12]

So did Philip Larkin, writing about a house of worship:

And that much never can be obsolete,
Since someone will forever be surprising
A hunger in himself to be more serious . . .[13]

I suspect that most of us feel, from time to time, a hunger to be more serious, which is why I have written this book.

Why now? Partly because I am troubled by the face that religion often shows to the postmodern world. Too often it appears on the news, and lodges in the mind, as extremism, violence and aggression. To be sure, religion is not the cause of conflict in the Balkans, the Middle East or elsewhere. Instead it forms the fault-line along which sides divide. But that in itself is serious. When political conflict is religionized, it is absolutized. What in politics are virtues – compromise, the willingness to listen to both sides and settle for less than one would wish in an ideal world – are, in religion, vices. Religion can therefore act not as a form of conflict-resolution but, rather, conflict-intensification. This work is my personal protest against suicide-bombers, religiously motivated terrorists and preachers of hate of whatever faith. The religious imperative to which I have tried to give voice in these pages is the one that says: create, do not destroy, for it is my world you are destroying, my creatures you are killing. The only force equal to a fundamentalism of hate is a counter-fundamentalism of love.

To this I add a further concern about religion generally. The prophets warned against a rift between the *holy* and the *good*, our duties to God and to our fellow human beings. It still exists today. There are those for whom serving God means turning inward – to the soul, the house of worship and the life of ritual and prayer. There are others for whom social justice has become a substitute for religious observance or God. The result, as I put it later in the book, is like a cerebral lesion between the two hemispheres of the brain. The message of the Hebrew Bible is that serving God and serving our fellow human beings are inseparably linked, and the split between the two impoverishes both. Unless the holy leads us outward toward the good, and the good leads us back, for renewal, to the holy, the creative energies of faith run dry. For six days, so the first chapter of Genesis tells us, God created a universe and pronounced it good. On the seventh day he made a stillness in the turning world and declared it holy. Unless we reconnect the holy and the good we do less than justice to the unity that is the hallmark of the monotheistic imagination.

Fortunately, we are not short of role-models of how it is done. The following pages are my tribute to the many people I have met throughout the Jewish communities of Britain and the Commonwealth who devote much of their time to service to others. These are my heroes. They rarely make the news. Their work is often unrecognized. But it makes all the difference, humanizing our all-too-often dehumanized world. According to Jewish tradition, when the Israelites had finished constructing the sanctuary in the wilderness, Moses blessed them with the words: 'May it be God's will that his presence lives in the work of your hands'.[14] This is my thanksgiving offering to the many people in whose work I have sensed the divine presence, the *Shekhinah*.

From them I have learned that to live is to give. Precisely because they take their responsibility for granted, they represent eloquent testimony to what a religious tradition at its best can do. By making extraordinary demands, it inspires ordinary people to live extraordinary lives. Some, said Shakespeare, are born great; others achieve greatness, while others have greatness thrust upon them. The last seems to me the story of Jewry: an unexceptional people, often stubborn, rebellious, fractious, capricious, not what anyone would instinctively call a community of saints, yet made great by being asked to do great things. Nor is this the story of Judaism alone.

This book is about the faith I love and the people I know, but this too I know: that goodness and virtue are widely distributed throughout humanity. Many times, I have been inspired by the community-building, life-transforming, hope-creating work of Christians, Muslims, Hindus, Sikhs, Buddhists, Jains, Zoroastrians, Bahai; indeed of every faith with whom it has been my privilege to come into contact. Equally, I value the moral force of many forms of secular humanism, from John Stuart Mill to Bertrand Russell and beyond. Experience has taught me the truth of the wise words of Rabbi Abraham Isaac Kook (1865–1935):

> The narrow-mindedness that leads one to see whatever is outside the bounds of one's own people . . . as ugly and defiled is a terrible darkness that causes general destruction to the entire edifice of spiritual good, the light of which every refined soul hopes for.[15]

This is not relativism. Rather, it represents an essential distinction between the holy and the good. The religious expressions of humankind (the holy) are incommensurable, but goodness – bringing blessing to lives other than one's own – is as near as we get to a universal language. Poverty, hunger, disease are evils in any culture, and those who heal them are giants of the spirit. If you spend your life searching for evidence that, as Kant put it, 'Out of the crooked timber of humanity, no straight thing was ever made', you will certainly find it. But if you spend it searching for fragments of light that lie, as Jewish mystics believed, scattered throughout the universe, you will find them also – and this is a no less just view of the human condition.

I have never been persuaded that a jaundiced view of humanity is more realistic than the alternative. To the contrary, I believe that all of us are made in the image of God and that each culture has a contribution to make to the human heritage. Nor do you have to be religious to be good. That became manifestly clear among those quiet heroes and heroines who saved lives during the Holocaust. What was common to them, as studies have shown, was not religious belief or any particular kind of upbringing. Most of them saw nothing special in what they did, even though many of them must have known that they were taking a risk that might cost them their lives. They were simply human, doing what human beings are expected to do.

In the pages that follow, I have interwoven with the analysis, stories of individuals I have met or in some cases, known through the testimony of others. Books about ethics are often somewhat abstract, but telling stories is one of the best ways of making a moral point. The Israeli thinker Avishai Margalit speaks of the difference between 'i.e.' and 'e.g.' philosophies: those that proceed by abstract reasoning and others that make their case by giving examples.[16] Judaism is full of stories (there is a Jewish saying: 'God created mankind because he loves stories'). The Bible itself is one of the key examples of *truth as story*, as opposed to the more usual Western model of *truth as system*. What I love about Jewish stories is that they are mostly about ordinary people. They are not like myth, epic tales of larger-than-life heroes, gods who act like men or men who act like gods. If ancient Greece spoke about the virtue of democracy, Judaism speaks about *the democracy of virtue* – the good that is real because it is done by people like us.

One of the great Jewish folk-traditions speaks of the *lamed-vovniks*, the 'thirty-six' hidden righteous people in whose merit the world exists. The most important thing about this group is that those who belong to it do not know they do. In the traditional tales, they are usually the people no one suspects of being special: the local woodcutter or horse-driver, the illiterate, the poor, the people who sit at the back of the synagogue unable to read the prayers. That is a tradition in need of reinstatement. It is easy to tell stories about figures of superhuman piety, but the essence of our humanity is that we are human – fallible, frail, prone to doubts, susceptible to despair, as were the great heroes and heroines of the Bible. In my work I have come across many *lamed-vovniks*, and meeting them has been a greater education than any ethics text. We need not only textbooks but textpeople. Hence the stories in this book.

It is also about concepts. I confess to a love for the drama of ideas. Ideas are what change people, for good or bad. They affect how we interpret the world and what happens to us. They frame our imaginative horizon, at times lifting people to great heights, at others leading them to great folly or violence. We tend to forget how 'common sense' is neither common nor mere sense. Our taken-for-granted assumptions about what and who we are, our place in the universe and the meaningfulness or meaninglessness of a life, are the product of much thought on the part of those who came before us. The moral life is like Molière's *bourgeois gentilhomme* who discovered that he had been speaking prose all

11

his life and never realized it. We absorb moral ideas the way we learn a language, unconsciously; but there is much to be said, once in a while, for stepping back and asking why we came to see the world the way we did.

The concept of an ethic of responsibility was not at all natural, nor can we take it for granted. It came about through intellectual discoveries, revolutionary in their time and still challenging today. Judaism has distinctive beliefs, not the least of which is the way in which God empowers us to exercise our freedom, under his tutelage, to create a social order that, by honouring human dignity, becomes a home for his presence. The Bible tells a story about this, and it is worth retelling.

Nor is Judaism a religion of pure obedience, submission to the divine will. In the story of Noah the Bible delivers a remarkably candid and unexpected *critique of pure obedience*. Noah does everything God commands him, but in the meanwhile the world is destroyed. Listening to the Bible with Jewish ears, we hear a more challenging demand, God's call to Abraham: 'Walk ahead of Me and be perfect' (Gen. 17:1). Don't wait, in other words, until I command you. Sometimes you need to take the initiative. The story of how the Bible encourages human initiative is little known and needs to be spelled out.

At the heart of the story I tell is a difficult idea, but one profoundly in keeping with the challenges of our time. God trusts us and empowers us. That means necessarily that he empowers us to make mistakes, to get it wrong. That is what it is to be human, and God does not ask us to be superhuman. 'There is none on earth so righteous as to do only good and never sin', says Ecclesiastes (7:20). We sin, but God forgives. We err, but through our errors we learn. We fall, but God lifts us. We fail, but – as Rabbi Tarfon said: 'It is not for you to complete the work, but nor are you free to desist from it'.[17] We do our best: that is all God asks. The ethics of Judaism are demanding, but they are also profoundly forgiving. A secular Jew, a brilliant novelist, once said to me: 'Isn't Judaism full of guilt?' 'Yes,' I replied, 'but it is also full of forgiveness.' There is no suggestion in Judaism that we are weak and therefore condemned to a life of shame. Even the most pessimistic of the prophets, Jeremiah, is a figure of hope. Despair is not a Jewish emotion.

Behind the ethic of responsibility is the daring idea that more than we have faith in God, God has faith in us. Despite his frequent disappointments, he does not give up on us and never will. The story of the Flood tells of how God was grieved by the evil men do to one another, and of how he tore up the script of that chapter of humanity to begin again with a righteous man named Noah. The surprising denouement of that story is that God himself regretted what he had done and vowed never again to ask of humanity more than it can reasonably fulfil. God neither destroys the world, nor does he give up on his hopes for humankind, but he now knows it will take time. That is what hope is in Judaism: a refusal to give up on your deepest ideals, but a refusal likewise to say, in a world still disfigured by evil, that the Messiah has yet come, and the world is saved. There is work still to be done, the journey is not yet complete, and it depends on us: we who now all too briefly stride upon the stage of time.

*   *   *

I have tried to make the book as simple and readable as I can. The reader should, however, be aware that there are quite complex things going on beneath the text. In order to construct an adequate account of Jewish social ethics, I have had to bring together law and theology, biblical interpretation and philosophical reflection, general principles and specific examples, narrative and analysis. There is little that is self-evident in the interpretations I offer. They can be challenged at almost any point. That is a given of a living tradition as complex and many-faceted as Judaism. To an unusual degree Judaism is a conversation scored for many voices. Its key texts are anthologies of arguments. 'These and those', say the sages, 'are the words of the living God'.[18] In the final analysis, 'A judge must rule on the basis of the evidence before him'.[19] One has to tell the story as best one can, knowing that there are other ways of narrating it that may differ in both substance and style.

In particular, Jewish ethics is something different from, though it is bounded by, Jewish law. This is a point made with great clarity by the thirteenth-century exegete Nahmanides in his comment to the biblical command to do 'the right and the good in the eyes of God' (Deut. 6:18). It is impossible, he explains, to specify in advance all the challenges of the moral life. They are too contextual and situational. Therefore the Bible does two things: it gives concrete examples ('Do not be a talebearer', 'Do not take vengeance', 'Do not stand idly by the blood of your neighbour') and general principles, like 'Love your neighbour as yourself' and 'Do the right and the good'. Formulating a Jewish ethic will always be a synthetic as well as analytic exercise, bringing together sources of diverse kinds, sketching the broad arch of biblical and post-biblical thought, trying to match the parts to the whole and the whole to the parts.

In particular, I have emphasized the active rather than the passive mode of Jewish thought: what we do, rather than how we respond to what is done to us. Judaism is not without its passive mode, its thankfulness for life, its trust in the midst of suffering, its willingness to wait patiently for the saving act of God. The best reason I can give for why I have written what I have is because, having tried to listen as attentively as I can to 'the still, small voice' in which the eternal infinite speaks to me here and now, this is what I heard. The real and present challenge to Jews specifically, humanity generally, is to wrestle with the ever more consequential challenges of human action. To believe either that we are accountable to no one, or that God will somehow intervene to save us from ourselves, is consistent but irresponsible, and this is not how I read my faith or understand the human condition.

The structure of the book is this: I begin by confronting the strongest challenge to religion as a force for alleviating the human condition, that of Karl Marx. I argue that far from being 'the opium of the people', Judaism is a religion of protest and what Herbert Schneidau called 'sacred discontent'.[20] In Chapters 3 to 9 I set out Judaism's key concepts of social ethics: justice, charity, love-as-action, sanctifying God's name, the 'ways of peace' and 'mending the world'. I also devote two chapters to the idea of collective responsibility, the first within the covenant of faith, the second, for humanity as a whole. Chapters 10 to 14 are about the theology that gives rise to these ideas. Chapters 15 to 20 are about the difference they make to the way we live a life.

'The evil men do lives after them', said Shakespeare's Mark Anthony, 'the good is oft interred with their bones'. Of course he knew it was not so; that is the ironic point of the speech. It was only when, some years ago, I was mourning for my late father that I learned what anyone who has sat *shiva* knows (in Judaism, we sit on low stools for a week – *shiva* – to mourn the death of a close relative, and it is the universal custom for family, friends and community to visit the mourners during this period to give them comfort). People who had known him, in many cases before I or my brothers were born, told us of his kindnesses to them and the things about him they admired: his integrity, his moral passion, his Jewish pride. It was then I experienced for myself what I had learned from all those other funerals at which I had officiated: that the good we do does live after us, and it is by far the most important thing that does.

I freely admit, there were times during those days when I wept, not just because he was gone, but because he wasn't there to hear and know the impact he had made on others. He had not had an easy life, and beneath his often radiant smile I sensed an enormous reservoir of pain. 'Why did you never say these things to him when he was alive?' I found myself thinking time and again. Yet that is the human condition, and we all know it. Only rarely do we catch a glimpse of the difference we make to other people's lives. Unless we are Mark Twain, we never get to read our own obituaries. But it was then that I knew beyond scepticism or doubt that *the greatest gift is to be able to give*, and the life we lead is measured by the good we do.

I have written this book not only for Jews but also as a Jewish voice in the conversation of humankind, for we all wrestle with questions about the meaning of our lives and the kind of world we will leave to those who come after us. At such times we need not only the passions of the present but the wisdom of our several traditions, lovingly handed on from generation to generation: the gift of the past to the future, and the offering each heritage can make to the moral imagination of humankind.

NOTES

1. Viktor Frankl, *The Doctor and the Soul: from psychotherapy to logotherapy* (London: Souvenir Press, 2004), p. 24.
2. Quoted in Rabbi Joseph B. Soloveitchik, *Halakhic Man*, trans. Lawrence Kaplan (Philadelphia: Jewish Publication Society of America, 1983), p. 91.
3. A. Williams, D. Haber, G. Weaver and J. Freeman, 'Altruistic Activity', *Activities, Adaptation and Ageing* (1998), 22:31.
4. L. Pegalis, *Frequency and Duration of Positive Affect: the dispositionality of happiness.* PhD dissertation, University of Georgia, Athens, Georgia, 1994.
5. H. Lepper, *In Pursuit of Happiness and Satisfaction in Later Life: a study of competing theories of subjective well-being.* PhD dissertation, University of California, Riverside, 1996. T. Rahman and A. Khaleque, 'The Purpose in Life and Academic Behaviour Problem Students', *Social Indicators Research* (1996), 39:59.
6. J. Gerwood, M. LeBlanc and N. Piazza, 'The purpose in life test and religious denomination', *Journal of Clinical Psychology* (1998), 54:49.
7. R. Kean, S. Van Zandt and N. Miller, 'Exploring factors of perceived social performance, health and personal control', *International Journal of Aging and Human Development* (1996), 43:297.
8. S. Hong and E. Giannakopoulos, 'Students' Perception of Life Satisfaction', *College Student Journal* (1995), 29:438.
9. M. Sirgy, D. Cole, R. Kosenko and H. L. Meadow, 'A life satisfaction measure', *Social Indicators Research* (1995), 34:237.
10. Hans Jonas, *The Imperative of Responsibility* (Chicago: University of Chicago Press, 1984).
11. James Lovelock, *The Ages of Gaia* (New York: Norton, 1988).
12. William Wordsworth, 'The world is too much with us', in M. H. Abrahams (ed.), *The Norton Anthology of English Literature*, sixth ed. (New York: Norton, 1993), p. 199.
13. Philip Larkin, 'Church Going', in *Philip Larkin: collected poems*, ed. Anthony Thwaite (London: Faber and Faber, 1988), p. 98.
14. *Sifre, Bamidbar* 143.
15. Abraham Isaac Kook, *Musar Avikha*, p. 96; English translation in Benjamin Ish Shalom and Shalom Rosenberg (eds.), *The World of Rav Kook's Thought* (Jerusalem: Avi Chai, 1991), p. 212.

16. Avishai Margalit, *The Ethics of Memory* (Cambridge, MA: Harvard University Press, 2002), p. ix.
17. Mishnah, *Avot* 2:16.
18. Babylonian Talmud, *Eruvin* 13a.
19. Ibid., *Baba Batra* 131a.
20. Herbert N. Schneidau, *Sacred Discontent: the Bible and Western tradition* (Berkeley: University of California Press, 1976).

Chapter 2

Faith as Protest

> Learn to do good,
> Seek justice,
> Aid the oppressed.
> Uphold the rights of the orphan,
> Defend the cause of the widow.
> (Isaiah 1:17)

Since this book is about religious ethics, we ought to confront at the outset the most compelling argument that religion is not a force for good. In one of the more famous passages of modern times, Karl Marx in 1844 delivered his verdict. Religion is, he said: 'the sigh of the oppressed creature, the feeling of a heartless world, the soul of soulless conditions. It is the opium of the people.'[1] Religious faith, Marx believed, was what reconciled people to their condition – their poverty, their disease and death, their 'station in life', their subjection to tyrannical rulers, the sheer bleakness of existence for most people most of the time.

Faith anaesthetized. It made the otherwise unbearable bearable. Things are as they are because that is the will of God. God made some people rich and others poor; some people rulers and the others ruled. Religion was the most powerful means ever devised for keeping people in their place and preserving the status quo. It robed their lives with ritual. It dignified their tears into prayer. It gave the social order metaphysical inevitability. So, if the world is to be changed, Marx concluded, religion must go:

> The abolition of religion as the illusory happiness of the people is at the same time the demand for their real happiness. The demand to give up the illusions about their condition is a demand to give up a condition that requires illusions. Criticism has plucked the

imaginary flowers from the chains so that man may throw off the chains and pluck real flowers. Religion is only the illusory sun around which man revolves so long as he does not revolve around himself.[2]

A century and a half later, we know what Marx himself could not, that the earthly paradise he envisaged turned, under Stalin, into one of the most brutal, repressive regimes in the history of humankind. The dream of utopia ended in a nightmare of hell.

Marx's family background was Jewish: his grandfather had been a rabbi.[3] His relationship to Judaism was, however, hostile,[4] and his description of religion fails as a description of the Hebrew Bible. Judaism is not a religion that reconciles us to the world. It was born as an act of defiance against the great empires of the ancient world, Mesopotamia and Egypt, which did what he accused all religions of doing – sanctifying hierarchy, justifying the rule of the strong over the weak, glorifying kings and pharaohs and keeping the masses in place. In the Bible God *removes* the chains of slavery from his people; he does not impose them. The religion of Israel emerged out of the most paradigm-shifting experience of the ancient world: that the supreme power intervened in history to liberate the powerless. It was in and as the voice of social protest that the biblical imagination took shape.

*   *   *

There is a scene that, in 4,000 years, has not lost its capacity to take us by surprise. God has just sent messengers, in the guise of three strangers passing by, to Abraham and Sarah to give them the news that Sarah will have a child. Sarah, by then ageing and post-menopausal, laughs in disbelief, but God assures her that it is true. The strangers take their leave, and at that point the scene should end. But it does not. What happens next is the birth of a new drama in the relationship between heaven and earth, quite literally a world-changing event:

> The Lord said, 'Shall I hide from Abraham what I am about to do, seeing that Abraham shall become a great and mighty nation, and all the nations of the earth shall be blessed in him? For I have chosen him so that he may instruct his children and his household after him to keep the way of the Lord by doing righteousness and justice, so that the Lord may bring about for Abraham, what He has promised him'.
>
> Then the Lord said, 'How great is the outcry against Sodom and Gomorrah and how very grave their sin! I must go down and see whether they have done altogether according to the outcry that has come to Me; and if not, I will know'. (Gen. 18:17–21)

It is a strange passage. Is God speaking to Abraham or not? If so, why? Does he expect Abraham to have anything to say about the cities of the plain? Could there be anything Abraham might know that God himself does not know? There cannot be. God knows and sees all, including things we can never know: the private thoughts of others, their intentions and motives, the impact of their actions on the moral ecology of the world. Yet Abraham overhears these words and responds with an astonishing address:

> Then Abraham came near and said: 'Will You indeed sweep away the righteous with the wicked? Suppose there are fifty righteous within the city: will You then sweep away the place and not forgive it for the fifty righteous who are in it? Far be it from You to do such a thing, to slay the righteous with the wicked, so that the righteous fare as the wicked! Far be it from You! Shall not the Judge of all the earth do justice?' (Gen. 18:23–5)

God accedes. If there are 50 righteous people in the city, he will not destroy it. Abraham does not let the matter rest. Calling himself 'dust and ashes' he none the less continues the argument relentlessly. What if there are 45, 40, 30, 20? Is there a precise calculus of justice? Eventually God and Abraham agree. If there are even ten righteous individuals (ten form a quorum; their virtue is public, not private), God will save the city. The dialogue ends.

The conversation has a sequel. Two of Abraham's visitors, by now identified as angels, arrive at Sodom where they are greeted and given hospitality by Abraham's nephew Lot: 'But before they lay down, the men of the city, the men of Sodom, both young and old, all the people to the last man, surrounded the house, and they called to Lot, "Where are the men who came to you tonight? Bring them out to us so that we may know them"' (Gen. 19:4–5). The text leaves us in no doubt that what they have in mind is a crime. They are intent on homosexual rape. Many evils are implicit in their threat: physical assault, sexual impropriety, an abuse of hospitality and a belief that strangers have no rights and may be mistreated at will. The narrative is pointedly telling us something else as well. The curiously reiterated phrases, 'young and old', 'all the people', 'to the last man', are intended to show us that as a matter of fact Abraham's conjecture was false. There were not ten righteous people in the city. There was not one. So the city and its surrounding towns are destroyed. Lot and his family alone are rescued, evidently by virtue of Abraham's merit. Abraham's prayer failed. Why then did he make it?

The answer is given at the beginning of the story, when God as it were thinks aloud in Abraham's hearing. There can be only one reason. God *wants* Abraham to respond. His very act of communication is an

19

invitation to Abraham to pray. Nor is this all: he gives Abraham guidance as to the *terms* in which he is to pray. He says, 'For I have chosen him so that he may instruct his children and his household after him to keep the way of the Lord by doing righteousness [*tzedakah*] and justice [*mishpat*]'. God wants Abraham to live by these values, and it is these two words that form the heart of Abraham's prayer. The word *tzaddik*, 'righteous', appears seven times in the course of Abraham's appeal (a sevenfold repetition is the Bible's way of signalling a key theme). The word *mishpat* forms the beginning and end of the most important sentence: 'Shall not the Judge [*ha-shophet*] of all the earth do justice [*mishpat*]?' Abraham has precisely followed God's cues.

But this only deepens the mystery. Why does God invite Abraham to pray? Why does he in effect teach him how to pray? It cannot be that Abraham knows anything that God does not know. Nor can it be that God expects him to raise any moral consideration he has neglected. For God is just and righteous. If he were not, he would not have told Abraham to live by justice and righteousness. Whichever way we look at it, the episode seems unintelligible – not just within our categories but within the narrative logic of the text itself.

Yet it is clearly not intended to be unintelligible. It is written in simple, lucid prose. It does not look or read like a riddle, a metaphysical conundrum. In fact, the story conveys a proposition at once simple yet utterly unexpected. It turns all conventional understandings of religion upside down. In Judaism, faith is a revolutionary gesture – the precise opposite of what Karl Marx took religion to be.

*　　　　　*　　　　　*

With monotheism a question was born. Why do the righteous suffer? Why do bad things happen to good people? Or, as the prophet Jeremiah later asked, 'Why does the way of the wicked prosper?' (Jer. 12:1). In polytheistic or secular cultures, the question does not arise. There is no single force governing the universe. Instead there are many conflicting powers. In ancient times, they were the sun, the sea, the storm, the wind, the god of rain and the goddess of the earth, the pantheon of greater and lesser deities. Today we would speak of the global economy, terror, technological progress, the international arena, the media and the biosphere. They control our lives but cannot be controlled. They are not the work of a single mind but the unpredictable outcome of billions of decisions. They clash, sometimes producing order, at others chaos, leaving human beings as victims or spectators of forces at best indifferent, at worst hostile to humankind. In such a world – or rather, in such a way of seeing the world – there is no justice because there is no supreme Judge.

The single greatest protest against such a universe is monotheism.

It was born in the faith that the world that gave birth to us is not indiffer-ent to our existence. Nor is it accidental that we alone of all life-forms ask questions. There is something at the heart of being – something that *is* the heart of being – that responds to us as persons, and *teaches us* to ask questions. We are here because someone wanted us to be. Nor are we condemned to ignorance as to who or what that someone is. For in its most radically humanizing gesture, the Hebrew Bible tells us that *God speaks.* The universe is not silent. And with those words from the One-who-speaks, a question takes shape in the mind of the one-who-listens.

Its classic expression takes the form of an apparent contradiction. God is all powerful and all good. But there is injustice in the world. One or other of these statements must, it seems, be false. Either God cannot prevent injustice, or he can but chooses not to. If he cannot, he is not all powerful. If he chooses not to, he is not all good. The alternative is that there is no injustice, and what *seems* to be wrong from our limited per-spective is in fact right if looked at from a wider or more long-term point of view. These – or so it seems – are the only alternatives: to deny the power or goodness of God or to deny the existence of unjustified evil.

The first view, that of Karl Marx, says simply that there is no God. There is therefore no reason to expect that history will be anything other than the tyranny of the strong over the weak, of might over right, of the 'will to power' over the will to good. Justice is (as Plato's Thrasymachus argued in *The Republic*)[5] whatever serves the interests of the most power-ful. This is a world of Darwinian natural selection. The strong survive. The weak perish. *Homino homini lupus est,* 'Man is wolf to man'. Nietzsche was its greatest exponent. For him, words like kindness, compassion and sympathy were either disingenuous or naïve. There is nothing in nature nor in the untutored human heart to lead us to confer on others a moral dignity equal to our own. We do what is in our interest and what we can get away with. All else is an illusion, wishful thinking. There is no justice because there is no Judge.

Against this, the second voice says No. God exists. There is a judge, therefore there is justice, and what seems to us injustice is not ultimately so. Those who suffer do so because they are being punished for their sins. In one version, they may be suffering for Adam's sin, which still stains humankind. It may be that suffering is not punishment for past vice but preparation for future virtue. It cures us of our pride. It teaches us strength and courage. It gives us sympathy with those who suffer, a sym-pathy we could not have, had we not suffered ourselves. The world, said Keats, is a 'vale of soul-making' ('Do you not see', he added, 'how neces-sary a world of pains and troubles is to school an intelligence and make it a soul?').[6] God exists, therefore injustice does not exist.

These are the conventional alternatives and there seems to be no other. The first is the road taken by all ancient polytheistic and modern

secular cultures. The second is most associated with the two great monotheisms that separated from Judaism and went into independent orbit:
Christianity and Islam. Judaism rejects both. But there seems to be no
logical space for it to occupy, for there is apparently no third option. That
is why it is a faith hard to understand and often misunderstood. Its answer
is not difficult, but it is revolutionary. It is that in creating humanity, God
empowers humanity. He grants dignity – radical, ontological dignity – to
the fact that human beings are not gods. Infinity confers a blessing on
finitude by recognizing that it is finite, and loving it because it is. God not
only speaks, he also listens, and in listening gives humankind a voice –
Abraham's voice.

        *   *   *

God exists, therefore there is justice. But it is *divine* justice – justice from
the perspective of one who knows all, sees all, and considers all: the universe as a whole, and time as a whole, which is to say, eternity. But we who
live in space and time cannot see from this perspective, and if we did, it
would not make us better human beings but worse.

To be a parent is to be moved by the cry of a child. But if the child is ill
and needs medicine, we administer it, making ourselves temporarily deaf
to its cry. A surgeon, to do his job competently and well, must to a certain
extent desensitize himself to the patient's fears and pains and regard
him, however briefly, as a body rather than as a person. A statesman, to do
his best for the country, must weigh long-term consequences and make
tough, even brutal decisions: for soldiers to die in war if war is necessary;
for people to be thrown out of jobs if economic stringency is needed.
Parents, surgeons and politicians have human feelings, but the very roles
they occupy mean that at times they must override them if they are to do
the best for those for whom they are responsible. To do the best for
others needs a measure of detachment, a silencing of sympathy, an anaes-
thetizing of compassion, for the road to happiness or health or peace
sometimes runs through the landscape of pain and suffering and death.

If we were able to see how evil today leads to good tomorrow – if we
were able to see from the point of view of God, creator of all – we would
understand justice but *at the cost of ceasing to be human.* We would accept
all, vindicate all, and become deaf to the cries of those in pain. God does
not want us to cease to be human, for if he did, he would not have created
us. We are not God. We will never see things from his perspective. The
attempt to do so is an abdication of the human situation. My teacher,
Rabbi Nahum Rabinovitch, taught me that this is how to understand the
moment when Moses first encountered God at the burning bush. 'Moses
hid his face because he was afraid to look at God' (Ex. 3:6). Why was he
afraid? Because if he were fully to understand God he would have no

choice but to be reconciled to the slavery and oppression of the world. From the vantage point of eternity, he would see that the bad is a necessary stage on the journey to the good. He would understand God but he would cease to be Moses, the fighter against injustice who intervened whenever he saw wrong being done. 'He was afraid' that seeing heaven would desensitize him to earth, that coming close to infinity would mean losing his humanity.[7] That is why God chose Moses, and why he taught Abraham to pray.

A Holocaust historian was once interviewing a survivor of the extermination camps. He was a hassidic rebbe (the name given by hassidim, Jewish mystics, to their leader). Astonishingly, he seemed to have passed through the valley of the shadow of death, his faith intact. He could still smile. 'Seeing what you saw, did you have no questions about God?' she asked.

'Yes', he said, 'Of course I had questions. So powerful were those questions, I had no doubt that were I to ask them, God would personally invite me to heaven to tell me the answers. And I prefer to be down here on earth with the questions than up in heaven with the answers'. He too belonged to this ancient Jewish tradition.

There is divine justice, and sometimes, looking back at the past from a distance in time, we can see it. But we do not live by looking back at the past. More than other faiths, the religion of the Hebrew Bible is written in the future tense. Ancient Israel was the only civilization to set its golden age in not-yet-realized time, because a free human being lives toward the future. There is divine justice, but God wants us to strive for *human* justice – in the short term, not just the long term; in this world, not the next; from the perspective of time and space, not infinity and eternity. *God creates divine justice, but only we can create human justice*, acting on behalf of God but never aspiring to be other than human. That is why he created us. It is why God not only speaks but listens, why he wants to hear Abraham's voice, not just his own. Creation is empowerment. That is the radical proposition at the heart of the Hebrew Bible. God did not create humankind to demand of it absolute submission to his all-powerful will. In revelation, creation speaks. What it says is a call to responsibility.

*   *   *

There is an aspect of Genesis 18, the text with which I began, which has not been adequately understood, yet it is fundamental not only to the encounter between Abraham and God, but to the whole message of the Hebrew Bible and its distinctive tone of voice.

The conversation about the cities of the plain does not take place in a vacuum. It is preceded by another episode. We recall that the purpose of the three visitors was to tell Abraham and Sarah that they were about to have a child. The two events seem to have nothing to do with one another. What does the prospect of a child have to do with the fate of Sodom or an argument about justice?

Yet this will not do. These are not two episodes but one. The text is explicit on this point. Between the first half and the second we read this verse: 'The men turned away and went towards Sodom, but Abraham *remained standing* before God' (Gen. 18:22). 'Remained standing' tells us that this is not a new scene but a continuation of what has gone before. The Hebrew Bible always announces a break in the narrative. 'And it came to pass that . . .' which means, in effect, the end of one scene and the beginning of the next. There is no such direction here. To the contrary, the text goes out of its way to signal a seamless transition, an unbroken conversation.

To make doubly certain we do not miss the point, the narrative explicitly links the two subjects. In the course of disclosing his plans for Sodom, God makes reference to the fact that Abraham is about to have a child: 'For I have chosen him *so that he may instruct his children* and his household after him to keep the way of the Lord by doing righteousness and justice'. Abraham's role, the task for which he has been chosen, is to be a father. That is what his name means: 'You shall be called Abraham for I will make you the father of many nations'. The second half of the chapter is thus intimately related to the first half. In inviting him to enter into a dialogue about the fate of Sodom, God is about to teach Abraham *what it is to be a father*.

All talk of God in the Bible is by way of metaphor. God, the prophets tell us, is a king, a judge, a shepherd, a husband, and many other images, each of which captures a fragment of the relationship between heaven and earth while none expresses all. Undoubtedly, though, the most powerful and consistent metaphor in the Bible is of God as a father. 'My child, my firstborn, Israel' (Ex. 4:22), says God when he is about to rescue his people from slavery. Sometimes the prophets, Isaiah especially, speak of God as a mother: 'Like one whom his mother comforts, so shall I comfort you' (Is. 66:13). Either way, however, though it is highly anthropomorphic, the entire biblical tradition tells us that if we seek to understand God – something we can never fully do by any act of the imagination – the best way to do so is to reflect on what it is to be a parent, bringing new life into being through an act of love, caring for it, protecting it while it is young, and then gradually withdrawing so that it can learn to walk, speak and exercise responsibility.

The use of a metaphor, however, may at times change the meaning of the metaphor itself, and that is the case here. Alongside a revolutionary concept of God, Judaism gave rise to an equally revisionary understanding of what it is to be a parent. In the ancient world, children were the property of their parents without an independent dignity of their own. That gave rise to the form of idolatry most repugnant to the Bible, child

24

sacrifice (against which the story of the binding of Isaac is directed: God wants Abraham *not* to sacrifice his child). It also set in motion the tragic conflict between sons and fathers dramatized in the myth of Oedipus, which Freud, wrongly I believe, saw as endemic to human culture.

The Hebrew Bible tells the long and often tense story of the childhood of humanity under the parenthood of God. But God does not want humankind to remain in childhood. He wants them to become adults, exercising responsibility in freedom. In Jewish law, the obligations of children to parents begin *only when they cease to be children* (at the age of 12 for girls, 13 for boys). Before then they have no obligations at all. Paradoxically, it is only when we become parents that we understand our parents – which is why the first recorded command in the Bible is that of parenthood ('Be fruitful and multiply'). A weak parent seeks to control his children. A true parent seeks to relinquish control, which is why God never intervenes to protect us from ourselves. That means that we will stumble and fall, but only by so doing does a child learn to walk. God does not ask his children not to make mistakes. To the contrary, he accepts that, in the Bible's own words, 'There is none on earth so righteous as to do only good and never to sin' (Eccl. 7:20). God asks us only to acknowledge our mistakes and learn from them. Forgiveness is written into the structure of the universe.

The connection between the two halves of the chapter lies in an utterly new understanding of what it is to be a parent. Abraham, about to become father to the first child of the covenant, is being taught by God what it means to raise a child. *To be a father – implies the Bible – is to teach a child to question, challenge, confront, dispute.* God invites Abraham to do these things because he wants him to be the parent of a nation that will do these things. He does not want the people of the covenant to be one that accepts the evils and injustices of the world as the will of God. He wants the people of the covenant to be human, neither more nor less. He wants them to hear the cry of the oppressed, the pain of the afflicted and the plaint of the lonely. He wants them *not* to accept the world that is, because it is not the world that ought to be. He is giving Abraham a tutorial in what it is to teach a child to grow by challenging the existing scheme of things. Only through such challenges does a child learn to accept responsibility; only by accepting responsibility does a child grow to become an adult; and only an adult can understand the parenthood of God.

To be a Jewish child is to learn how to question. Four times the Mosaic books refer to children asking questions (the 'four sons' of the Haggadah).[8] The most significant family ritual, the seder service of Passover, begins with the questions asked by a child. Against cultures that see unquestioning obedience as the ideal behaviour of a child, Jewish tradition, in the Haggadah, regards the 'child who has not learned to ask' as the lowest, not the highest, stage of development (Solomon ibn Gabirol said, 'A wise question already contains half the answer'). A famous verse in Judaism's holiest prayer, the Shema, is usually translated as 'You shall teach these things diligently to your children' (Deut. 6:7). The great eleventh-century commentator Rashi (Rabbi Shlomo Yitzhaki), however, translates the verb not as 'you shall teach diligently' but as 'you shall *sharpen*'.[9] Education, in Judaism, is active, not passive. It is about honing the mind, sharpening the intellect, through question and answer, challenge and response.

Judaism is God's perennial question-mark against the condition of the world. That things are as they are is a fact, not a value. Should it be so? Why should it be so? Only one who asks whether the world should be as it is, is capable of changing what it is. That is why Marx was wrong. Biblical faith is not a conservative force. It does not conceal the scars of the human condition under the robes of sanctity and inevitability. There may be – there is – divine justice in or beyond history, but God does not ask us to live by the standards of divine justice for if we could understand divine justice we would no longer be human. We are God's children, not God. By teaching Abraham how to be a child, challenging, questioning, defending even the wicked in the name of human solidarity, God was instructing him in what it is to be human, keeping 'the way of the Lord by doing righteousness and justice'.

God exists, therefore the universe is just. But we are merely human, and God has empowered us to seek the justice that is human – not justice from the point of view of the universe and eternity but from the point of view of the fallible, frail, ephemeral, vulnerable beings that we are. We who live in space and time cannot but see injustice. We cannot know the rewards of a life beyond the grave. We cannot judge the remote consequences of an event all too vividly present in the here and now. Our pain is not made less by the belief that it is necessary for the good of the whole. Still less is it made bearable by the belief that it is justified as punishment for sin. That – as Job's comforters belatedly discovered – is not a form of comfort but a double affliction. In the book of Job, the comforters who defend the justice of God are condemned by God himself, because He asks of us *not* to take his part but to be human, the essence of which is acknowledging that we are not God.

God in making humanity conferred on us the right and duty to see things from a human point of view. If evil exists within our horizons, then it is real no matter how limited those horizons are. Making us human, not divine, God calls on us to judge and act within the terms of our humanity. 'The Torah was not given to ministering angels', said the sages.[10] It was given to human beings, and the justice it asks us to fight for is human justice. That is why God empowered Abraham to challenge him on the fate of Sodom and the cities of the plain.

God knew that there were no righteous in the city. But Abraham did not and could not know. Had he said nothing – had he accepted the divine decree – justice would have been done, but not seen to be done, not at any rate in a way intelligible to us on earth. There had to be a fair trial, an advocate for the defence, a plea in mitigation. That was Abraham's role and his courage – the courage God invited him to show. For the faith Abraham was being asked to initiate would be one that in every generation strove for justice in human terms. It is not a faith that accepts the status quo as God's will. On the contrary, it is a faith in which God invites human beings to become his partners in the work of redemption; to build a society on the basis of a justice that people understand as such; a human world, without hubris (the attempt to be more than human) or nemesis (a descent into the less-than-human).

'The Torah speaks in the language of human beings', said Rabbi Ishmael,[11] meaning, it is addressed to us within the parameters of our understanding. 'It is not in heaven', said Moses at the end of his life, 'nor is it beyond the sea' (Deut. 30:12–13). There is plenary truth in heaven; on earth, we live among its reflections and refractions. We could not understand God's justice without being gods ourselves. God does not ask us to be anything other than we are, finite beings whose knowledge is limited, whose life-span is all too short, and whose horizons are circumscribed. It is within those limits that God asks us to create a justice we can understand: a human justice that may and must fall short of the divine but which is no less significant for that. For God, in creating us, gave our lives significance. We may be no more than an image, a faint reflection, of God himself, but we are no less.

*   *   *

Opium of the people? Nothing was ever less an opiate than this religion of sacred discontent, of dissatisfaction with the status quo. It was Abraham, then Moses, Amos, and Isaiah, who fought on behalf of justice and human dignity – confronting priests and kings, even arguing with God Himself. That note, first sounded by Abraham, never died. It was given its most powerful expression in the book of Job, surely the most dissident book ever to be included in a canon of sacred scriptures. It echoes again and again in rabbinic midrash, in the *kinot* (laments) of the Middle Ages, in hassidic tales and the literature of the Holocaust. In Judaism, faith is not acceptance but protest, against the world that is, in the name of the world that is not yet but ought to be. Faith lies not in the answer but the question – and the greater the human being, the more intense the question. The Bible is not metaphysical opium but its opposite. Its aim is not to transport the believer to a private heaven. Instead, its impassioned, sustained desire is to bring heaven down to earth. Until we have done this, there is work still to do.

There are cultures that relieve humankind of responsibility, lifting us

27

beyond the world of pain to bliss, ecstasy, meditative rapture. They teach us to accept the world as it is and ourselves as we are. They bring peace of mind, and that is no small thing. Judaism is not peace of mind. 'The righteous have no rest, neither in this world nor the next', says the Talmud.[12] I remain in awe at the challenge God has set us: to be different, iconoclasts of the politically correct, to be God's question-mark against the conventional wisdom of the age, to build, to change, to 'mend' the world until it becomes a place worthy of the divine presence because we have learned to honour the image of God that is humankind.

Biblical faith demands courage. It is not for the faint-hearted. Its vision of the universe is anything but comfortable. However free or affluent we are, on Passover we eat the bread of the affliction and taste the bitter herbs of slavery. On Sukkot (Tabernacles) we sit in shacks and know what it is to be homeless. On the Sabbath we make our living protest against a society driven by ceaseless production and consumption. Every day in our prayers (Psalm 146) we speak of God who 'brings justice to the oppressed and food to the hungry, who sets captives free and opens the eyes of the blind, who straightens the backs of those who are bent down . . . who watches over the stranger and gives heart to the orphan and the widow'. To imitate God is to be alert to the poverty, suffering and loneliness of others. Opium desensitizes us to pain. The Bible sensitizes us to it.

It is impossible to be moved by the prophets and not have a social con-science. Their message, delivered in the name of God, is: accept responsibility. The world will not get better of its own accord. Nor will we make it a more human place by leaving it to others – politicians, columnists, protestors, campaigners – making them our agents to bring redemption on our behalf. The Hebrew Bible begins not with man's cry to God, but with God's cry to us, each of us, here where we are. 'If you are silent at this time', says Mordekhai to Esther, 'relief and deliverance will come from elsewhere . . . but who knows whether it was not for such a time as this that you have attained royalty?' (Esth. 4:14). That is the ques-tion God poses to us. Yes, if we do not do it, someone else may. But we will then have failed to understand why we are here and what we are sum-moned to do. The Bible is God's call to human responsibility.

NOTES

1. Karl Marx, 'Towards a critique of Hegel's philosophy of right: introduc-tion'. Quoted in Don Cupitt, *The Sea of Faith* (London: BBC, 1984), p. 144.
2. Ibid.
3. George Steiner, in his *In Bluebeard's Castle: some notes towards the redefinition of culture* (London: Faber and Faber, 1971), pp. 29–48, argues that the socialism of Marx, Trotsky and Ernst Bloch has its roots in biblical

messianism. There is, however, a difference in kind between religious and secular messianism. On the latter, see J. L. Talmon, *The Origins of Totalitarian Democracy* (London: Penguin, 1986).

4. See Sander L. Gilman, *Jewish Self-Hatred: anti-Semitism and the hidden language of the Jews* (Baltimore: Johns Hopkins University Press, 1986), pp. 188–207.

5. *The Republic*, 338c; G. R. F. Ferrari (ed.), trans. Tom Griffith (Cambridge: Cambridge University Press, 2000), p. 15.

6. John Keats, 'Letter to George and Georgiana Keats, 14 February–3 May, 1819', in *The Letters of John Keats, 1814–1821*, ed. Hyder Edward Rollins (Cambridge, MA: Harvard University Press, 1999).

7. Nahum Rabinovitch, *Darkah shel Torah* [Hebrew] (Jerusalem: Maaliyot, 1999), pp. 185–91.

8. Ex. 12:26; 13:8, 14; Deut. 6:20.

9. Rashi, *Commentary* to Deut. 6:7.

10. Babylonian Talmud, *Berakhot* 25b.

11. Ibid., 31b.

12. Babylonian Talmud, *Moed Katan* 29a.

Chapter 3

Charity as Justice

The Kaminker Rebbe once resolved to devote a whole day to reciting Psalms. Towards evening, he was still reciting when a messenger came to tell him that his mentor, the Maggid of Tzidnov, wanted to see him. The rebbe said he would come as soon as he was finished, but the messenger returned, saying that the Maggid insisted that he come immediately. When he arrived, the Maggid asked him why he had delayed. The rebbe explained that he had been reciting Psalms. The Maggid told him that he had summoned the rebbe to collect money for a poor person in need. He continued: 'Psalms can be sung by angels, but only human beings can help the poor. Charity is greater than reciting Psalms, because angels cannot perform charity.'

(Hassidic tale)[1]

If you want to understand a culture, listen to the stories it tells. The following, set in the early nineteenth century, was told by the Yiddish writer J. L. Peretz.[2] To understand it, one has to remember the tensions between the hassidim, the Jewish mystics of Eastern Europe, and their highly intellectual opponents, the mitnagdim, of Lithuania. The Lithuanians thought the mystics ignorant and superstitious and frowned on their leaders, known as rebbes, whom they saw as wonder-workers, not scholars.

Every Friday morning before dawn, the Rebbe of Nemirov would disappear. He could be found in none of the town's synagogues or houses of study. The doors of his house were open but he was not there. Once a Lithuanian scholar came to Nemirov. Puzzled by the Rebbe's disappearance, he asked his followers, 'Where is he?' 'Where is the Rebbe?' they replied. 'Where else but in heaven? The people of the town need peace, sustenance, health. The Rebbe is a holy man and therefore he is surely in heaven, pleading our cause.'

The Lithuanian, amused by their credulity, determined to find out for himself. One Thursday night he hid himself in the Rebbe's house. The next morning before dawn he heard the Rebbe weep and sigh. Then he saw him go to the cupboard, take out a parcel of clothes and begin to put them on. They were the clothes, not of a holy man, but of a peasant. The Rebbe then reached into a drawer, pulled out an axe and went out into the still dark night. Stealthily, the Lithuanian followed him as he walked through the town and beyond, into the forest. There he began chopping down a tree, hewing it into logs and splitting it into firewood. These he gathered into a bundle and walked back into the town.

In one of the back streets, he stopped outside a run-down cottage and knocked on the door. An old woman, poor and ill, opened the door. 'Who are you?' she said.

'I am Vassily', the Rebbe replied. 'I have wood to sell, very cheap, next to nothing.'

'I have no money', replied the woman.

'I will give it to you on credit', he said.

'How will I be able to pay you?' she said.

'I trust you – and do you not trust God? He will find a way of seeing that I am repaid.'

'But who will light the fire? I am too ill.'

'I will light the fire', the Rebbe replied, and he did so, reciting under his breath the morning prayers. Then he returned home.

The Lithuanian scholar, seeing this, stayed on in the town and became one of the Rebbe's disciples. After that day, when he heard the people of the town tell visitors that the Rebbe ascended to heaven, he no longer laughed, but added: 'And maybe even higher.'

Moses Maimonides, the austere twelfth-century sage, was not a man to confuse law with narrative. Yet in his law code, the *Mishneh Torah*, he is moved to a note of wonder: 'We have never seen nor heard of an Israelite community that does not have an alms fund.'[3] Powerless, stateless and often living under conditions of great poverty, Jews throughout the centuries of their dispersion created a communal equivalent of a welfare state. They did so voluntarily, because it was a mitzvah (religious deed), because it is what Jews do, and because they knew that no one else would do it for them. As Maimonides notes in another aside:

All Jews and those attached to them are like brothers, as it is said, 'You are the children of the Lord your God' – and if a brother will not show mercy to his brother, then who else will have mercy on him? And to whom can the poor of Israel look for help? To those nations who hate and persecute them? They can look for help only to their brethren.[4]

Earlier, the sages had already noticed an ironic fact about the Pentateuch (the Five Books of Moses). When the Israelites in the wilderness were asked by Aaron to give their ornaments to make a golden calf, they did so. When they were asked by Moses to contribute to the building of the sanctuary, they did so with such generosity that he had to order them to stop. The first, the Golden Calf, was their greatest sin, the second, the sanctuary, their greatest act of service. They had only one feature in common: a willingness to give. 'Who can understand this people?' a midrash asks. 'When they are asked to make a contribution to the making of a golden calf, they give. When they are asked to contribute to the construction of the sanctuary, they give.'[5] *Tzedakah* lies close to the core of what it is to be a Jew. So much so that the rabbis said, 'If someone is cruel and lacks compassion, there are sufficient grounds to suspect his lineage.' Not to give is prima facie evidence that one is not a Jew.

*   *   *

The word *tzedakah* is untranslatable because it joins together two concepts that in other languages are opposites, namely *charity* and *justice*. Suppose, for example, that I give someone £100. Either he is entitled to it, or he is not. If he is, then my act is a form of justice. If he is not, it is an act of charity. In English (as with the Latin terms *caritas* and *iustitia*) a gesture of charity cannot be an act of justice, nor can an act of justice be described as charity. *Tzedakah* means both.

It arises from Judaism's theological insistence on the difference between possession and ownership. Ultimately, all things are owned by God, creator of the world. What we possess, we do not own – we merely hold it in trust for God. The clearest statement of this is the provision in Leviticus: 'The land must not be sold permanently because the land is Mine; you are merely strangers and temporary residents in relation to Me.' If there were absolute ownership, there would be a difference between justice (what we are bound to give others) and charity (what we give others out of generosity). The former would be a legally enforceable duty, the latter, at best, the prompting of benevolence or sympathy. In Judaism, because we are not owners of our property but guardians on God's behalf, we are bound by the conditions of trusteeship, one of which is that we share part of what we have with others in need. What would be regarded as charity in other legal systems is, in Judaism, a strict requirement of the law and can, if necessary, be enforced by the courts.

The nearest English equivalent to *tzedakah* is the phrase that came into existence alongside the idea of a welfare state, namely *social justice* (Friedrich Hayek regarded the concept of *social* justice as incoherent and self-contradictory).[6] Behind both is the idea that no one should be without the basic requirements of existence, and that those who have more than they need must share some of that surplus with those who have less. This is fundamental to the kind of society the Israelites were charged with creating, namely one in which everyone has a basic right to a dignified life and equal worth as citizens in the covenantal community under the sovereignty of God.

Tzedakah, as we saw in an earlier chapter, first appears in the book of Genesis, in the only passage in which the Torah explains why God singled out Abraham to be the founder of a new faith:

> Then the Lord said, 'Shall I hide from Abraham what I am about to do? Abraham will surely become a great and powerful nation, and all the nations of the earth will be blessed through him. For I have chosen him so that he will direct his children and his household after him to keep the way of the Lord by doing what is right and just [*tzedakah u-mishpat*], so that the Lord will bring about for Abraham what He has promised him.' (Gen. 18:17–19)

The 'way of the Lord' is defined here by two words, *tzedakah* and *mishpat.* Each is a distinctive form of justice. *Mishpat* means retributive justice: the rule of law through which disputes are settled by right rather than might, the weighing of evidence and hearing both sides rather than vigilantism and revenge. Law takes out of private hands and places within society as a whole the determination of innocence and guilt. It establishes a set of rules, binding on all, by means of which the members of a society act in such a way as to pursue their own interests without infringing on the rights and freedoms of others. Law has the highest dignity in Judaism, because it is the most basic institution of a free society. It is no coincidence that in the Hebrew Bible, God reveals himself primarily in the form of laws, for Judaism is concerned not just with *salvation* (the soul in its relationship with God) but also with *redemption* (society as a vehicle for the divine presence). A law-governed society is a place of *mishpat.*

Mishpat alone, however, cannot create a decent society. To it must be added *tzedakah,* distributive justice. One can imagine a society which fastidiously observes the rule of law, and yet contains so much inequality that wealth is concentrated into the hands of the few, and many are left without the most basic requirements of a dignified existence. There may be high unemployment and widespread poverty. Some may live in luxury while others go homeless. That is not the kind of order the Torah contemplates. There must be justice not only in how the law is applied, but also in how the means of existence – wealth as God's blessing – are distributed. That is *tzedakah.*

The command itself is set out somewhat tangentially in the Pentateuch, in the context of the seventh year, 'the year of release' in which outstanding debts were cancelled so that the poor would not be held captive by their poverty. The danger was, of course, that lenders might be reluctant to make loans as the year of release approached, fearing that they would never be repaid. Against this the Torah insists:

> If there is a poor man among your brothers in any of the towns of the land that the Lord your God is giving you, do not be hard-hearted or tight-fisted towards your poor brother. Rather be open-handed and freely lend him whatever he needs . . . Give generously to him and do so without a grudging heart; then because of this the Lord your God will bless you in all your work and in everything you put your hand to. There will always be poor people in the land. Therefore I command you to be open-handed towards your brothers and towards the poor and needy in the land. (Deut. 15:7–11)

Why, if *tzedakah* is so central an institution in Judaism, is it set out so briefly in the Torah? The answer lies in the nature of the society for which it legislates. In biblical times this was primarily agricultural. Therefore, the Torah sets out its programme of *tzedakah* in terms of an agrarian order.

There was, as we noted, the 'year of release' when debts were cancelled. In the seventh year of service, slaves went free. There was the Jubilee in which ancestral lands returned to their original owners. There were the 'corner of the field', the 'forgotten sheaf', the 'gleanings' of grain and wine harvest, and the tithes in the third and sixth years that were given to the poor. In these ways and others the Torah established an early form of welfare state – with one significant difference. It did not depend on a *state*. It was part of *society*, implemented not by power but by moral responsibility and the network of obligations created by the covenant at Sinai. It was a gracious structure.

The genius of the sages lay in their ability to sustain this social vision in a quite different age and economic order. They took the verses cited above as scriptural warrant for wide-ranging rabbinic legislation on *tzedakah*. *Tzedakah* refers to more than gifts of produce; it includes gifts of money – the medium of exchange in all advanced societies whatever their economic base. Thus what in biblical times was a relatively minor provision became – when Israel was no longer a nation in its own land, and when most of its people no longer lived and worked on farms – the very lifeblood of its system of distributive justice.

*　　　　　*　　　　　*

What distinguishes the concept of *tzedakah* is, firstly, an absolute refusal on the part of the sages to romanticize poverty. It is not, for them, a blessed state. It is an unmitigated evil. 'Poverty', they said, 'is a kind of death.'[7] 'Poverty in a person's house is worse than fifty plagues.'[8] 'Nothing is harder to bear than poverty, for one who is crushed by poverty is like one to whom all the troubles of the world cling and upon whom all the curses in Deuteronomy have descended. If all the troubles were placed on one scale and poverty on the other, poverty would outweigh them all.'[9]

These are the statements of people who knew hardship from personal experience. Many of the sages were poor themselves. Hillel lacked the small sum needed to secure entrance to the house of study.[10] Hanina ben Dosa is said to have survived on a kilo of carobs from one week to the next.[11] They knew that poverty does not dignify, nor does it refine the soul. It deadens the sensibilities, turns a person in on himself, crushes the spirit and humiliates the soul. 'If there is no meal', said the sages, 'there can be no Torah.'[12] Maimonides explained simply: it is impossible to turn the mind to higher things when you are hungry or thirsty or without shelter or in pain.[13] On this the rabbis would have agreed with Marx, that statements in praise of poverty are indefensible defences of the status quo by those with privilege and power.

The whole tenor of the Torah is based on the idea that God is to be found in the physical world and its blessings. We are commanded to serve God in joy out of the abundance of good things, not through self-denial. One Talmudic teacher went so far as to say that in the world to come a person will have to face judgement for every legitimate pleasure he denied himself in this life.[14] Asceticism – always a temptation in the religious life – was never embraced by the Jewish mainstream. On the contrary, it was an implicit disavowal of this world which God created and pronounced good. Jewish teachings on poverty have a refreshing directness and sense of reality. Having regard for the poor did not mean in Judaism embracing poverty oneself. No poor person was ever helped by knowing that a saint had joined his ranks. He was helped by being given the chance not to be poor.

Equally robust was the rabbinic refusal to see inequalities in society as the will of God. On this, the Talmud records a fascinating debate between Rabbi Akiva and the Roman governor of Israel, Tineius Rufus:

> Tineius Rufus asked Rabbi Akiva, 'If your God loves the poor, why does He not provide for them?'
>
> Rabbi Akiva replied, 'So that we may be saved through them from the punishment of Gehenna [i.e. charity atones].'
>
> Rufus said, 'On the contrary, it is this that will condemn you to Gehenna. I will make my point clear by a parable. A king of flesh and blood became angry with his slave, put him in prison, and ordered that he be given neither food nor drink. A certain man went [to the prison] and gave him food and drink. When the king

hears what the man did, will he not be angry with him? And after all you are no more than God's slaves, as it is written, "For to Me the children of Israel are slaves"' (Lev. 25:55).

Rabbi Akiva replied, 'I will prove my point with another parable. A king of flesh and blood became angry with his child, put him in prison, and ordered that he be given neither food nor drink. A certain man went [to the prison] and gave him food and drink. When the king hears what the man did, will he not reward him? And after all we are called [God's] children, as it is written, "You are children of the Lord your God"' (Deut. 14:1).[15]

There is nothing inevitable or divinely willed about social and economic inequality. Judaism rejects the almost universal belief in antiquity and throughout the Middle Ages that hierarchy and divisions of class are written into the structure of society. What human beings have created, human beings can rectify.

It followed that everyone should be provided with the basic requirements of a dignified life. The sages inferred this from the biblical phrase, 'be open-handed and freely lend him *whatever he needs*'. Needs included food, housing, basic furniture, and if necessary, funds to pay for a wedding. To this end, each community organized *tzedakah* funds, contributions to which could be coerced by communal sanction. From earliest rabbinic times there were such institutions as the *tamchui*, or mobile kitchen, which distributed food daily to whoever applied, and the *kuppah*, or community chest, which distributed money weekly to the poor of the city, together with specific funds for clothing, raising dowries for poor brides and providing burial expenses for the poor. Post-biblical Judaism was faithful to one of the Bible's most powerful imperatives, that a society is judged by what it contributes to the welfare of the least advantaged, 'the widow, the orphan, the poor and the stranger'. The religious basis for this is given majestic expression in the saying of one of the early Talmudic sages:

Rabbi Johanan said: 'Wherever you find the greatness of the Holy One, blessed be He, there too you will find His humility . . . Thus it is written in the Torah, "For the Lord your God is the God of gods and Lord of lords, the great, mighty and awesome God . . ." and immediately afterwards it says, "He upholds the cause of the fatherless and widow, and loves the stranger, giving him food and clothing." Likewise it says in the Prophets, "Thus speaks the High and exalted One . . . I live in a high and holy place but also with him who is contrite and lowly in spirit, to revive the spirit of the lowly and the heart of the contrite." It is stated a third time in the Holy Writings, "Sing to God, sing praises to His name, extol Him who rides the clouds . . ." and immediately afterwards it says, "Father of the fatherless, a judge of widows, is God in His holy habitation."[16]

Greatness, even for God, certainly for us, is not to be above people but to be with them, hearing their silent cry, sharing their distress, bringing comfort to the distressed and dignity to the deprived. The message of the Hebrew Bible is that civilizations survive not by strength but by how they respond to the weak; not by wealth but by how they care for the poor; not by power but by their concern for the powerless. What renders a culture invulnerable is the compassion it shows to the vulnerable.

Most striking is the psychological dimension of *tzedakah* legislation. Poverty not merely deprives; it *humiliates,* and a good society will not allow humiliation.[17] Nowhere do we see this more clearly than in Maimonides' famous summary of the eight levels of *tzedakah*:

There are eight degrees of charity, one higher than the other.

The highest degree, exceeded by none, is that of one who assists a poor person by providing him with a gift or a loan or by accepting him into a business partnership or by helping him find employment – in a word, by putting him in a situation where he can dispense with other people's aid. With reference to such aid it is said, 'You shall strengthen him, be he a stranger or a settler, he shall live with you' (Lev. 25:35), which means: strengthen him in such a manner that his falling into want is prevented.

A step below this stands the one who gives alms to the needy in such a way that the giver does not know to whom he gives and the recipient does not know from whom he takes. This exemplifies doing a good deed for its own sake. One example was the Hall of Secrecy in the Temple, where the righteous would place their gift clandestinely and where poor people from noble families could come and secretly help themselves to aid. Close to this is dropping money in a charity box . . .

One step lower is where the giver knows to whom he gives, but the poor person does not know from whom he receives. Thus the great sages would go and secretly put money into poor people's doorways . . .

A step lower is the case where the poor person knows from whom he is taking, but the giver does not know to whom he is giving. Thus the great sages would tie coins in their scarves, which they would fling over their shoulders, so that the poor could help themselves without suffering shame.

Lower than this, is where someone gives the poor person a gift before he asks.

Lower still is one who gives only after the poor person asks.

Lower than this is one who gives less than is fitting, but does so with a friendly countenance.

The lowest level is one who gives ungraciously.[18]

This exquisitely calibrated ethic is shot through with psychological insight. What matters is not how *much* you give, but *how* you do so. Anonymity in the giving of aid is essential to dignity. The poor must not be embarrassed. The rich must not be allowed to feel superior. We give, not to take pride in our generosity, still less to emphasize the dependency of others, but because we belong to a covenant of human solidarity, and because that is what God wants us to do, honouring the trust through which he has temporarily lent us wealth in the first place.

Especially noteworthy is Maimonides' insistence that giving somebody a job, or the means to start a business, is the highest charity of all. What is humiliating about poverty is dependence itself: the feeling of being beholden to others. One of the sharpest expressions of this is to be found in the Grace after Meals, when we say, 'We beseech You, God our Lord, let us not be in need of the gifts of men or of their loans, but only of Your helping hand . . . so that we may not be put to shame nor humiliated for ever and ever.'[19] The greatest act of *tzedakah* is one that allows the individual to become self-sufficient. The highest form of charity is one that enables the individual to dispense with charity. From the point of view of the giver, this is one of the least financially demanding forms of giving. It may not cost him anything at all. But from the point of view of the recipient, it is the most dignifying, because it removes the shame of receiving. Humanitarian relief is essential in the short term, but in the long run, job creation and economic policies that promote full employment are more important.

Protecting dignity and avoiding humiliation were systematic elements of rabbinical law. So, for example, the rabbis ruled that even the richest should be buried plainly so as not to shame the poor.[20] On certain festive days girls, especially those from wealthy families, had to wear borrowed clothes, 'so as not to shame those who do not have'.[21] The rabbis intervened to lower the prices of religious necessities so that no one would be excluded from communal celebrations. Work conditions had to be such that employees were treated with basic respect. Here, the proof text was God's declaration, 'For to Me the children of Israel are servants' (Lev. 25:55) – meaning that they were not to be treated as servants of any human being. Freedom presupposes self-respect, and a free society will therefore be one that robs no one of that basic human entitlement.

One detail of Jewish law is particularly noteworthy: even a person dependent on *tzedakah* must himself or herself give *tzedakah*.[22] On the face of it, the rule is absurd. Why give X enough money so that he can give to Y? Giving to Y directly is more logical and efficient. What the rabbis understood, however, is that *giving is an essential part of human dignity*. As an African proverb puts it: the hand that gives is always uppermost; the hand that receives is always lower. The rabbinic insistence that the community provide the poor with enough money so that they themselves can give is a profound insight into the human condition.

So too is their understanding of wealth. As I noted in the first chapter, a series of research projects has shown that happiness is correlated not with what we possess, but with what we give. The privilege of wealth lies not in what it allows us to do for ourselves, but what it enables us to do for others. The sages told the following story:

> Our masters taught: it is related of King Monabaz [king of Adiabene in the first century CE who converted to Judaism] that during years of scarcity he spent all his own treasures and the treasures of his fathers on charity. His brothers and other members of his family reproached him: 'Your fathers stored away treasures, adding to the treasures of their fathers, and you squander them!' He replied: 'My fathers stored away for the world below, while I am storing away for the world above. My fathers stored away in a place where the hand of others can prevail, while I have stored away in a place where the hand of others cannot prevail. My fathers stored away something that produces no fruit, while I have stored away something that does produce fruit. My fathers stored away treasures of money, while I have stored away treasures of souls.'[23]

Judaism represents a highly distinctive approach to the idea of equality, namely that it is best served not by equality of income or wealth, nor even of opportunity. Nor is it sufficient that we each have equal standing before God at times of prayer, and before the law in cases of dispute. A society must ensure equal dignity – the Hebrew phrase is *kavod habriyot*, 'human honour' – to each of its members. 'The great concern of Moses', wrote Henry George, 'was to lay the foundation of a social state in which deep poverty and degrading want should be unknown.'[24]

This is a constant theme of the prophets. Amos, one of the first literary prophets, says in his most famous oracle, 'They sell the righteous for silver, and the needy for a pair of shoes. They trample on the heads of the poor as upon the dust of the ground, and deny justice to the oppressed' (Amos 2:7). Isaiah says, 'The Lord enters into judgement with the elders and princes of His people: "It is you who have devoured the vineyard, the spoil of the poor is in your houses. What do you mean by crushing My people, by grinding the face of the poor?" says the Lord God of hosts' (Is. 3:15). Jeremiah says simply of the reforming king Josiah, 'He judged the cause of the poor and needy; then it was well. Is this not to know Me? says the Lord' (Jer. 22:16).

At the end of his long and detailed analysis of early Israel, Norman Gottwald comes to the conclusion that its faith is 'the distinctive self-consciousness of a society of equals'. Israel, he says, '*thought* it was different because it *was* different: it constituted an egalitarian social system in the midst of stratified societies.'[25] To be sure, that equality was never total and was always at risk. That is the constant refrain of the prophets – themselves testimony to Judaism's underlying egalitarianism in their willingness to confront kings and 'speak truth to power'. Yet Jewry did succeed, more than most, in sustaining the dignity of its members through suffering and poverty. One vignette is revealing – Melvin Urofsky's description of Brandeis's reaction to the East European Jewish immigrants to the United States when he first encountered them in his role as mediator of the New York garment-workers' strike of 1910:

> While going through the lofts, he heard numerous quarrels between workers and their bosses, and was amazed that they treated one another more like equals than as inferiors and superiors. In one argument an employee shouted at the owner, '*Ihr darft sich shemen! Past dos far a Yid?*' ('You should be ashamed! Is this worthy of a Jew?'), while another time a machine operator lectured his employer with a quotation from Isaiah: 'It is you who have devoured the vineyard, the spoil of the poor is in your houses. What do you mean by crushing My people, by grinding the face of the poor? says the Lord God of hosts.'[26]

J. L. Peretz's story ('and maybe even higher') captures one vital fact about the role of *tzedakah* in the religious life. Justice-as-charity is a religious act, not merely a social one. We worship God not only in prayer, but also by how we act in the world. The nineteenth-century biblical commentator R. Zvi Hirsch Mecklenburg gave a striking interpretation of Genesis 1. That chapter sets out creation as a series of stages in which God says, 'Let there be . . .' and there is, and 'God saw that it was good.' Mecklenburg notes that the word 'that' in biblical Hebrew more often means 'because'. God saw, not '*that* it was good' but '*because* he is good'.[27] *To be good is to do good.* God created the world so that others could enjoy it. Goodness is not an attribute of the soul but a way of acting and creating: creating happiness for other people, mitigating their distress, removing even a fraction of the world's pain. We worship God *spiritually* by helping his creations *physically*. That is why, when the Temple was destroyed and the sacrifices came to an end, *tzedakah* became a substitute:

> R. Dostai son of R. Yannai taught: Consider the difference between the Holy One and a king of flesh and blood. If a man brings a present to the king, it may or may not be accepted. Even if it is

accepted, it remains doubtful whether the man will be admitted into the king's presence. Not so with the Holy One. A person who gives even a small coin to a beggar is deemed worthy of being admitted to behold the divine presence, as it is written, 'I shall behold Your face through charity, and when I awake, shall be satisfied with Your likeness' (Ps. 17:15).

R. Eleazar used to give a coin to a poor man and only then recite his prayer, because, he said, it is written, 'I, through charity, shall behold Your face.'[28]

Charity is a form of prayer, a preliminary to prayer. With its combination of charity and justice, its understanding of the psychological as well as material dimensions of poverty and its aim of restoring dignity and independence, not just meeting needs, *tzedakah* is a unique institution. Deeply humanitarian, it could not exist without the essentially religious concepts of divine ownership and social covenant. To know God is to act with justice and compassion, to recognize his image in other people and to hear the silent cry of those in need. The Mishnaic sage R. Judah bar Ilai gave this poetic expression:

There are ten strong things in the world:
Rock is strong, but iron breaks it.
Iron is strong, but fire melts it.
Fire is strong, but water extinguishes it.
Water is strong, but the clouds carry it.
The clouds are strong, but the wind drives them.
The wind is strong, but man withstands it.
Man is strong, but fear weakens him.
Fear is strong, but wine removes it.
Wine is strong, but sleep overcomes it.
Sleep is strong, but death stands over it.
What is stronger than death?
Acts of charity (*tzedakah*), for it is written, '*Tzedakah* delivers from death.' (Prov. 10:2)[29]

A later sage noted something strange about the geography of the Holy Land. There are two seas in Israel: the Dead Sea and the Sea of Galilee. The latter is full of life: fish, birds, vegetation. The former, as its name suggests, contains no life at all. Yet they are both fed by the same river, the Jordan. The difference, he said, is that the Sea of Galilee receives water at one end and gives out water at the other. The Dead Sea receives but does not give. The Jordan ends there. To receive without reciprocating is a kind of death. To live is to give.

The story is told of the great fifteenth-century Jewish diplomat and scholar Don Isaac Abrabanel (1437–1508), chancellor to King Ferdinand and Queen Isabella of Castile, that he was once asked by the king how much he owned. He named a certain sum.

'But surely', the king said, 'you own much more than that.'

'You asked me', Abrabanel replied, 'how much I owned. The property I have, I do not own. Your majesty may seize it from me tomorrow. At best I am its temporary guardian. The sum I mentioned is what I have given away in charity. That merit alone, neither you nor any earthly power can take away from me.'

We own what we are willing to share. That is *tzedakah*: charity as justice.

NOTES

1. Cited in Reuven Bulka, *Work, Life, Suffering and Death* (Northvale, NJ: Jason Aaronson, 1998), p. 185
2. I summarize the story to remove the deliberately archaic and satirical style in which Peretz relates it. An English translation can be found in J. H. Hertz, *A Book of Jewish Thoughts* (London: Oxford University Press, 1926), pp. 230–3.
3. *Mishneh Torah, Mattenot Ani'im* 9:3.
4. Ibid., 10:2.
5. Jerusalem Talmud, *Shekalim* 1:5; *Yalkut Shimoni, Terumah* 368.
6. Friedrich Hayek, *The Fatal Conceit* (London: Routledge, 1988), pp. 106–19.
7. Babylonian Talmud, *Nedarim* 7b.
8. Babylonian Talmud, *Baba Batra* 116a.
9. *Shemot Rabbah* 31:14.
10. Babylonian Talmud, *Yoma* 35b.
11. Babylonian Talmud, *Ta'anit* 24b.
12. Mishnah, *Avot* 3:17.
13. Maimonides, *The Guide for the Perplexed*, III:27.
14. Jerusalem Talmud, *Kiddushin* 4:12.
15. Babylonian Talmud, *Baba Batra* 10a.
16. Babylonian Talmud, *Megillah* 31a.
17. See Avishai Margalit, *The Decent Society* (Cambridge, MA: Harvard University Press, 1996).
18. *Mishneh Torah, Mattenot Ani'im* 10:7–14. For a readable and engaging contemporary presentation, see Julie Salamon, *Rambam's Ladder: a meditation on generosity and why it is necessary to give* (New York: Workman, 2003).
19. *The Authorised Daily Prayer Book of United Hebrew Congregations of the Commonwealth*, centenary edition (London: United Synagogue, 1992), p. 730.
20. Babylonian Talmud, *Moed Katan* 27b.
21. Mishnah, *Ta'anit* 4:8.
22. *Mishneh Torah, Mattenot Ani'im* 7:5; see also ibid., *Shekalim* 1:1.

23. Babylonian Talmud, *Baba Batra* 11a.
24. Henry George, *Moses: a lecture* (Berlin: J. Harrwitz, 1899).
25. Norman Gottwald, *The Tribes: a sociology of the religion of liberated Israel 1250–1050 BCE* (London: SCM Press, 1980), p. 693.
26. Melvin Urofsky, *American Zionism from Herzl to the Holocaust* (Garden City: Anchor Press, 1975).
27. Zvi Hirsch Mecklenburg, *Ha-Ktav veha-Kabbalah* (Jerusalem: Am Olam, 1969), p. 3b.
28. Babylonian Talmud, *Baba Batra* 10a.
29. Ibid.

Chapter 4

Love as Deed

For I desire loving-kindness, not sacrifice,
Acknowledgement of God, rather than burnt offerings.
(Hosea 6:6)

In 1966 an 11-year-old black boy moved with his parents and family to a white neighbourhood in Washington. Sitting with his two brothers and two sisters on the front step of the house, he waited to see how they would be greeted. They were not. Passers-by turned to look at them but no one gave them a smile or even a glance of recognition. All the fearful stories he had heard about how whites treated blacks seemed to be coming true. Years later, writing about those first days in their new home, he says, 'I knew we were not welcome here. I knew we would not be liked here. I knew we would have no friends here. I knew we should not have moved here . . .'

As he was thinking those thoughts, a white woman coming home from work passed by on the other side of the road. She turned to the children and with a broad smile said, 'Welcome!' Disappearing into the house, she emerged minutes later with a tray laden with drinks and cream cheese and jelly sandwiches which she brought over to the children, making them feel at home. That moment – the young man later wrote – changed his life. It gave him a sense of belonging where there was none before. It made him realize, at a time when race relations in the United States were still fraught, that a black family could feel at home in a white area and that there could be relationships that were colour-blind. Over the years, he learned to admire much about the woman across the street, but it was that first spontaneous act of greeting that became, for him, a definitive memory. It broke down a wall of separation and turned strangers into friends.[1]

The young man, Stephen Carter, is now a law professor at Yale, and he eventually wrote a book about what he learned that day. He called it *Civility*. The name of the woman, he tells us, was Sara Kestenbaum, and she

44

died all too young. He adds that she was a religious Jew. 'In the Jewish
tradition', he notes, such civility is called '*hessed* – the doing of acts of
kindness – which is in turn derived from the understanding that human
beings are made in the image of God.' Civility, he adds, 'itself may be
seen as part of *hessed*: it does indeed require kindnesses toward our
fellow citizens, including the ones who are strangers, and even when it is
hard'.[2] Reflecting on the loss of civility in contemporary society he
comes to the conclusion that it needs the encouragement of a religious
tradition:

> Nothing in contemporary secular conversation calls us to give up
> anything truly valuable for anybody else . . . Only religion offers a
> sacred language of sacrifice-selflessness-awe that enables believers
> to treat their fellow citizens as fellow passengers. But even if religion
> is the engine of civility, it has too few serious practitioners, which is
> why those who are truly moved by it to love their fellow human
> beings are so special. I learned that truth in 1966, and, to this day, I
> can close my eyes and feel on my tongue the smooth, slick sweetness
> of the cream cheese and jelly sandwiches that I gobbled on that
> summer afternoon when I discovered how a single act of genuine
> and unassuming civility can change a life for ever.[3]

Carter's point is, of course, general. Many religious traditions emphasize
acts of kindness, and generosity of spirit is part of what makes us human.
But I found his story moving. I never knew Sara Kestenbaum, but years
after I had read Carter's book I gave a lecture to the Jewish community in
the part of Washington where she had lived. I told them Carter's story,
which they had not heard before. But they nodded in recognition. 'Yes',
one said, 'that's the kind of thing Sara would do.'

*　　　　　*　　　　　*

What is *hessed*? It is usually translated as 'kindness' but it also means
'love' – not love as emotion or passion, but love expressed as deed. Theologians define *hessed* as *covenant love*. Covenant is the bond by which two
parties pledge themselves to one another, each respecting the freedom
and integrity of the other, agreeing to join their separate destinies into a
single journey that they will travel together, 'fearing no evil, for You are
with me' (Ps. 23:4). Unlike a contract, it is an open-ended relationship
lived toward an unknown future. In one of the loveliest lines in the
prophetic literature God says to Israel through Jeremiah, 'I remember
the kindness [*hessed*] of your youth, the love of your betrothal – how you
were willing to follow Me through the desert in an unsown land' (Jer. 2:2).
Hessed is the love that is loyalty, and the loyalty that is love. It is born in the

45

generosity of faithfulness, the love that means being ever-present for the other, in hard times as well as good; love that grows stronger, not weaker, over time. It is love moralized into small gestures of help and understanding, support and friendship: the poetry of everyday life written in the language of simple deeds. Those who know it experience the world differently from those who do not. It is not for them a threatening and dangerous place. It is one where trust is rewarded precisely because it does not seek reward. *Hessed* is the gift of love that begets love.

More even than *tzedakah*, the concept of *hessed* in Judaism is learned from the acts of God himself:

> R. Hama son of R. Haninah said, What does [the Torah] mean when it says, *You shall walk after the Lord your God* (Deut. 13:5)? Is it possible for a human being to walk after the divine presence? Does it not say, *For the Lord your God is a consuming fire* (Deut. 4:24)? Rather, the meaning is: you shall walk after the attributes of the Holy One, blessed be He.
>
> Just as He clothes the naked, as is written, *And the Lord God made for Adam and his wife garments of skin and clothed them* (Gen. 3:21), so shall you clothe the naked.
>
> Just as He visits the sick, as is written, *And the Lord appeared to him by the oaks of Mamre* (Gen. 18:1), so you visit the sick.
>
> Just as the Holy One, blessed be He, comforts the mourners, as is written, *And it came to pass after the death of Abraham, that God blessed Isaac his son* (Gen. 25:11), so you comfort mourners.
>
> Just as the Holy One, blessed be He, buries the dead, as is written, *And He buried him [Moses] in the valley* (Deut. 34:6), so you bury the dead.[4]

Where *tzedakah* is a gift or loan of money, *hessed* is the gift of the person. It costs less and more: less because its gestures often cost little or nothing, more because it takes time and attention, existential generosity, the gift of self to self. More than anything else, *hessed* humanizes the world. The biblical vignettes cited by the Talmud belong to an age when, outside Israel, the gods were seen as powers to be found in nature, terrifying in their capacity to create havoc and destruction, at best indifferent, at worst hostile to humankind. That God is to be found in acts of *hessed*, loving care, must have been almost unintelligible, yet that is how the patriarchs and matriarchs experienced the divine presence. It is also how they communicated it.

Sara Kestenbaum's welcoming gesture belongs to a long tradition that began in the famous scene in Genesis, when Abraham, sitting at the entrance of his tent in the heat of midday, sees three strangers passing by, runs to greet them and brings them food to eat and water to drink (Gen.

18:1–3). He did not know that they were angels. The text describes them at that point simply as 'men', as if to imply that Abraham and Sarah were the kind of people who treated all visitors as if they might be angels. That is no small part of why they were chosen to be the grandparents of a new kind of faith.

'You are', said God through the prophet Isaiah, 'My witnesses' (Is. 43:10) – not by seeking to convert those of another faith, but simply by reaching out to embrace the image of God in another human being, by seeing the divine Other in the human other, because that is how God reveals himself. Abraham and Sarah, say the sages, brought God into the world without metaphysical arguments or theological proofs, awesome miracles or military victories, but by welcoming strangers and giving them food and shelter. When their guests were about to leave, they would begin to thank the couple but they would reply, 'Don't thank us; thank God whose blessings we have shared.'[5] That was all, and it was enough.

Hessed is born in the phrase in the second chapter of Genesis, 'It is not good for man to be alone.' The duality of the human condition is not just that we are body conjoined with soul, 'the dust of the earth' joined to 'the breath of God'. It is also that we are self-conscious and therefore capable of being lonely, not just alone. *Homo sapiens* is uniquely creative yet also uniquely vulnerable. There is something incomplete within the self that seeks completion in an other. That cannot be achieved by power, forcing the other to do our will, for that humiliates the other by treating him or her as an extension of ourselves. It can only be achieved by conferring dignity on the other, by bringing him or her a gift that – whatever its tangible form – is really the offer of our person. *Hessed* is the redemption of solitude, the bridge we build across the ontological abyss between I and Thou.

*   *   *

In the long centuries between the destruction of the Second Temple and the dawn of European Emancipation, Jewish communities were largely built around *hessed* activities, each of which had its own *chevrah* or fellowship. In seventeenth-century Rome, for example, there were seven societies dedicated to the provision of clothes, shoes, linen, beds and warm winter bed-coverings for children, the poor, widows and prisoners. There were two societies providing trousseaus, dowries and the loan of jewellery to poor brides. There was one for visiting the sick, another bringing help to families who had suffered bereavement, and others to perform the last rites for those who had died – purification before burial, and the burial service itself. Eleven fellowships existed for educational and religious aims, study and prayer; another raised alms for Jews living in the Holy Land; others were involved in the various activities associated with the circumcision of newborn boys. Yet others provided the poor with the means to fulfil certain commands, such as mezuzot for their doors, oil for the Hanukkah lights and candles for the Sabbath.[6]

Particular concern was taken to visit the sick, an activity invested with immense sensitivity and religious depth. The following passages from the *Shulhan Arukh,* Joseph Caro's authoritative code of law, give some sense of the reverence in which the command was held:

1. It is a religious duty to visit the sick. Relatives and close friends should enter at once, others after three days. If the illness is serious, both groups can visit him at once.
2. Even a distinguished person should visit a humble one. The more one visits the more praiseworthy it is, provided only that the visits do not become a burden to the patient . . .
3. One who visits the sick should not sit upon a bed or chair or on a stool but should sit in front of the patient, for the divine presence rests above a sick person . . .
4. One should not visit the sick during the first three hours of the day, for every patient's illness is alleviated in the morning, and consequently he (the visitor) will not trouble himself to pray for him; and not during the last three hours of the day, for then his illness grows worse and one will give up hope of praying for him.[7]

The treatment of the sick was a fundamental priority. Doctors would treat the poor without charge. Communal funds – they came to be known as *hekdesh,* the same term used in an earlier age for donations to the Temple – were put aside for the maintenance of hospices. In late medieval times the Jewish communities of Turkey, Italy, Germany, Poland and the Netherlands maintained hospitals, communal physicians, nurses, midwives and visitation societies.[8] The sages ruled that communities were permitted to divert gifts or legacies given for the building of a synagogue to the construction of a hospital or any other form of aid to the sick.

Another concern, going back to the Bible, was for the welfare of widows and orphans, those least able to take care of themselves. Often, communities would appoint senior figures to look after their affairs, managing what funds they had, monitoring their resources, and ensuring that their needs were taken care of. In some communities these were known as the 'fathers of orphans'. The rabbi of the town was also charged with responsibility. In Hesse-Cassel, for example, each newly appointed spiritual leader had to take an oath on assuming office, containing the following paragraph:

I wish to take faithful care of Jewish widows and orphans in all matters under my jurisdiction, and see to it that they [the orphans] be placed by the authorities under capable and reliable guardians, that they be raised in the observance of Jewish law and ceremonies, and that their property be administered faithfully and suffer from no embezzlement.[9]

Another dimension of *hessed*, one that linked Jewish communities in a global network of mutual responsibility, was the ransoming of captives. This too goes back to Abraham, who fought a war to release his nephew Lot, and it became a persistent and tragic feature of Jewish life. At times it placed huge financial burdens on Jewry, made all the worse by the fact that, knowing that others would come to their aid, bandits and governments alike became all the readier to seize Jews as a sure way of earning ransom money. Communities wrestled with this dilemma – how to honour their duty without at the same time encouraging the very phenomenon they were fighting against – but in the end duty prevailed. The thought of leaving their brothers and sisters without help was, for Jews, ultimately unthinkable. They shared, indeed their very peoplehood was defined by, mutual responsibility. Israel Abrahams tells the story of one typical episode:

> When towards the end of the fifteenth century Alfonso V of Portugal captured the African seaports, Arzilla and Tangier, he carried off 250 Jews of both sexes and every age, and sold them as slaves throughout the kingdom. The Portuguese Jews applied to Yechiel of Pisa, financier and philanthropist, and he generously assisted his brethren. Lisbon Jews formed a representative committee of twelve members, and the famous statesman-scholar Don Isaac Abrabanel himself travelled over the whole country and redeemed the Jewish slaves, often at a high price. The ransomed Jews and Jewesses, adults and children, were clothed, lodged, and maintained until they had learned the language of the country and were able to support themselves.[10]

Lastly, of course, there was hospitality. By an ingenious reading of the opening verses of Genesis 18, in which Abraham is first visited by God, then by three passers-by, the sages concluded that Abraham interrupted his conversation with God to look after the needs of his visitors, from which they concluded, 'Greater is hospitality than receiving the divine presence itself.'[11] *Hessed* in its many forms became synonymous with Jewish life and one of the pillars on which it stood. Divine command and historical exigency met: Jews performed kindnesses to one another because it was 'the way of God' and also because they or their families had had intimate experience of suffering and knew they had nowhere else to turn. It provided an access of grace in dark times. More than that, it compensated for the loss of the Temple and its rites:

Once, as R. Yohanan was walking out of Jerusalem, R. Joshua followed him. Seeing the Temple in ruins, he cried, 'Woe to us that this place is in ruins, the place where atonement was made for Israel's iniquities.' R. Yohanan said to him: 'My son, do not grieve, for we have another means of atonement which is no less effective. What is it? It is deeds of loving-kindness, about which Scripture says, "I desire loving-kindness and not sacrifice"' (Hos. 6:6).[12]

Through *hessed*, Jews humanized fate as once, they believed, God's *hessed* had humanized the world.

*   *   *   *   *

Hessed is a different kind of virtue from *tzedakah*. The sages identified some of the differences:

Our masters taught: loving-kindness [*hessed*] is greater than charity [*tzedakah*] in three ways. Charity is done with one's money, while loving-kindness may be done with one's money or with one's person. Charity is done only to the poor, while loving-kindness may be given both to the poor and to the rich. Charity is given only to the living, while loving-kindness may be shown to the living and the dead.[13]

The distinction goes deeper than this, however, and touches on a fundamental principle of Judaism. One way of approaching it is by looking at two key passages in which the Hebrew Bible sets out the terms of the covenant, the first in Genesis, the second in the book of Hosea. In Genesis God says, 'For I have chosen him [Abraham] so that he will direct his children and his household after him to keep the way of the Lord by doing what is *right* and *just*' (18:19). As we saw in the previous chapter, the key words, *tzedakah* and *mishpat*, are about justice. In the book of Hosea God adds two other terms:

I will betroth you to Me for ever.
    I will betroth you to Me in righteousness and justice [*tzedek u-mishpat*], in love and compassion [*hessed ve-rahamim*].
    I will betroth you in faithfulness, and you will know the Lord. (Hos. 2:19–20)

Jewish men say these words each weekday as we wind the tefillin-strap around our finger as a symbolic wedding-ring.
    Something changed in the religious situation from the days of Abraham to the time of Hosea. *Hessed* and *rahamim*, love and compassion,

50

had been added to the vocabulary of the religious life. That cannot be because Abraham was unaware of the notion of *hessed*. He knew it and practised it. When he sent his servant to find a wife for Isaac, the servant chose an act of *hessed* as a test of who would be appropriate: the woman who, when he approached her asking for water, would give it not only to him but also to his camels. Abraham valued and lived a life of *hessed*, but it had not yet become part of the structure of the covenant. Why so?

Judaism has a unique dual structure of ethics. On the one hand there is the covenant of Noah, which binds all humanity on the basis of seven fundamental commands (I discuss these in Chapter 9). On the other is the Abrahamic and later Sinai covenant that binds Jews by a more detailed and demanding system of commands. Judaism is constituted by this basic tension between the universal and the particular. Its way of life is intensely particular, yet its God and ultimate gaze are universal, concerned with all humankind, indeed all creation. How are we to understand the significance of this duality?

Helpful in this context is the distinction suggested by the Israeli philosopher Avishai Margalit between *morality* and *ethics*. Morality refers to the universal principles we use in dealings with humanity in general: our relationships with strangers. Ethics, by contrast, refers to our relationships with those with whom we share a special bond of shared memory and belonging: family, friends, fellow countrymen, or people with whom we share a faith. The two systems have a different tonality: 'Morality is greatly concerned, for example, with respect and humiliation . . . Ethics, on the other hand, is greatly concerned with loyalty and betrayal . . .'[14] This is the best way of understanding the difference between *tzedek* and *mishpat* on the one hand, *hessed* and *rahamim* on the other. *Tzedek* and *mishpat* belong to morality. *Hessed* and *rahamim* belong to ethics. The former are about justice, the latter about loving attention, for which the simplest English term is *care*. Justice is and must be impersonal. 'You shall not recognize persons in judgement', says Deuteronomy (16:19). The beauty of justice is that it belongs to a world of order constructed out of universal rules through which each of us stands equally before the law. *Hessed*, by contrast, is intrinsically personal. We cannot care for the sick, bring comfort to the distressed or welcome a visitor impersonally. If we do so, it merely shows that we have not understood what these activities are. Justice demands disengagement (Adam Smith spoke of adopting the standpoint of an 'impartial spectator'). *Hessed* is an act of engagement. Justice is best administered without emotion. *Hessed* exists only in virtue of emotion, empathy and sympathy, feeling-with and feeling-for. We act with kindness because we know what it feels like to be in need of kindness. We comfort the mourners because we know what it is to mourn. *Hessed* requires not detached rationality but emotional intelligence.

Abraham and Sarah, founders of a faith, did not yet live among fellow believers. Outside their own household there were few if any. Their role in history was to relate to a world that did not share their vision. The sages interpreted the phrase 'Abraham the Hebrew [*ha-ivri*]' as meaning, 'the rest of the world was on one side [*ever*] and he on the other'.[15] Their mode of engagement was with a world of strangers. Therefore they were charged with living by a morality for strangers, namely *tzedek* and *mishpat*. By the time of the prophet Hosea, centuries later, Israel was no longer a family but a nation in covenant with one another and with God. They were bound in a web of thick relationships anchored in shared memory, a common code, a joint faith and collective aspiration. They had not only a morality but also an ethic. They were not only strangers but neighbours and friends, brothers and sisters in a society envisaged as an extended family. Therefore, in addition to the universals of morality they were bound also by the particularities of ethics, the code of care, defined by the words *hessed* and *rahamim*. That is the historical change Hosea notes in his description of God's love.

Hessed is one of the Torah's most important framing devices. The Mosaic books, as the sages noted, begin and end with an act of kindness on the part of God. He makes clothes for Adam and Eve as they are about to leave paradise. He personally attends to the burial of Moses after he has taken him to the top of Mount Pisgah to see from afar the land to which he has been travelling for 40 years but will not be destined to enter. The significance of these scenes of tender concern on the part of God are not incidental to the narrative but of its essence. God is He-who-cares. He has given his word, his book, to a people so that it will become a nation-that-cares.

Hessed also makes an appearance at two crucial points in Israel's history. It is the central theme of the encounter between Abraham's servant and Rebekah, the woman who will give birth to the son who will give his name to the people Israel. It is also the central motif of the book of Ruth (the word *hessed* appears three times in the book, as it does in the scene where Rebekah and Abraham's servant meet): 'R. Ze'era said, the scroll of Ruth tells us nothing of the laws of cleanness or uncleanness, of what is prohibited or permitted. Why then was it written? To teach you how great is the reward of those who do deeds of kindness.'[16] The kindness that brought Ruth and Boaz together gave birth, seven generations later, to Israel's greatest king, David. These strategically placed episodes – events that prefigure Israel's birth, first as a family, then as a kingdom – tell us that despite the Torah's insistence on justice as the foundation of society, there is something prior to justice and to society itself, namely the gossamer strands of kindness that link self to self in bonds of love.

The Torah is an extended wrestling with the question of human association. Each of us is the image of God, but each of us is also incomplete, and therefore we seek the company of others. Out of this come the gradually widening forms of association: marriage, the family, the tribe, the community, society and the state. One of the key questions the Torah addresses is: how do we create associations that honour both self and other, 'I' and 'Thou'? To this there have been, and still are, two primary answers: economics and politics, the market and the state. People come together in order to trade. This creates the market. They also come together to defend themselves against enemies without and chaos within. This creates the state. Economics is about the production and distribution of wealth. Politics is about the concentration and distribution of power. But neither is adequate to the fundamental dilemma: how do I create a lasting relationship of mutuality and trust with an other while honouring his or her freedom and dignity? If I pay another to do my will (economics) I have not created an enduring bond. Likewise if I coerce the other by the use, real or threatened, of force (politics). In both cases, what is operative is the self-interest of two persons, not a sharing of their concerns into a conjoint 'We'.

The Torah gives a third answer – covenant – and we are now in a position better to understand its centrality and depth. In the second half of the twentieth century a whole series of disciplines – sociobiology, games theory and the Iterated Prisoner's Dilemma, economics, sociology and political theory – converged on a central idea that ran counter to classical economics, Darwinian biology and the theory of rational action. The idea, from Adam Smith's *Wealth of Nations* onward, had been that progress was made by individuals acting to maximize their own private satisfactions. Seeking our own survival or gain, we were led as if by an 'invisible hand' to create an order in which the totality – the economy, society or the ecosystem – gained as a whole.

It was the discovery of a paradox known as the Prisoner's Dilemma that showed how individuals, each acting in their own best interest, created an outcome that was bad, not good, for all concerned. Two men, arrested on suspicion of a crime, would inform on each other with the result that both would suffer prolonged prison sentences. The form of the dilemma was not important, but the insight it afforded was. In addition to competition, any group in order to flourish needs to develop habits of cooperation – and these in turn depend on trust. Economists call this 'social capital'. Sociobiologists call it 'reciprocal altruism'. Political theorists speak of community or civil society. I use the phrase *covenantal relationships*.[17]

The difference between politics and economics on the one hand, and covenantal relationships on the other, can be seen by a simple arithmetic thought-experiment. If I have total power and then share it with nine others, I am left with only a tenth of what I had to begin with. If I have a thousand pounds and share it with nine others, again I am left with a tenth of what I had. But if I share with nine others, not power or wealth but *friendship* or *kindness* or *influence* or *love*, I find I have not less, but more. These 'spiritual goods' are unique in that the more we share, the more we have.

The great Jewish institutions – the home, the synagogue, the community and the school – are all like this. They are environments in which we are bound to one another not by transactions of power or wealth but by *hessed*, covenant love. These are the places where we learn the intimate grammar of reciprocity, the delicate choreography of ethical intelligence, the knowledge that love given is not given in vain, and that by sharing our vulnerabilities we discover strength.

That is the point the Torah is making when it sets at key moments in its narrative, stories of *hessed*. Societies are only human and humanizing when they are a community of communities built on face-to-face encounters – covenantal relationships. Emmanuel Levinas was right to see the concept of 'face' as fundamental to our humanity.[18] Society is faceless; *hessed* is a relationship of face to face. The Pentateuch repeatedly emphasizes that we cannot see God face to face. It follows that we can only see God in the face of another. There it is hidden enough yet sufficiently real for us to construct a humanizing relationship. A British politician once asked me how I would define community. I replied, 'A community is where they *know your name* and where they *miss you when you are not there.*' Community is society with a human face.

There is a strange and lovely detail in the construction of the sanctuary. The holiest item of its furniture was the ark. It contained the holiest of objects, the tablets on which were written God's word, both the second set that remained whole, and the first that were shattered into fragments. Above the ark were two figures, cherubim. The Torah says that 'their faces were turned to one another' (Ex. 25:20). Ostensibly this was a great risk. The Israelites had been told not to make any likeness that might be worshipped as a god, an idol. The sanctuary itself was constructed in the aftermath of such an episode, the making of the Golden Calf. Why then were figures introduced into the Holy of Holies?

The sages say they were like children,[19] or, in another interpretation, that they were intertwined like lovers.[20] It was *between the two cherubs* that God spoke to Moses. The message of this symbol was so significant that it was deemed by God himself to be sufficient to outweigh the risk of misunderstanding. *God speaks where two persons turn their face to one another* in love, embrace, generosity and care. God's presence is everywhere. But not everywhere are we ready to receive it. When we open our 'I' to another's 'Thou' – that is where God lives. We discover God's image in ourself by discerning it in an other. God lives in *the between* that joins self to self through an act of covenantal kindness. That is *hessed*, the physical deed in which soul touches soul and the universe acquires a personal face.

*   *   *

At the third Sabbath meal, as the day grew dark and the mood intense, one of the hassidim turned to the Rebbe with a question he had long wanted to ask but had not had the courage to do so until now: 'Rebbe, why does the Messiah not come?'

'Why do you ask, my son?'

'Because', he replied, 'in the past perhaps we were not ready. The world was not ready. The hour was not right. But now, after the Holocaust, and the return of Jews to their land, has the time not come?'

'What do you mean?' the Rebbe asked, his face unchanging but his gaze intent.

The hassid continued: 'What I mean is – do we not read in the holy Talmud that at the end of days the Holy One, blessed be He, will bring against the Jewish people a king whose decrees will be as harsh as Haman's – and did that not happen? Was not Hitler just such a king and were his decrees not just as harsh? And did not our holy teacher Moses say that at the end of exile God will gather us in? Did he not say, "Even if you have been banished to the most distant land under the heavens, from there the Lord your God will gather you and bring you back"? And has this too not occurred, now that Jews have returned to Israel from more than a hundred different lands? Why then does the Messiah not come?'

'I will tell you, my son', said the Rebbe. 'How *could* the Messiah come? Consider: If he were a hassid of one sect, the hassidim of the other sects would not recognize him. If he were a hassid of any kind, the mitnagdim, their opponents, would not recognize him. If he were Orthodox, the Reform Jews would not recognize him. If he were religious, the secular Jews would not recognize him. How then can he come?

'And now', continued the Rebbe, 'I will tell you a great secret.' The Rebbe dropped his voice to a whisper. '*It is not we who are waiting for the Messiah. It is the Messiah who is waiting for us.* He has been here all the time. It is we who are not yet ready for him.'

Before the hassid could reply, the Rebbe continued: 'And now let me ask you a question. What would you do if the Messiah *did* arrive? Would you not greet him as a long-lost, long-awaited friend? Would you not invite him in as a royal guest and do the utmost to pay him honour and be honoured beyond measure by his presence?'

'Of course', replied the hassid. 'Can the Rebbe doubt it?'

'Well,' said the Rebbe, 'I will tell you what you must do and teach others to do. Regard every person – familiar or a stranger, young or old, learned or unlearned, observant or unobservant – as if he or she might

55

be the Messiah, for the Messiah will surely come in disguise. If only we would do this, we would find that, without our realizing it, the Messiah had come.'

That, if only we understood it, is the meaning of *hessed* and its power to bathe the world in the light of the divine presence.

NOTES

1. Stephen Carter, *Civility* (New York: Basic Books, 1999), pp. 61–3.
2. Ibid., p. 71.
3. Ibid., p. 75.
4. Babylonian Talmud, *Sotah* 14a.
5. *Sifre*, Deut. 32; *Genesis Rabbah* 39:14.
6. Israel Abrahams, *Jewish Life in the Middle Ages* (London: Edward Goldston, 1932), pp. 348–63.
7. *Shulhan Arukh Yoreh Deah* 335.
8. Salo Baron, *The Jewish Community* (Philadelphia: Jewish Publication Society of America, 1945), vol. 2, pp. 325–33.
9. Ibid., p. 330.
10. Abrahams, *Jewish Life*, pp. 360–1.
11. Babylonian Talmud, *Shabbat* 127a.
12. *Avot de-Rabbi Natan* 4.
13. Babylonian Talmud, *Sukkah* 49b.
14. Avishai Margalit, *The Ethics of Memory* (Cambridge, MA: Harvard University Press, 2002), p. 8. The argument is modelled on the famous distinction made by Clifford Geertz in his *The Interpretation of Cultures* (London: Fontana, 1993), pp. 3–32, between 'thin' and 'thick' moral concepts. For Margalit, morality is 'thin', ethics 'thick'.
15. *Genesis Rabbah* 42:8.
16. *Ruth Rabbah* 2:14.
17. I tell the story in my *The Politics of Hope*, second ed. (London: Vintage, 2000), pp. 233–44, and *The Dignity of Difference* (London: Continuum, 2003), pp. 142–60.
18. Emmanuel Levinas, *Humanism of the Other* (Urbana and Chicago: University of Illinois Press, 2003). Levinas' philosophy on this point is discussed in Jeffrey Bloechl (ed.), *The Face of the Other and the Trace of God* (New York: Fordham University Press, 2000).
19. Babylonian Talmud, *Hagigah* 13b.
20. Babylonian Talmud, *Yoma* 54a.

Chapter 5

Sanctifying the Name

The Jew should remember that the glory of God is, as it were,
entrusted to his care and that every Israelite holds the honour of his
faith and of his entire people in his hands.

(J. H. Hertz)[1]

I first came to know the Feuersteins when, early in my rabbinical career, I
spent time in Boston, Mass. I was impressed by many of the families there
and their ability to combine Jewish learning and strong religious observance with a thoroughgoing engagement in the wider society in the
academic world, business, law, and medicine. One of the great challenges
for any faith is how to maintain a creative dialogue between 'the world'
and 'the holy' so that each enriches the other. The Boston Jewish community was a fine example of how it can be done.

In this environment, the Feuersteins had an honoured place. They
were respected business people: generous philanthropists, admired for
their leadership within the community. I cherished an interpretation
Mo Feuerstein offered (he had heard it, I think, from Rabbi Joseph
Soloveitchik) of one of the most difficult lines in the Bible: 'I was young
and now am old, yet I have never seen the righteous forsaken or their
children begging for bread' (Ps. 37:25). Edmund Blunden, the First
World War poet, wrote an ironic commentary on it:

> I have been young, and now am not too old;
> And I have seen the righteous forsaken,
> His health, his honour and his quality taken.
> This is not what we were formerly told.[2]

The verb 'seen' [*ra'iti*] in this verse, said Feuerstein, is to be understood
in the same sense as in the book of Esther: 'How can I bear to see [*ra'iti*]

57

disaster fall on my people?' (Esth. 8:6). 'To see' here means 'to stand still and watch'. The verse should thus be translated, 'I was young and now am old, but I never merely *stood still and watched* while the righteous was forsaken or his children begged for bread.' It was a lovely insight, central to the theme of this book.[3]

Back in Britain I heard little of the Feuersteins until a news-cutting caught my eye. In late 1995, the textile mill the family owned in Lawrence suffered a devastating fire – the worst in Massachusetts for more than a century. By then, most of the textile mills in New England had closed. There was cheaper labour to be had in Mexico, India or Asia. Many assumed that the owner, Aaron Feuerstein, by then 70 years old, would simply take the opportunity to collect the insurance and close the mill. What caught the headlines was his principled decision not to do so. The business was a major employer in the town – 1,800 people worked in it – and he felt a strong sense of responsibility to them and their families. He announced, first, that the mill would be rebuilt; second, that for the next 60 days all employees would be paid their full salaries; third, that their health insurance had already been paid. It would be good to be able to say that virtue was rewarded. In strictly economic terms it was not: the business faced ongoing difficulties. But Aaron Feuerstein kept his word and became known as 'the *mensch* of Malden Mills'.[4]

Everyone knew that he was a religious man, and that he had religious reasons for doing what he did. 'You are not permitted to oppress the working man', he said when explaining his decision, 'because he's poor and needy, amongst your brethren and amongst the non-Jews in your community.' There is a colloquial Jewish phrase for such conduct: *Kiddush ha-Shem*, literally 'sanctifying the name' of God. It refers to behaviour that creates respect for God. The Talmud associates it with the command, 'You shall love the Lord your God' (Deut. 6:5), which it interprets as meaning, among other things, 'You shall cause the Lord your God to be loved':

> 'And you shall love the Lord your God' – this means that the name of Heaven shall be beloved because of you. If someone studies Scripture and Mishnah and attends on the disciples of the wise, is honest in business and speaks pleasantly to people, what do people say about him? Happy the father who taught him Torah, happy the teacher who taught him Torah, woe to the people who have not studied Torah, for this man has studied Torah – and see how fine are his ways and how righteous his deeds. Of him does Scripture say, 'And he said to me: You are My servant Israel in whom I will be gloried' (Is. 49:3).
>
> But if someone studies Scripture and Mishnah and attends on the disciples of the wise, but is dishonest in business and discourte-

ous in his relations with people, what do people say about him? Woe to him who studied Torah, woe to the father who taught him Torah, woe to his teacher who taught him Torah, for this man has studied Torah – and see how corrupt are his deeds and how ugly his ways. Of him does Scripture say, 'Men said of them, These are the people of the Lord, and are gone forth out of His land.' (Ezek. 36:20)[5]

The significance of this principle is often forgotten. A Jewish lawyer once said to me, 'You have written many books about Judaism but none that answers the question that most concerns me: How am I to serve God in my daily life? I know what it is to serve God at home and in the synagogue. But how do I serve him at work? There is nothing religious about being a lawyer, advising my clients on how best to manage their affairs, drawing up contracts, defending people against whom allegations have been made. I do this five days a week. It takes up the major part of my time. But I cannot see how, doing what I do, I am performing a religious act, advancing the cause of Judaism, or honouring my Creator.'

This question made a deep impact on me. The person who asked it is an exceptional human being, though he would be the last to admit it. He achieved distinction in his legal studies, attended several Jewish academies and is a Judaic scholar of real depth. He is one of the finest fathers I have met, and spends much of his free time studying Talmud with his children. He gives a large part of his salary away to charity, which he does in secret. Generally acknowledged to be one of the best lawyers in his field, he is a man of integrity and high principle who inspires admiration and trust in those for whom he works. He makes no secret of his religious commitments, wears a yarmulka at all times, and keeps Jewish law at all times.

His question was therefore odd, because the answer was so obvious. His work, character and life are a living advertisement for God, and that itself is an ongoing task of the religious life. What we are and do inevitably colour people's perception of faith and God, and to be a positive role-model is an essential element of Judaism. That is something we do or fail to do all the time. So I want in this chapter to explore the idea of 'sanctifying the name'. This will, however, turn out to be far from simple because it brings together several different dimensions from different eras of Jewish life.

*　　　　　*　　　　　*

The command of *Kiddush ha-Shem*, sanctifying God's name, and its opposite *Hillul ha-Shem*, desecrating the name, have their source in the book of Leviticus: 'Be careful regarding My commandments and keep them; I am the Lord. Do not desecrate My holy name. I must be sanctified among the

Israelites. I am the Lord and I am making you holy and bringing you out of Egypt to be your God. I am God' (Lev. 22:32). In its immediate context what this means is that the boundaries separating holy and profane must not be confused. The priests must take care in their sacred vocation. The laws concerning sacrifices in the sanctuary must be scrupulously observed. We recall God's words to Moses at the burning bush: 'Remove your shoes, for the place where you are standing is holy ground.' The sacred is God's domain and must be treated with reverence and respect. In Leviticus, the command has the restrictive meaning of honouring the integrity of sacred times and places.

In the book of Ezekiel, however, the phrase is used in a far broader sense. The prophet speaks about history and about how the fate of Israel is intertwined with, as it were, the standing of God in the world. He says in God's name:

> I dispersed [the Israelites] among the nations, and they were scattered through the countries . . . And wherever they went among the nations they *profaned My holy name*, for it was said of them, 'These are the Lord's people, and yet they had to leave His land.' I had *concern for My holy name*, which the house of Israel profaned among the nations where they had gone. Therefore say to the house of Israel, 'This is what the Sovereign Lord says: It is not for your sake, O house of Israel, that I am going to do these things, but *for the sake of My holy name*, which you have profaned among the nations where you have gone. I will show *the holiness of My great name*, which has been profaned among the nations, the name you have profaned among them. Then the nations will know that I am the Lord, declares the sovereign Lord, when I show Myself holy through you before their eyes.' (Ezek. 36:19–23)

Here, the sanctification or desecration of God's name has to do with how God is perceived by 'the nations'. This in turn relates to the history of Israel. When they are exiled, this is a desecration of God's name. When they return, it is a sanctification. There is an intense inner conflict here between the demands of justice and the perception, on the part of the nations, of the God of Israel. The people, implies Ezekiel, may have deserved punishment, but this has negative consequences for how God is perceived by the world. Israel knows that it suffers because it has failed to honour the terms of its covenant, but that is not how 'the nations' see it. For them, each nation had its own god. The defeat of a nation was therefore a defeat of its god. Israel's exile, as they saw it, was a sign that Israel's God was unable to protect his own people. Hence God's name was desecrated.

The difference between Leviticus and Ezekiel is that in Leviticus the emphasis is on the word *sanctify*, whereas in Ezekiel it is on the word *name*. It is not God who is sanctified or desecrated – that is impossible – but his 'name' may be. The idea of a 'name' in the biblical sense is what today we might call reputation, standing, or public image. It is clear throughout the Bible that this is an issue of real concern. God tells Moses, 'I will harden Pharaoh's heart, that I may multiply My signs and marvels in the land of Egypt . . . and *the Egyptians shall know* that I am the Lord . . .' (Ex. 7:3–5). Foretelling the encounter at the Red Sea, he says, 'Then I will stiffen Pharaoh's heart and he will pursue them, that I may assert My authority against Pharaoh and all his host; and *the Egyptians shall know* that I am the Lord' (Ex. 14:18). Moses invokes this idea when he prays to God to forgive the people, first when they make the Golden Calf: 'Why should Egypt be able to say that You took them out with evil intentions, to kill them in the hill country and wipe them out from the face of the earth. Withdraw Your display of anger, and refrain from doing evil to Your people' (Ex. 32:12). He uses a similar logic when God threatens to destroy the people for their rebellion following the demoralizing report of the spies: 'Moses said to the Lord, "If You put all these people to death at one time, the nations who have heard this report about You will say, 'The Lord was not able to bring these people into the land He promised them on oath; so He slaughtered them in the desert'"' (Num. 14:15–16). There is a theological issue here in need of explanation. Why should God be concerned about how the nations perceive him? Truth is not made by public opinion. Faith is not the pursuit of popularity. What difference does it make whether the nations believe that God is powerful or power-less? Let us hold these questions, fundamental though they are, for a moment, noting simply that Ezekiel has highlighted a second facet of 'sanctifying the name', namely, God's standing in the world as evidenced by the history of the people of the covenant.

Moving to the rabbinic literature, we immediately enter new and darker territory. By now, under the Greeks and Romans, 'sanctifying God's name' has come to mean *martyrdom*. Here is Maimonides' summary of the key provisions of the law:

> All the members of the house of Israel are commanded to sanctify the great name of God . . . Should an idolater arise and coerce an Israelite to violate any of the commandments mentioned in the Torah under the threat of death, the Israelite is to commit the transgression rather than suffer death, for concerning the commandments it is said 'which, if a man do them he shall live by them' (Lev. 18:5) – [meaning:] live by them not die by them . . .
>
> This rule applies to all the commandments except the prohibitions against idolatry, inchastity, and murder. With regard to these,

if an Israelite is told 'transgress one of them or else you will be put to death', he should suffer death rather than transgress . . .

This applies at a time free from religious persecution. But when there is such persecution, such as when a wicked king arises like Nebuchadnezzar and his confederates, and issues decrees against Israel with the purpose of abolishing their religion or one of the precepts, then it is the Israelites' duty to suffer death and not violate *any* of the commandments, whether the coercion takes place in the presence of ten Israelites or in the presence of idolaters.[6]

What is poignant about these rules is that they are the result of a decision on the part of the sages to *limit* martyrdom rather than encourage it. There is considerable evidence, not only from the Hellenistic period but also from Europe at the time of the Crusades, that Jews were ready to go to their deaths rather than embrace another faith or culture – and to do so far beyond the strict requirement of the law. Here 'sanctifying the name' takes on a third meaning – to show, *in extremis*, that you love God more than life itself.

There is a fourth sense, implicit in an episode in the book of Joshua during the Israelites' conquest of the land. The Gibeonites, anxious for their safety after hearing of the Israelite victories at Jericho and Ai, resort to a deception. They put on worn clothes and shoes and come to the Israelites looking as if they have travelled a long way. They say that they 'have come from a very distant country', and propose a peace treaty, to which Joshua accedes. Three days later the Israelites discover that the Gibeonites in fact live close by. They urge Joshua and the leaders to abrogate the treaty since it was undertaken on false pretences. The leaders refuse to do so on the grounds that it would undermine trust in an oath taken in God's name. A word having been given should not be withdrawn:

But the Israelites did not attack [the Gibeonites] because the leaders of the assembly had sworn an oath to them by the Lord, the God of Israel. The whole assembly grumbled against the leaders, but all the leaders answered, 'We have given them our oath by the Lord, the God of Israel, and we cannot touch them now.' (Josh. 9:18–19)

The Babylonian Talmud[7] explicitly attributes this to the principle of 'sanctifying the name'. Here the principle is that an act which may be legally or morally justified nevertheless should not be done because of the bad 'name' it might create. This too was taken up in rabbinic law, with the unusual stipulation that much depends on circumstance and the people involved. The greater the individual, the more scrupulous he or she must be:

There are other things that are a profanation of the name of God. When a person, great in the knowledge of the Torah and reputed for his piety does things which cause people to talk about him, even if the acts are not express violations, he profanes the name of God. For example, if such a person makes a purchase and does not pay promptly . . . or if he indulges immoderately in jesting, eating or drinking among ignorant people, or if his way of addressing people is not gentle, or he does not receive people affably but is quarrelsome and irascible. The greater the person, the more scrupulous he should be in all such things, doing more than the strict letter of the law requires.

If a person is scrupulous in his conduct, gentle in his conversation, pleasant towards his fellow creatures, affable in manner when receiving them, not retorting even when affronted, but showing courtesy to all, even to those who treat him with disdain, conducting his commercial affairs with integrity, not readily accepting the hospitality of the ignorant nor frequenting their company . . . such a person has sanctified God's name.[8]

Closely related to this is the idea of *exemplary conduct* or its opposite. When Moses and Aaron, provoked by the Israelites demanding water, strike the rock instead of speaking to it, God says to them: 'You did not have enough faith in Me to *sanctify* Me in the presence of the Israelites' (Num. 20:12). Later he says to Moses, 'you broke faith with Me . . . and you did not *sanctify* Me among the Israelites' (Deut. 32:51). The precise nature of their offence is obscure, and the interpretations are legion. According to Maimonides, Moses was assumed to be acting on divine instruction and thus wrongly conveyed to the Israelites by his own anger that God was angry with the people.[9] One way or another, Moses failed to act as a fitting role-model.

Particular emphasis appears, in some of the literature, on the impression Jewish conduct makes on non-Jews. Thus the Talmud[10] says that Joseph, resisting attempted seduction by Potiphar's wife, 'sanctified the name'. The story is told of Rabbi Shimon ben Shetach (first century BCE) who bought an ass from an Arab. When his servants brought it home, they discovered a valuable jewel in its harness. R. Shimon immediately ordered them to return it on the grounds that he had intended to buy the ass, not the jewel. He told his disciples: 'Do you consider me a barbarian? I would prefer that a Gentile say, "Blessed be the God of the Jews" than all the money in the world.'[11]

In Jewish law, behaviour that might otherwise be permitted, but could give rise to adverse perceptions on the part of Gentiles, is forbidden on the grounds of 'desecration of the name'. So, for example, whereas in Jewish law workers may eat part of the produce on which they are working, they are forbidden to do so when working for a Gentile in case he or she considers such conduct as theft.[12] A synagogue menorah that is the gift of a Gentile may not be exchanged for something else, even to fulfil a commandment, whereas if it were the gift of a Jew it may. The Gentile may see the act as ingratitude or impropriety; therefore it is forbidden.

The common factor in these cases is not the act in itself but *the way it may be perceived.* This is the reason for the exceptional severity with which 'desecrating the name' is regarded:

> There are transgressions that are forgiven immediately, and others pardoned only after a time . . . All this applies only if at the time of the transgression one did not desecrate God's name. If he did, then even though he repents, and the Day of Atonement comes and he is still penitent, and he suffers afflictions, his atonement is not complete until he dies.[13]

'Profaning God's name' is a wrong that cannot be righted in one's lifetime, because what has been harmed is not just the victim, nor the perpetrator, but the very standing of God in the eyes of the world.

*　　　　　*　　　　　*

How do these various strands fit together? What have guarding sacred times and places, martyrdom, exemplary conduct and avoiding the appearance of wrongdoing to do with the role of God in history and his standing in the eyes of the world? At stake is the very nature of God and the definition of the children of Israel as 'a kingdom of priests and a holy nation'.

The structure of Jewish spirituality is built on a difficult but sane and humane idea. The Hebrew Bible begins, not with the story of Israel, or even its prehistory in the days of the patriarchs and matriarchs, but with humanity as a whole. God makes the human person in his image but is repeatedly disappointed, first with Adam and Eve, then with Cain, then with the generation of the Flood. In grief ('God regretted that He had made man on earth, and was pained to His very core'), he de-creates life on earth to begin again with a single righteous man, Noah. This time he resolves never to set the bar of virtue so high that humanity is bound to fail: 'Never again will I curse the ground because of man, even though every inclination of his heart is evil from childhood' (Gen. 8:21). God has not changed; neither has man. What have changed are the terms of their relationship.

This is the point at which the Hebrew Bible confronts what Paul and Christianity were later to call 'original sin', but in a quite different way.

God makes a covenant with all humanity, based on the prohibition of murder ('Whoever sheds the blood of man, by man shall his blood be shed'). The sages were eventually to identify seven 'Noahide' laws, but the principle is essentially the same. God no longer makes maximal demands: he makes minimal ones. This is what contemporary philosophers call a 'thin' morality, the basic requirements of human conduct as such.

God does not condemn humankind; he does not hold it guilty or incapable of good. Instead, he lowers his requirements to the level at which virtue is humanly achievable. Enough, he seems to say, that you honour the sanctity of life and the basic human decencies. But that is not the end of the story. If it were, the Bible would be merely one work of moral philosophy among many others, articulating the 'thin' principles universal to the human condition. Instead it makes a surprising move. God asks one individual – eventually a family, a tribe, a collection of tribes, a nation – to serve as an exemplary role-model, to be as it were a living case-study in what it is to live closely and continuously in the presence of God. This is – as Jewish history testifies – a weighty and risk-laden responsibility.

Since God is beyond nature, his people will have a fate that, in conspicuous ways, cannot be explained in natural terms (Nietzsche saw this most clearly, writing 'The Jews are the most remarkable nation of world history . . . They defined themselves *counter* to all those conditions under which a nation was able to live').[14] Abraham and Sarah begin their journey by severing their natural ties to land and home. Sarah, Rebekah and Rachel are naturally infertile: their children are born by a miracle. Unnaturally, the Israelites become a nation in exile. Their prophet, who speaks the word of God, is a man naturally inarticulate ('I am not a man of words,' says Moses, 'I am slow of speech and tongue'). They receive their constitution in the desert before they have even entered their land. Naturally small, weak and exposed, their survival depends on exceptional dedication to their mission. Indeed, they are the only nation in history, with the possible exception of the United States, to be defined *by* a mission. Uniquely, their laws and covenant come from God, and their history testifies to a power greater than themselves. Indeed post-biblical Jewish history exemplifies this even more than biblical history itself, in the way Jewry survived, its identity intact, through almost twenty centuries of dispersion and persecution. Something within points to something beyond.

That is the meaning of 'a holy nation'. The holy, in the Bible, simply means *God's domain* – those points in time and space at which his presence is peculiarly visible. That is what Isaiah means when he says of Israel: 'You are My witnesses – declares the Lord – that I am God' (Is. 43:10). It is also what Moses means in one of his closing addresses: 'The Lord will establish you as His holy people, as He promised you on oath, if you keep the commands of the Lord your God and walk in His ways. Then *all the peoples on earth will see that you are called by the name of God* and they will fear you' (Deut. 28:9–10). There is no assertion in the Bible that the Israelites are inherently better or more moral than others. Their vocation represents not a privilege but a responsibility. It confers no material advantages, only the religious life itself. Nor is there any implication that God is not accessible to others. On the contrary, he is the creator and sustainer of all. Job, the supreme example of a righteous man, is not a Jew. At his prayer at the dedication of the Temple, Solomon asks God to hear the prayers of 'the foreigner who does not belong to Your people Israel . . . so that all the peoples of the earth may know Your name and fear You, as do Your people Israel' (1 Kings 8:41–3). Israel is called on to be the opposite of a master-race, for it is not a race but a covenant into which one may convert, nor is it to seek mastery over men but to become, instead, a servant of God. There is nothing in the particularism of Israel to contradict the universalism of the human condition as the image and likeness of God.

Israel's role is to be an example: no more, no less. That is how Maimonides' son Abraham interprets, in his father's name, the phrase 'a kingdom of priests':

> The priest of any congregation is its leader, its most honoured individual and the congregation's role-model through whom they learn to follow in the right path. [In calling on Israel to be a 'kingdom of priests' it was as if God said to them], 'Become leaders of the world through keeping My Torah, so that your relationship to [humanity] becomes that of a priest to his congregation, so that the world follows in your path, imitates your deeds and walks in your ways.'[15]

In a similar vein, R. Ovadiah Sforno writes: 'In this fashion you will be the treasure of all [humanity] by being a kingdom of priests to understand and teach the entire human race to call on the name of God and serve Him with one accord.'[16] The great nineteenth-century Jewish thinkers made essentially the same point. Rabbi Naftali Zvi Yehudah Berlin states that the purpose for which the people of Israel was brought into existence was 'to be an illumination to the nations to cause them to arrive at knowledge of the Lord of the universe'.[17] Rabbi Jacob Ettlinger writes that 'not for [Israel] alone did the Torah become a light illuminating the darkness but rather for the entire world'.[18] Rabbi Samson Raphael Hirsch adds that 'As the priest among the people, so should [Israel] among mankind uphold the vision of God and humanity and by so doing be a holy nation.'[19]

If Israel's role is to be an example, then its conduct must never be less than exemplary. That is the meaning of 'sanctifying the name'. When Israel honours its holy times and places, when Jews act in such a way as make people positively aware of God, and when they are willing to die rather than compromise their faith, they act as witnesses to the divine presence within the affairs and history of humankind. When they sin and suffer exile, it is as if the divine presence is hidden, not only from them but in an important sense from the human arena. God's name – the awareness people have of him – is eclipsed and thereby desecrated.

The concept of 'sanctifying the name' introduces into ethics a simple but surprising principle. We are God's ambassadors on earth. The way we live affects how others see him. God needs us. The idea sounds paradoxical but it is true. Wittingly or unwittingly, the way we live tells a story. If we live well, becoming a blessing to others, we become witnesses to the transformative power of the divine presence. God lives within the human situation to the extent that we live his will. As a radio converts waves into sound, so a holy life translates God's word into deed. We become his transmitters. That is why 'sanctifying the name' is a metaprinciple of Judaism.

Not everything in Jewish ethics can be specified in the form of law. This is a point compellingly made by Nahmanides in his comment on the biblical command to do 'the right and the good in the sight of God' (Deut. 6:18):

At first [Moses] stated that you are to keep [God's] statutes and His testimonies which He commanded you. Now he goes on to add that even where He has not commanded you, be careful to do what is good and right in His eyes, for He loves the good and the right. This is a great principle, for it is impossible to mention in the Torah all aspects of a person's conduct with neighbours and friends, all his various transactions, and the ordinances of all societies and countries. But since He mentioned many of them – *Do not go up and down as a talebearer, Do not take vengeance or bear a grudge, Do not stand idly by the blood of your neighbour, Do not curse the deaf, Rise up before the hoary head,* and the like – he reiterated in a general way that, in all matters, one should do what is good and right, including compromise [not insisting on your rights] and going beyond the strict letter of the law.[20]

There is no precise, exhaustive formula capable of telling us, in advance, what constitutes the right and the good in every conceivable situation. The moral life is too subtle and situational. Therefore, the Torah provides a combination of general rules and specific examples. Rabbi Naftali Zvi Yehudah Berlin analyses the phrase 'a kingdom of priests' along similar lines:

This refers to behaviour toward other people by doing the right and the good. However, the Torah does not spell out in detail what the right and the good are, because not every situation, place and time are the same. This is therefore not a condition of Judaism since it has no fixed law. It is, however, the will of God.[21]

This, then, is Judaism's answer to the question posed by the lawyer who asked: how can I serve God while practising my profession? It is precisely in our day-to-day relationships, at work or among friends, in our dealings with people and the integrity, sensitivity and generosity we bring to bear on them, that we most add or subtract to the respect those around us have for the values by which we live. Here, the greatest of biblical commands – to sanctify and not desecrate God's name – have their arena, their impact and influence. There is no greater religious achievement than to have sanctified God's name, and no greater a sin than to have lessened the respect in which it is held. Because of a single act in which he failed to sanctify God's name, Moses forfeited the chance to reach the destination he had spent his life as a leader journeying toward: the promised land. 'Sanctifying the name' is no mere marginal addendum to the script of Jewish life but its very point: to bring God's presence into the world by making others aware that God's word sanctifies life.

*　　　　　*　　　　　*

I end with two poignant moments in the history of this idea. The first occurred in the Warsaw ghetto uprising when, in April 1943, hearing that they were about to be exterminated, the inmates of the ghetto fought back, holding several divisions of the German army at bay for longer than did the whole of France. On the night of the uprising, an elderly rabbi, R. Isaac Nissenbaum, addressed his followers in these words:

> This is a time for the sanctification of life, *kiddush ha-hayyim*, and not for the holiness of martyrdom, *kiddush ha-Shem*. Previously, the Jew's enemy sought his soul, and the Jew sanctified his body in martyrdom [i.e. he denied his enemy what he wished to take from him]. Now the oppressor demands the Jew's body, and the Jew is therefore obliged to defend it, to preserve his life.[22]

He believed that the ghetto uprising was a turning-point in modern Jewish history, the moment when the long history of Jewish martyrdom was about to be transformed. In the past, Jews had sanctified God's name by being willing to die for their faith. Now they were being summoned to fight for the right to live for their faith.

There is another scene from the Warsaw ghetto that I find almost unbearably moving. Janusz Korczak, one of the heroes of the twentieth century, had trained in Poland as a physician. Early in his career, he was drawn to the plight of underprivileged children. He wrote books about them and became a kind of Polish Dickens. In 1911 he founded an orphanage for Jewish children in Warsaw which became so successful that he was asked to create one for Catholic children as well, which he did. He had his own radio programme which made him famous throughout Poland. They called him the 'old doctor'. He had revolutionary views about the young. He believed in trusting them and giving them responsibility. He got them to produce their own newspaper, the first children's paper in Poland. He turned schools into self-governing communities. He wrote some of the pioneering works of child psychology, including one called *The Child's Right to Respect*.[23]

He used to say, 'Children . . . have a right to be taken seriously. The unknown person inside each of them is our hope for the future.' He believed that in each child there burned a moral spark which if nurtured could defeat the darkness at the core of human nature. When the time came for the children under his care to leave, he used to say to them: 'I cannot give you God for you must find him in quiet contemplation in your own soul. I cannot give you love of man, for there is no love without forgiveness, and forgiving is something everyone must learn to do on his own. I can give you one thing only: a longing for a better life, a life of truth and justice. Even though it may not exist now, it may come tomorrow if you long for it enough.'[24]

In 1940 he and the orphanage were driven into the Warsaw ghetto, and in 1942 the order came to transport them to Treblinka. Offered the chance to escape, he refused, and in one of the most poignant moments of those years, he walked with his 200 orphans to the train that took them to the gates of death, inseparable from them to the end in the dignity of love. His life, and death, were a *kiddush ha-Shem*. He saw God's image in children the world had abandoned. He kept his faith with them and with God to the very end.

NOTES

1. J. H. Hertz, *The Pentateuch and Haftorahs* (London: Soncino, 1977), p. 519.
2. Edmund Blunden, 'Report on Experience', in *The Penguin Book of English Verse*, ed. John Hayward (London: Penguin, 1956), pp. 450–1.
3. I include this interpretation in Jonathan Sacks, *The Chief Rabbi's Haggadah* (London: HarperCollins, 2003), pp. 66–7.
4. The story is told in Jack Canfield, Mark Victor Hansen and Rabbi Dov Peretz Elkins (eds.), *Chicken Soup for the Jewish Soul* (Deerfield Beach, FL: Health Communications, 2001), pp. 97–9.

5. Babylonian Talmud, *Yoma* 86a. See also Maimonides, *Sefer haMitzvot*, positive command 3.
6. Maimonides, *Mishneh Torah, Yesodei ha-Torah* 5:1–3.
7. Babylonian Talmud, *Gittin* 46a.
8. Maimonides, *Mishneh Torah, Yesodei ha-Torah* 5:10.
9. Maimonides, *Eight Chapters*, 4; Raymond Weiss and Charles Butterworth, *Ethical Writings of Maimonides* (New York: Dover, 1975), pp. 73–4.
10. Babylonian Talmud, *Sotah* 10b.
11. Jerusalem Talmud, *Baba Metsia* 2:5; *Deuteronomy Rabbah* 3:3. *Pnei Mosheh* to Jerusalem Talmud ad loc. explicitly relates Shimon ben Shetach's comments to the principle of *Kiddush ha-Shem*.
12. The details are set out in *Talmudic Encyclopaedia* (Hebrew) (Jerusalem: Talmudic Encyclopaedia Publications, 1976), vol. 15, pp. 340–60.
13. *Mishneh Torah, Teshuvah* 1:9–12.
14. Nietzsche, *Twilight of the Idols and The Anti-Christ*, trans. R. J. Hollingdale (Harmondsworth: Penguin, 1968), p. 134.
15. *Perush Rabbi Avraham ben HaRambam* to Ex. 19:6.
16. Sforno, *Commentary* to Ex. 19:6.
17. See *Ha-amek Davar, Introduction* (*Kidmat ha-Emek*); *Introduction* to Ex., and *Commentary* to Ex. 12:51.
18. Jacob Ettlinger, *Minchat Ani*, Bamidbar. I am indebted, for these references, to J. David Bleich, '*Tikkun Olam*: Jewish Obligations to non-Jewish society', in David Shatz, Chaim Waxman and Nathan Diament (eds.), *Tikkun Olam: social responsibility in Jewish thought and law* (Northvale, NJ: Jason Aronson, 1997), pp. 61–102.
19. Samson Raphael Hirsch, *Horeb: a philosophy of Jewish laws and observances*, trans. Isidor Grunfeld (London: Soncino, 1962), no. 613; vol. 2, pp. 465–7.
20. Nahmanides, *Commentary* to Deut. 6:18.
21. *Ha-amek Davar* to Ex. 19:6.
22. Quoted in Emil Fackenheim, *To Mend the World* (New York: Schocken, 1982), p. 223.
23. Janusz Korczak, E. P. Kulawiec and Gizela Gawronski, *When I Am Little Again and The Child's Right to Respect* (Lanham: University Press, 1992); Sandra Joseph (ed.), *A Voice for the Child* (London: Thorsons, 1999).
24. Joseph, *A Voice for the Child*, p. 144.

Chapter 6

Mending the World

When God created the world, He provided an opportunity for the work of His hands – man – to participate in His creation. The Creator, as it were, impaired reality in order that mortal man could repair its flaws and perfect it.

(R. Joseph Soloveitchik)[1]

The late David Baum was one of the most unusual men I ever met. To picture him one has to think of Harpo Marx. David was his clone – short, full of energy, with the same shock of curly silver hair and an impish, mischievous smile. He was a religious Jew, who saw care for children as a sacred task. But he carried his faith lightly. He was full of fun. He was a man who took God so seriously that he did not need to take himself seriously at all.

David was a paediatrician, one of the finest in Britain. He developed new techniques of child care. Among them were the 'silver swaddler' he invented to protect premature babies, and the technique he developed for pasteurizing human milk. He worked tirelessly to create the Royal College of Paediatrics and Child Health, and became its first president. He chose as its motto the words from Psalm 127, 'Children are God's heritage and His reward to us' and was immoderately proud of the Hebrew poster he had made of these words – designed by his son, a religious artist living in Safed, Israel. He helped build the first children's hospice in Britain (he invited Sister Helen, the nun who initiated the project, to his son's bar mitzvah. 'What should I wear?' she asked him. 'Come in your habit,' he replied, 'God will enjoy that!').

Not content to confine his work to Britain, he went to Brazil, Ethiopia and Thailand and helped doctors there to improve levels of child care. He did the same in Moscow, as a result of which he became a friend of

President Mikhail Gorbachev. He was deeply concerned with the fate of refugee children during the 1999 war in Kosovo, and it was in the course of a sponsored bicycle ride to raise money to build a health-care centre there that he suffered the heart attack that killed him at the tragically young age of 59.

David was a religious Zionist. Though he lived in Bristol, he left instructions that he was to be buried in Israel, in Rosh Pinah. One of the last projects in which he was involved was the creation of a state-of-the-art child-care centre for Palestinian children in Gaza. He explained to people that this was what Zionism meant for him: to want the best for Israel's children but no less for the children of Israel's neighbours. Love, decency and care know no religious or ethnic boundaries.

He used to tell a story – taken from the American anthropologist Loren Eiseley[2] – that summed up his attitude to life. An old man was walking on the beach at dawn when he noticed a young man picking up starfish stranded by the retreating tide, and throwing them back into the sea one by one. He went up to him and asked him why he was doing this. The young man replied that the starfish would die if left exposed to the morning sun. 'But the beach goes on for miles, and there are thousands of starfish. You will not be able to save them all. How can your effort make a difference?' The young man looked at the starfish in his hand and then threw it to safety in the waves. 'To *this one*', he said, 'it makes a difference.'

David loved that story because he knew that we do not have to redeem the world all together in one go. We do it one day at a time, one person at a time, one act at a time. A single life, said the sages, is like a universe. Save a life and you save a world. Change a life and you begin to change the world.

There is a name for this idea in Judaism: *tikkun olam*, mending or perfecting the world. Of all the ideas in Judaism's ethics of responsibility it is the least halakhic, the least rooted in law. Its origins, we will see, are mystical. Not everything of religious significance in Judaism can be expressed in precise formulas: laws, codes of conduct, guidelines that do not change from one generation to the next, one situation to the next. *Tikkun olam* is something each of us does differently. It is an expression of the faith that it is no accident that we are here, in this time and place, with these gifts and capacities, and this opportunity to make a positive difference to the world. This belief is known as divine providence (in Hebrew, *hashgahah peratit*): the idea that God is operative in our lives *as individuals*, not only, as the Greek philosophers believed, concerned with universals. We are here because someone wanted us to be and because there is a task that only we can fulfil. No two people, places, times and circumstances are the same. Where *what I can do* meets *what needs to be done* – there is God's challenge and our task.

*   *   *

To understand how the concept of *tikkun olam* arose we have to travel back in time to one of the turning-points in Jewish history: the Spanish expulsion and its aftermath. For centuries Spain had been the home of medieval Jewry's golden age. Under relatively liberal regimes, Jews had risen to eminence in business, the sciences and public life. Their expertise was sought in finance, medicine and diplomacy. They sustained a rich intellectual and cultural life. Jewish learning flourished. Spanish Jewry was noted for its achievements in Jewish law, mysticism and philosophy. But the Jews of Spain were also well versed in the wider culture and made significant contributions to its poetry, politics, astronomy, medicine and cartography.

They were never totally secure. There were periodic attempts to convert them to Christianity. In 1263 the Jewish community was summoned to a public disputation. The Jewish spokesman, Nahmanides, successfully refuted the arguments of his opponent, but he had to pay a price. Two years later he was sentenced to exile. Then, in 1391, there was a volcanic explosion of anti-Jewish feeling. Throughout Spain there were riots. Synagogues were burned, houses and businesses looted, and many Jews killed.

For the first time, significant numbers of Jews converted to Christianity. The next hundred years saw wave after wave of conversionary activity, accompanied by anti-Jewish legislation. Jews who converted were offered equal citizenship. Those who remained Jewish were confined to special areas, forced to wear distinctive clothing, barred from public life and forbidden to mix with Christians. Eventually, in 1492, the remaining Jews were expelled.

The trauma was intense. For medieval Jewry, Spain was the one country that seemed to signal that Jews could find a place where they were not persecuted, humiliated and deprived of rights. The length and intensity of the anti-Jewish activity when it came was deeply disturbing, not only in the suffering it caused but because it seemed to close the door on hope itself. The great Jewish statesman and biblical scholar Isaac Abrabanel has left us a vivid picture of how Jews felt:

> In the days of the redemption . . . I shall relate how I used to say in those days [i.e. the times of despair that followed the expulsion] . . . all the prophets who prophesied about my redemption and salvation are false . . . Moses, may he rest in peace, was false in his utterances, Isaiah lied in his consolations, Jeremiah and Ezekiel lied in their prophecies, and likewise all the other prophets . . . Let people remember all the despairing things they used to say at the time of the exile.[3]

Some of the exiles travelled to the small hill town of Safed in northern Israel where, together with other Jewish scholars, they wrote one of the most glorious chapters in the history of Jewish spirituality. The group included the talmudist Rabbi David ibn Abi Zimra (Radbaz), the mystic Moses ben Jacob Cordovero, Joseph Caro, author of one of Judaism's greatest law codes, the *Shulhan Arukh*, and the mystical poets, Shlomo Alkabetz and Eliezer Azikri. Among their innovations was a new ceremony, *Kabbalat Shabbat* ('Welcoming the Sabbath'), which eventually found a permanent place in the Jewish prayer book. Dressed in white robes, they would go out into the fields on Friday afternoon, reciting Psalms and welcoming the Sabbath as if it were a bride.

Many of these figures produced works of genius, but they acknowledged one in particular as a towering figure in their midst: Rabbi Isaac ben Solomon Luria (1534–72), known as the *Ari*. Luria had grown up in Egypt, acquiring expertise in both Jewish law and mysticism (the kabbalah). He had spent two years on an island in the Nile, pondering the great mystical text, the Zohar, and came to Safed to study with Moses Cordovero. Although he was only there for the last two years of his short life, he attracted a devoted following and a legendary reputation. It is hard to summarize his teachings, which were complex and profound.[4] He committed few of them to writing, and instructed his disciple Rabbi Hayyim Vital to keep them secret after his death. Their impact, though, was too great to be hidden, and within decades had added a new vocabulary to the lexicon of Jewish thought.

There are certain questions that, once asked, seem obvious, yet it takes a special genius to formulate them for the first time. That was the case with Rabbi Luria. He posed a question, seemingly naïve in its simplicity yet far-reaching in its consequences: *If God exists, how does the world exist?* If God is infinite, filling the world with his presence and every place with his glory, how is there room – physical or metaphysical – for anything else? Two things cannot coexist at a single time in a single space. Infinity must always crowd out finitude. How then is there a universe?

Luria's radical answer was the doctrine known as *tzimtzum*, a word that means contraction, self-effacement, withdrawal or concealment. God, he said, *contracted into himself* to leave a space for the world. The universe that unfolded day by day during the six phases of Genesis 1 was necessarily only the second stage of creation. The first was the act of divine self-effacement, a withdrawal into himself on the part of God. The Hebrew word for 'universe' and 'eternity', *olam*, comes from the root *'-l-m* which also means 'hiding' or 'concealment'. Only when God is hidden can the universe exist.

To this must be added a second idea, *shevirat ha-kelim* ('breaking of the vessels'), a catastrophe theory of creation. God, in making the world, could not leave it devoid of his presence. He therefore sent forth rays of his light (strangely, this is not unlike the 'background radiation' discov-

74

ered by scientists in 1965 which eventually proved the Big Bang theory of the birth of the universe). The light was, however, too intense for its containers, which thereby broke, scattering fragments of light throughout the world. It is our task to gather up these fragments, wherever they are, and restore them to their proper place. Hence the third idea: *tikkun*, healing a fractured world. Each religious act we do has an effect on the ecology of creation. It restores something of lost harmony to the cosmos. Or, to use another term from Lurianic kabbalah, it 'unifies the divine name' and helps mend the breach between God's essence and his indwelling presence (*Shekhinah*) which is currently in exile.

This is a vision of cosmic catastrophe progressively healed by individual deeds which, though they seem small and local, 'mend the world'. Lurianic kabbalah spoke to a Jewry shattered by persecution. It still does, as a metaphor for a post-Holocaust world. The world is fractured, filled with 'broken vessels'. However, by a life suffused with the love of God, it is possible to redeem these fragments and restore them to their proper place as containers of divine light. Lurianic kabbalah explained catastrophe without diminishing it, transforming its negative energies into a force for healing and restoration.

＊　　　　　＊　　　　　＊

How did Rabbi Isaac Luria come by these ideas? They represent the synthesis of several elements long present in Judaism but never before brought together in quite this way. The first is the phrase *tikkun olam* itself. It appears in a series of Mishnaic teachings, where it serves as the explanation of certain laws relating, among other things, to divorce, the freeing of slaves, and the redemption of captives.[5] Common to these provisions is that they address areas in which the law contains anomalies which, if not rectified, would have adverse consequences for individuals or for society as a whole. *Tikkun olam* is, in this sense, a jurisprudential principle which we might translate as 'for the better ordering of society'. It is a legal maxim directing attention to the long-term impact of rules, not merely their application to particular cases. Within Jewish law, *tikkun olam* is a concept of limited scope, not a theory of the cosmos.

The phrase, however, also appears in one of Judaism's best-known prayers, *Alenu*, said at the end of each of the daily services. The paragraph in which it occurs is one of the great universalistic statements of the prayer book:

Therefore it is our hope, O Lord our God, that we may soon see the glory of Your power, to remove abominations from the earth so that idols are utterly cut off, to perfect the world [*le-takken olam*] under the sovereignty of the Almighty. Then all humanity will call on Your

75

name . . . For the kingdom is Yours and You will reign for all eternity in glory as it is written in your Torah, 'The Lord shall reign for all eternity', and as it is said, 'The Lord shall be king over all the world; on that day will the Lord be One and His name One.'[6]

The idea here is indeed cosmic – but it has little if anything to do with human action. The prayer is an expression of the prophetic vision of the end of days, envisaging a time when all humanity will acknowledge the One God and serve him with one accord so that his 'name' (the way God is known by different cultures) will be one. This outcome is part of a historical process which is divine rather than human. It is God, not us, who will perfect the world. *Alenu* is not a call to action, but a prayer.

In choosing the phrase *tikkun olam*, Rabbi Luria was thus bringing together two ideas, one from Jewish law, the other from Jewish prayer, neither of which had the sense that he attached to it. None the less, Lurianic kabbalah does express an idea fundamental to Judaism, spanning the whole of history from creation to the 'end of days'.

The first chapter of Genesis sets out creation in seven phases or days. It is intended less as a protoscientific document than as a spiritual—metaphysical affirmation whose fundamental concern is with *order*. On the first three days God creates a series of domains (day and night, heaven and earth, sea and dry land). On the second three days he fills each domain with its appropriate objects (sun and moon, birds and fish, animals and humankind). The result is ontological harmony – the still point of the turning world – expressed on the seventh day, the Sabbath, the first thing God calls holy. The word 'good' appears seven times in this chapter (three-, five- and sevenfold repetitions are always thematic markers in the Pentateuch). The verb *b-d-l*, to separate or divide, appears five times. R. Samson Raphael Hirsch notes that the phrase '*very* good', which appears at the end of the sixth day, has an ecological dimension – each aspect of creation was good in itself; *very* good in the harmonious integration of the whole.[7]

God creates order; man creates chaos. That is the message of the early chapters of Genesis. Each element of creation has its proper place. The Hebrew word *averah*, like its English equivalent 'transgression', signifies that sin involves crossing a boundary, entering forbidden territory, failing to respect the separation between different spaces and times. Adam and Eve transgress the boundary between permitted and forbidden foods; Cain transgresses the boundary of human life itself. The punishment or consequence of sin is *exile*. The measure-for-measure result of an act in the wrong place is that the agent finds him- or herself in the wrong place, in exile, not at home in the world. So Adam and Eve are exiled from Eden, Cain from habitation – and eventually the Israelites from their land.

Justice in the Hebrew Bible is thus more than a matter of law. It *restores a broken order*. By suffering the wrong he inflicted on others, the wrong-doer comes to feel remorse. He or she repairs the damage they have done. Exile ends in homecoming, and something of the lost harmony of the world is restored. Jewish mysticism thus shares with the non-mystical side of Judaism a fundamental vision of *order disrupted and repaired*.

There is, however, one feature of Lurianic kabbalah of far-reaching significance, because it bridges a gap in the basic structure of Jewish thought. The prophets and sages, virtually without exception, shared a vision of 'the end of days' (the messianic age, the world to come) in which restoration would be far-reaching and macrocosmic. At one level, the political–historical, it would be the return of Jews to their land and the renewal of the covenant between God and Israel. At a deeper, spiritual–metaphysical level it would mean the end of war and strife and the dawn of a universal sense of the presence of God, as in Isaiah's great vision:

> They will neither harm nor destroy
> On all My holy mountain,
> For the earth will be full of the knowledge of the Lord
> As the waters cover the sea. (Is. 11:9)

The question is, *how do we get from here to there*, from historical to messianic time? That was always a difficult question in Judaism. On the one hand, redemption comes from God; on the other, without human initiative, there is nothing through which God can act. The history of Zionism is a good example. Many of the early Zionists (Hess, Pinsker, Herzl) were secular. For them, the return of Jews to their land was something that Jews must do for themselves without relying on either prayer or God. For their part, many of the religious leaders of East European Jewry believed that redemption can only be brought about by God. Zionism was, from a religious perspective, misconceived, an attempt to wrest history from divine to human hands, thereby 'forcing the end'.

The significance of Lurianic kabbalah is that it is a *redemption of small steps*, act by act, day by day. Each act mends a fracture of the world. The way from here to there, like the journey of the Israelites through the wilderness, takes time. There are setbacks on the way – sins, rebellions, false turns. A journey of a few days takes 40 years. But there are no short cuts, no miraculous leaps. This seems to me an immensely helpful way of resolving one of the most significant lacunae in Jewish thought.

The controversy in the early years of the Zionist movement was like the disagreement, almost 2,000 years earlier, between the Sadducees and Essenes, as described by Josephus. The Essenes believed in fate. God alone wrote the script of history. The Sadducees believed in choice. Human history is written by human hands. The Pharisees alone, says Josephus, believed in interaction through which God and man become co-authors.[8] Rabbinic Judaism is the legacy of the Pharisees, but for profound historical reasons, Jews had tended to spiritualize redemption to discourage political activism to hasten the 'end of days'. One reaction against this was the series of messianic movements that made their appearance throughout the Middle Ages, culminating in the one associated with Shabbatai Zevi in the seventeenth century. If the journey from here to redemption can only be conceived as a single giant leap brought about by God, pent-up longing can sometimes explode in false messianism, the feeling that exile is about to end. Lurianic kabbalah is an alternative way of thinking about redemption as the slow, patient process of transforming the world, in which each act plays a part.

One thing I must make clear. *Tikkun olam* as R. Isaac Luria conceived it, is a mystical and spiritual idea. It is *not* social action. For the kabbalists, we mend the world not by healing the sick and feeding the hungry, but by prayer and the observance of the commands. Jewish mysticism is about the commands linking us to God, not those relating us to other people. To be sure, each of our acts has an effect on the 'upper worlds', the deep structure of reality, but this is not through normal channels of causation. *Tikkun olam* in the Lurianic sense is about the soul, not the world; the spirit, not the body; metaphysical fracture, not poverty and disease. Lurianic kabbalah is at best a metaphor, not a prescription, for the forms of social action I have described in this book. But it remains a compelling metaphor none the less. It suggests that our acts make a difference. They repair fractures in the world. They restore a lost order. They rescue fragments of the divine light. They mend the damage done by the evil men – even the imperfections that are part of creation itself. Our moral imagination is shaped by such metaphors.[9] Lurianic kabbalah is not afraid to look at catastrophe without concluding that the world is irreparable, evil endemic, that history is a meaningless sequence of events and the human situation irredeemable. Out of broken fragments, it shapes a mosaic of hope.

*　　　　　*　　　　　*

It is anachronistic to read back into ancient sources ideas that made their appearance many centuries later. That certainly applies to the concept of 'progress' as that word has been used in the West since the eighteenth century. It belongs to the historic transformation of Europe set in motion by the rise of science (testing hypotheses by experiment and observation), the secularization of knowledge and the growth of technology.

Judaism's classic texts, biblical and rabbinic, do not speak of massive transformations in our understanding of the universe, our ability to control nature, create economic growth, cure disease or eliminate poverty. They are silent on these subjects because they were not, until relatively recently, part of the horizon of human possibility.

That said, we find in both biblical and post-biblical sources, the attribution of a remarkable dignity to human action. It is there at the beginning. God charges humankind, in the Bible's first chapter, 'Be fruitful and multiply; fill the earth and subdue it. Rule over the fish of the sea and the birds of the air and over every living creature that moves on the ground' (Gen. 1:28). In the magnificent eighth Psalm the poet says:

> When I behold Your heavens, the work of Your fingers,
> The moon and stars that You set in place,
> What is man that You are mindful of him,
> Mortal man that You take note of him?
> Yet You have made him little less than the angels
> And adorned him with glory and majesty. (Ps. 8:3–5)

Homo sapiens is the one creation that is itself creative. To a degree unique among life-forms, human beings are not confined to adapting to their environment. They are capable of adapting the environment to themselves.

Max Weber, the nineteenth-century sociologist, traced the roots of Western scientific rationality back to the Hebrew Bible. For the first time in history, God was conceived of as something apart from and above nature. The universe was demythologized or, in his word, 'disenchanted', stripped of its overlay of magic and mystery. Without this vision of God, man and nature, the scientific revolution would simply not have happened – as indeed it did not happen in long-established, sometimes technically advanced civilizations such as that of China.

There can be no doubt, however, that the Jewish imagination does not value technology as such. Genesis 4 attributes the invention of musical instruments to Jubal, and of bronze and iron tool-making to Tubal-Cain, without endowing either with special significance. The description of the invention of brick-making in the story of the Tower of Babel is, if anything, anti-technological. No sooner have human beings mastered a new technique, the Bible seems to say, than they are ready to storm the heavens and take the place of God. Ancient Mesopotamia and Egypt, by far the most sophisticated cultures of their age, are the very places the people of the covenant move away from – Mesopotamia in the days of Abraham, Egypt in the time of Moses. The Hebrew Bible embodies serious concerns about technology as a source of hubris on the one hand, social control and human enslavement on the other. In Judaism, power must always be subordinate to purpose, science to ethics, technology to human dignity. The *why* matters more than the *how*.

Yet we find great openness to scientific knowledge in the Talmud. At one point, comparing Jewish and Greek astronomy, it states with astonishing lack of concern, 'Their view seems more correct than ours.'[10] Crucial to both biblical and rabbinic thought is the distinction between *Torah* (divine teaching) and *hokhmah* (human wisdom). The sages regarded wisdom as part of the heritage of humankind. It had nothing to do with revelation. It could be found in many cultures, the property of many nations. The sages said, 'If you are told there is wisdom among the nations, believe it.'[11] They invested it with religious dignity, going so far as to coin a blessing to be pronounced over seeing 'one of the sages of the nations'.[12] This sharp differentiation between religious and scientific knowledge meant that Judaism was untroubled and unthreatened by secular disciplines as such.

No less significant was the idea, articulated by some of the sages, that God had deliberately left creation incomplete, to leave room for the work of man. That is the idea behind this remarkable passage, a confrontation between a Roman governor and one of the great sages of the Mishnaic period, R. Akiva:

The wicked tyrant Rufus once asked Rabbi Akiva, 'Which are more pleasing, the works of God or those of human beings?' Rabbi Akiva replied, 'The works of human beings.' Rufus asked, 'Behold the heavens and the earth – can human beings make anything like them?' Rabbi Akiva replied, 'Do not bring an argument from things which are altogether beyond human capacity. Speak only of things which human beings can do.' Rufus replied, 'Why do you circumcise your children?' Rabbi Akiva said, 'I knew this was the point of your question. That is why I pre-empted you and said that the works of human beings are more pleasing than those of God.' Rabbi Akiva then brought out ears of wheat, and cakes, and said, 'These are the work of God and those the work of human beings. Are the cakes not more agreeable than the ears of wheat?'[13]

To be sure, the text is polemical in intent, countering a Roman suggestion that circumcision was barbaric: had God wanted children to be circumcised, he would have created them without a foreskin. None the less, the assertion is radical. Creation is God's unfinished symphony, and he has entrusted its completion to us.

Equally characteristic of the rabbinic literature is the refusal on the part of the sages to see the sufferings and injustices of the world as given, unchangeable, part of the divine will. This refusal is constitutive of

Judaism. There may be poverty in every age, but that does not make it God's will for the world. There may be injustice, but we may not be silent in the face of it. The unsentimental clear-sightedness of rabbinic Judaism here reaches heroic heights. Jews did not believe, with the Manichaeans or Gnostics, that the physical world is a vale of tears to be transcended. It is the world God made and pronounced good. On the other hand its failings, inequities and corruptions are neither inevitable nor to be accepted with resignation. It is this ability to hold together a sense of the goodness of creation and the evil it contains, thanking God for the one, working in God's name against the other, that marks Judaism as an activist, future-oriented faith. *Tikkun olam* involves the recognition that the world *does* need repair, rather than Stoic acceptance or ascetic denial. Hence the positive endorsement of scientific progress by R. Joseph Soloveitchik in his essay, 'The Lonely Man of Faith':

Men of old who could not fight disease and succumbed in multitudes to yellow fever or any other plague with degrading helplessness could not lay claim to dignity. Only the man who builds hospitals, discovers therapeutic techniques, and saves lives is blessed with dignity . . . The brute is helpless, and therefore not dignified. Civilized man has gained limited control of nature and has become in certain respects her master, and with his mastery he has attained dignity as well. His mastery has made it possible for him to act in accordance with his responsibility.[14]

To be human is to be creative, a master of fate, not its slave.

To this must be added the idea, noted above, of the universality of *hokhmah*, human wisdom. Revelation is particular; scientific knowledge is not. This stance allowed the sages to recognize and salute the technical and medical achievements of their age. Exceptional in this context, though not unique, is the tribute paid by R. Israel Lipschutz (*Tiferet Yisrael*, 1782–1860) to great benefactors of humanity and the religious significance of their work:

We find that many of the pious [of the nations] did more than recognize the Creator, and believe in the divine revelation of Torah, and perform acts of kindness to the Jewish people, but also that they conferred benefit on humanity as a whole. Among them were [Edward] Jenner who discovered [smallpox] vaccine, thus saving tens of thousands of people from sickness, death and disfigurement; [Sir Francis] Drake who brought the potato to Europe, mitigating famine on several occasions; and [Johannes] Gutenberg who invented printing. Some of them were not rewarded in this world at all, like [Johannes] Reuchlin who risked death to prevent the burning of Talmuds . . . and died, heartbroken, in poverty. Is it possible to imagine that these great deeds went unrewarded in the world to come. God forbid! Surely we know that the Holy One, blessed be He, does not withhold the reward of any creature . . . The advantage of the [other] nations over Israel is that they, through their own free choice and efforts made themselves – and this is certainly a greater [human] achievement than Israel, who were led toward perfection by the force of God and who therefore cannot claim the credit for what God did for them in the merit of their ancestors.[15]

Here 'perfecting the world' is seen in its full universal scope: the human project as such through which we use our creative gifts to 'confer benefit on humanity as a whole'. It is from this tradition Rabbi Soloveitchik speaks when he states as a self-evident truth that

> We have always considered ourselves to be an inseparable part of humanity and we were ever ready to accept the divine challenge, 'Fill the earth and subdue it.' We have never proclaimed the philosophy of *contemptus* or *odium seculi*. We have steadily maintained that involvement in the creative scheme of things is mandatory.[16]

I have tried to show some of the complex tributaries that converge in the idea of *tikkun olam*, 'mending the world', some theological, others mystical, combining in the imperative to ameliorate the human situation by constructive engagement with the world. It is not a concept given to precise definition, still less is it spelled out in the crisp imperatives of Jewish law. But it bestows religious dignity on those, Jewish and non-Jewish alike, who work to eliminate the evils of the world, as David Baum sought to do, an act at a time, a life at a time. Each generation, said the sages, has its own seekers and search, its own leaders and challenges.[17] So each of us has our own task, our unique gifts, our singular contribution to make. For each of us there is something no one else could do, and it is not least for this that we were created.

As long as there is hunger, poverty and treatable disease in the world there is work for us to do. As long as nations fight, and men hate, and corruption stalks the corridors of power; as long as there is unemployment and homelessness, depression and despair, our task is not yet done, and we hear, if we listen carefully enough, the voice of God asking us, as he asked the first humans, 'Where are you?'

Hassidim tell the story of the second Lubavitcher Rebbe (the 'Mitteler' Rebbe) who was once so intent on his studies that he failed to hear the cry of his baby son. His father (R. Shneur Zalman of Ladi) heard, and went down and took the baby in his arms until he went to sleep again.

Then he went into his son, still intent on his books, and said, 'My son, I do not know what you are studying, but it is not the study of Torah if it makes you deaf to the cry of a child.' To live the life of faith is to hear the silent cry of the afflicted, the lonely and marginal, the poor, the sick and the disempowered, and to respond. For the world is not yet mended, there is work still to do, and God has empowered us to do it – with him, for him and for his faith in us.

NOTES

1. Joseph B. Soloveitchik, *Halakhic Man*, trans. Lawrence Kaplan (Philadelphia: Jewish Publication Society of America, 1983), p. 101.
2. Loren Eiseley, *The Star Thrower* (New York: Times Books, 1978).
3. Don Isaac Abrabanel, *Zevah Pesah* (Constantinople, 1505); cited in H. H. Sasson (ed.), *A History of the Jewish People* (Cambridge, MA: Harvard University Press, 1976), p. 692.
4. The classic scholarly presentation is Gershom Scholem, *Major Trends in Jewish Mysticism* (London: Thames & Hudson, 1955), pp. 244–86.
5. Mishnah, *Gittin* 4:2, 4–9; 5:3; 9:4; *Eduyot* 1:13.
6. *The Authorised Daily Prayer Book* (London: United Synagogue, 1992), pp. 134–6.
7. Samson Raphael Hirsch, *Commentary* to Gen. 1:31; trans. Isaac Levy (Gateshead: Judaica Press, 1982), pp. 37–40.
8. Josephus, *Wars* ii, 8, 14; *Antiquities* xiii, 5, 9. In *Antiquities* xviii, 1, 3, he adds that the Pharisees believe 'that it was God's good pleasure that there should be a fusion and that the will of man with his virtue and vice should be admitted to the council-chamber of fate'.
9. See George Lakoff and Mark Johnson, *Metaphors We Live By* (Chicago: University of Chicago Press, 2003).
10. Babylonian Talmud, *Pesahim* 94b.
11. *Eikhah Rabbah* 2:13.
12. *The Authorised Daily Prayer Book*, pp. 749–50.
13. *Tanhuma, Tazria* 5.
14. Joseph B. Soloveitchik, *The Lonely Man of Faith* (New York: Doubleday, 1992), p. 17.
15. *Tiferet Yisrael* to Mishnah, *Avot* 3:14.
16. Joseph B. Soloveitchik, 'Confrontation', in Norman Lamm and Walter Wurzburger (eds.), *A Treasury of Tradition* (New York: Hebrew Publishing Company, 1967), p. 69.
17. Babylonian Talmud, *Sanhedrin* 38b, *Avodah Zarah* 5a.

Chapter 7

Like a Single Soul

A man in a boat began to bore a hole under his seat. His fellow passengers protested. 'What concern is it of yours?' he responded, 'I am making a hole under my seat, not yours.' They replied, 'That is so, but when the water enters and the boat sinks, we too will drown.'
(Rabbi Shimon bar Yohai)[1]

We were being driven back from a conference taking place in the Catskills, and to while away the time, our driver told us a story. One Friday afternoon, a friend of his was driving along the highway to join his family for Sabbath – the Catskills were where many New York Jews had holiday homes. He saw a motorist stranded by the roadside, his car immobilized by a flat tyre. He was wearing a yarmulka. Naturally the driver assumed that he too was heading for the Catskills and was concerned that he might not be able to change the wheel in time to reach his destination before the Sabbath began. He stopped, and helped the man change the tyre. As he was parting, the owner of the other car removed his yarmulka and put it in his pocket. 'Why are you doing that?' said the first. 'Don't you wear it all the time?'

'Oh no', said the other, 'You see, I'm not Jewish.'

'Then why were you wearing a yarmulka?'

'Simple', he replied. 'I know that if someone is in trouble and is wearing a yarmulka, a Jew will stop to help him.'

I hope it needs neither yarmulka nor Jewishness to help someone in need. But the story provides a point of entry into one of the fundamental principles of Judaism, attributed in the rabbinic literature to the sage and mystic, R. Shimon bar Yohai:

'A [holy] nation' – this teaches that they [the Jewish people] are like one body with one soul [the midrash identifies *goi*, a nation, with the word *geviyah*, a body], and thus it says, 'Who is like your

84

people Israel, a nation one on earth.' When one sins, all are punished, as it says, 'Did not Akhan ben Zerah sin in the matter of devoted things, and wrath fell upon all the congregation of Israel, and he did not perish alone for his iniquity' (Josh. 22:20). When one is injured, all feel the pain.[2]

To emphasize the point he offered another analogy: '"Israel is a scattered sheep"' (Jer. 5:17). Why are the Israelites compared to a sheep? Just as if you strike a sheep on its head or on one of its limbs, all its limbs feel it, so, if one Israelite sins, all Israelites feel it.'[3] The phrase the sages used to express this idea was 'All Israelites are sureties for one another.'[4] Judaism is not just a code of *individual* responsibility. Each of us is responsible for others also. The covenant creates a bond of *collective* responsibility. This is a well-known idea. Less well known is the intense historical drama out of which it emerged. In this chapter I want to tell the story of a moment of crisis in the very definition of what it is to be a Jew, and of the stunning leap of imagination to which it gave rise. Jewish history is a living testimony to the power of ideas, and few were more influential or fateful than this. To unravel the story, however, we must begin with a very strange text indeed.

*   *   *

The book of Leviticus reaches a climax with an account of the blessings and curses attendant on Israel's obedience, or lack of it, to the terms of the covenant. The blessings are relatively brief. The curses are, by contrast, set out at length and with elemental power. They are terrifying. To this day we recite them in a low voice, barely above a whisper. In them we hear the dark side of covenant, its awesome responsibility and the dangers to which it exposes the people. As the prophet Amos said, 'You only have I known of all the families of the earth: *therefore* I will punish you for all your iniquities' (3:2). The curses of Leviticus describe the punishment. This is part of the passage:

> As for those of you who are left, I will make their hearts so fearful in the lands of their enemies that the sound of a windblown leaf will put them to flight. They will run as though fleeing from the sword, and they will fall, even though no one is pursuing them. *They will stumble over one another* as though fleeing from the sword, even though no one is pursuing them. So you will not be able to stand before your enemies. (Lev. 26:36–7)

The italicized phrase became the proof-text of the rabbinic doctrine of collective responsibility: '"They shall stumble over one another" – one *because* of another. This teaches that all Israel are sureties for one another.'[5] This is the sole source in the rabbinic literature for the principle. It first appears in the *Sifra*, a halakhic midrash of the Mishnaic period, and is quoted several times in the Babylonian Talmud. I want to stay with it for a moment to capture its counterintuitive quality, its singular strangeness.

In the first place, the proof-text has nothing to do with responsibility, collective or otherwise. 'Stumbling over one another' is not a description of a nation bound by mutual suretyship. It is an account of panic. In their hurry to escape, people fall over one another. Each is concerned with his own safety, not the common good. Whatever prompted the rabbinic interpretation, it was not the plain sense of the verse.

Moreover, it is not about the normal life of Israel at all. The passage of which it is a part does not describe Israel going about its business in fidelity, or lack of it, to God. It is a vision of defeat and despair. The nation is in the process of being defeated by its enemies. The people are fleeing as refugees. Normal life is in ruins. How can a passage that speaks of exile and dislocation serve as the basis of a code of conduct?

The third difficulty is the most fundamental. *It should not be necessary to search for a proof-text for the idea that the Jewish people are bound by a collective fate*, that each is responsible for the others. This is a commonplace of the Bible. Its entire vision of Israel's history is predicated on it. Whenever Moses speaks about the blessings and curses attached to the covenant, he speaks about the nation as a whole, moving seamlessly from singular to plural, the 'you' of individuals to the 'you' of the nation as a whole. One example will stand for many: 'Now, if you will carefully obey My commandments which I command you today . . . then I will provide rain in your land in its proper time . . . and you will eat and be satisfied . . . Beware lest your heart be lured away . . . for you will then soon perish from the good land which the Lord is giving you' (Deut. 11:13–17).

The governing assumption throughout the Hebrew Bible is that when Israel is rewarded, it is rewarded collectively. When it is punished, it is punished collectively. It experiences fate as a people, which is to say, together. In the book of Joshua, when a single individual, Akhan son of Zerah, sins by appropriating part of the spoil from Jericho, the entire people suffer a setback and are defeated in their next military engagement. As Joshua reminds the people years later, 'When Akhan son of Zerah acted unfaithfully regarding the devoted things, did not wrath come upon the whole community of Israel?' (Josh. 22:20).

Judaism is a collective faith. Despite its principled attachment to the dignity of the individual, its central experiences are not private but communal. We pray together. On 9 Av (the anniversary of the destruction of the Temple), we mourn together. On the Day of Atonement we confess together. There are moments when the fate of the individual is expressly separated from that of the group, but they are rare. At the time of the Korah rebellion, when divine anger threatened the entire people, Moses prayed, 'If one man sins, will You be angry with the whole congregation?' (Num. 16:22). But for the most part the assumption of biblical thought is that the people prosper together and suffer together, because 'All Israel are responsible for one another.' No proof-text should be necessary for this idea, or if it is, then there is an *embarrass de richesse* of them.

More specifically, the place to which the sages should have drawn our attention is the covenant at Mount Sinai. It was there that the Israelites became an *edah*, a body politic, as opposed to an *am*, a people with shared ancestry and history. Their assent to the covenant turned them into a nation under the sovereignty of God whose written constitution was the Torah. Indeed, we find just this idea in the early rabbinic sources. Here is one, in the name of R. Judah the Prince in *Mekhilta*, a halakhic midrash to the book of Exodus:

'I am the Lord your God' (Ex. 20:2) – this tells us the merit of Israel. When they all stood at Mount Sinai to receive the Torah they resolved, as with a single mind, to accept the kingdom of God with joy. And not only this, but they pledged themselves, each for the other. Nor was it for overt acts alone that the Holy One, blessed be He, intended to reveal Himself to them in order to make a covenant with them, but also the secret deeds. But they said to Him, 'For overt acts we will make a covenant with You, but not for the secret ones, lest one of us should sin in secret and the whole community be held liable', as it is said, 'The secret things belong to the Lord our God, but the things that are revealed belong to us and our children' (Deut. 29:28).[6]

At Mount Sinai, the Israelites accepted the principle of mutual responsibility, with one proviso, that liability was restricted to acts committed in public or, at least, generally known. The logic is straightforward. If I know that you are engaged in wrongdoing, I may reasonably be expected to try to stop you. If I do not know, how can I be held responsible? Thus, according to R. Judah, for overt sins there is collective responsibility; for sins committed in secret, only personal responsibility.

The rabbinic literature discusses the various covenant ceremonies, of which there were three: the first at Mount Sinai, the second when Moses, at the end of his life, renewed the covenant with the next generation, the third in the days of Joshua after the Israelites had crossed the Jordan and entered the land. There are also some complicated calculations of how many covenants were involved. According to R. Shimon ben Judah, 'There is not a single precept of the Torah over which there were not made 603,550 covenants, equivalent to the number of those who came out of Egypt.'[7] The point is a strong one. In the ancient world, covenants were normally made by and between kings on behalf of their respective nations. Israel's covenant with God, the rabbis insisted, was not like this at all. It was a covenant made with each individual. Indeed, on each occasion in the Bible when a covenant ceremony is described, it involves a national assembly of the entire population. Each gave his or her individual consent to the covenant; each pledged his or her responsibility for the fate of the nation as a whole.

The mystery, therefore, is: why, at some stage in the Mishnaic period between the first and third centuries CE did the rabbis locate the principle of collective responsibility *in one of the curses of Leviticus?* Of all possible sources, it seems the least appropriate. Why did the rabbis not cite any of the other myriad texts that testify to this idea? Why choose instead a verse which speaks about Israel in exile in the land of their enemies? Only once we feel the full incongruity of the rabbis' choice of text will we have an intimation of the depth of crisis into which Jewish life was plunged in the first century CE with the destruction of the Second Temple.

*   *   *

It is easy to think of collective responsibility as a distinctively religious idea, and an unusual one. For it is far from obvious that if you sin, I should bear part of the blame and punishment. It is your sin not mine, your responsibility not mine. Each of us is surely separately accountable for our own lives and no one else's. In fact, though, the idea is neither strange nor difficult to understand. To be the citizen of a state, or a resident in a neighbourhood, is inevitably to be involved in collective fate of some kind. If my neighbours let their properties deteriorate, the value of my house declines. If our fellow citizens allow moral standards to disintegrate, the resulting lawlessness affects us all. What happens to me is only partly determined by what I do. It is also determined by what others do. With or against our will, we are affected by those around us.

Inevitably, then, we are caught up in a wider framework of responsibility. However, this requires one of two conditions: physical proximity or an overarching political structure. Physical proximity is what binds us together as neighbours. A political structure is what binds us together as fellow citizens. That is why, during virtually the whole period covered by the Hebrew Bible, collective Jewish responsibility was self-evident and taken for granted. During that period Israel was an *am*, a people living together in a bounded physical space. It was also an *edah*, a political entity, at times under the leadership of judges, later under the rulership of kings. The Israelites were geographically concentrated and politically defined. They were neighbours and fellow citizens.

The destruction of the Second Temple, the loss of political autonomy under the Romans and the gradual dispersion of Jews to other lands therefore constituted an immense and potentially terminal crisis for Israel's existence as a nation. Suddenly the possibility became real that the Jewish people might no longer be either an *am* or an *edah*. It had lost its political structures. Dispersed, it was no longer geographically concentrated. This had happened only once before, many centuries earlier. After the death of King Solomon, the Israelites were divided into two kingdoms. The northern kingdom was conquered by the Assyrians. The population was deported, and eventually assimilated and disappeared, becoming known to history as the 'lost Ten Tribes'. The southern kingdom was later conquered by the Babylonians. But the exile was short enough for Jews not to lose hope of return.

The sheer scale of the defeat following the destruction of the Second Temple, and the later Bar Kochba rebellion, made it clear that this time exile and the loss of power would be prolonged. The prospect for the future of the Jewish people was, by any realistic standards, dim. How could Jews sustain their collective identity – the bond of shared belonging and responsibility – if they were neither neighbours nor fellow citizens? It was not only the Temple that lay in ruins. So too, or so it seemed, lay the whole concept of Jewish peoplehood. Lacking any of the normal preconditions of an *am* or *edah*, in what sense were Jews still a nation?

*   *   **

To understand precisely what was at stake we have to move forward many centuries to two figures: one from the seventeenth century, the other from the nineteenth. The first was Benedict (Barukh) Spinoza (1632–77), a child of Spanish marranos who had eventually resettled in Amsterdam. Spinoza carried with him the scars of marrano identity, neither fully Jewish nor fully Christian, distrusted by both, and encountering religion in the guise of persecution.[8] Of a philosophical temperament, and one of the first great theorists of liberalism (John Locke was the other), he argued both for a separation of religion and state, and for a religion that would itself be non-doctrinal.

Spinoza was early suspected of heretical opinions and in 1656 was formally excommunicated by the Jewish community of Amsterdam. In 1670 he published, anonymously, his treatise on religion, the *Tractatus Theologico-Politicus*. It caused a scandal not only in Jewish but also in Christian circles. To many readers it seemed to represent atheism. What concerns us here, however, is his view of Judaism. Central to his argument was the proposition that Judaism had long ceased to be binding for Jews. The laws of Moses, he contended, were like other legal systems. They were meant for a self-governing people in its own land. The 'election of the Jews' – their covenant with God – 'had regard to nothing but temporal physical happiness and freedom, in other words, autonomous government, and to the manner and means by which they obtained it'.[9] It followed that 'they were only valid while that kingdom lasted'.[10] As soon as Israel ceased to be a self-governing nation, Jews were no longer bound by the laws of God but by the laws of the nation among whom they lived. For Spinoza, with the loss of the Second Temple, the covenant was at an end. Jews were no longer chosen, nor a people, nor a nation.

Spinoza abandoned Judaism. But his argument was taken up two centuries later by one of the most radical proponents of Reform Judaism in Germany, Samuel Holdheim. Writing in 1848 to a group of sympathizers in Hungary, he argued:

> Now that the Jews have become integral elements of other peoples and states . . . all laws and institutions of Judaism which were based upon the election of a particular Jewish people – yes, of a particular Jewish state – and hence by their very nature implied exclusiveness and particularism, and served merely to strengthen the nationalistic sentiment . . . have lost all religious significance and obligation, and have given way to the national laws and institutions of such lands and peoples to which the Jews belong by birth and civic relationship.[11]

This was precisely Spinoza's case, with one difference. Holdheim did not advocate that Jews cease to be Jews. He merely maintained that virtually the whole of Jewish law was inoperative.

Though both these testimonies come from a later period in Jewish history, they define exactly the crisis faced by Jews in the wake of the destruction of the Second Temple. There is clear evidence from the Babylonian Talmud that this claim was made in Jewish circles at this time. The Babylonian Talmud, when dealing with historical catastrophe, is deliberately oblique. For the most part it does not describe the historical events of its time directly, for fear, perhaps, of demoralizing its readers. Instead it projects the crisis back to an earlier period, in this case to the Babylonian exile six centuries earlier. It states that the Jewish exiles in effect rejected Judaism. The prophet Ezekiel who lived at that time refers to them when he says: 'You say, "We want to be like the nations, like the peoples of the world, who serve wood and stone"' (Ezek. 20:32). The Talmud interprets their argument as follows: 'They came before the prophet and said: "Our master Ezekiel, if a servant is sold by his master, does the master still have any claim over him?"'[12] This is Spinoza's argument, anticipated and presented with stark simplicity. If another nation rules over Israel, then God does not. When he rescued them from Egypt, he became their sovereign in place of Pharaoh. But when he failed to rescue them from the Babylonians, he forfeited his sovereignty. No one can serve two masters. When Israel lived in God's land it was God's people. When it was forced into exile, it was no longer his people and he could have no legitimate claim to their loyalty or obedience.

It is impossible to exaggerate the depth of despair into which Jewish life was plunged by the Roman empire, first when the Temple was destroyed, then, some 60 years later, with the suppression of the Bar Kochba revolt and the subsequent Hadrianic persecutions. Jewry lost its most basic institutions, its autonomy and national life. There were no more kings or prophets. There was no Temple, no sacrifice, no central site of collective worship. Little by little, Israel ceased to be the home of most Jews. The intellectual centre moved to Babylon. There were significant Jewish communities elsewhere: in Egypt and many parts of Europe.

The Talmud records an extraordinary passage, dating from the Hadrianic persecutions of the second century:

> From the day that a government has come into power which issues cruel decrees against us and forbids us the observance of the Torah and its precepts, and does not allow us to enter into 'the week of the son' [i.e. circumcision], we ought by rights to bind ourselves not to marry and have children, so that the seed of Abraham our father would come to an end of itself.[13]

The Jewish people, some believed, was nearing its end. Israel was no longer a nation in the conventional sense: a people living in a single territory under the same government. It was in exile, but a more profound, scattered exile than Jews had ever known before. It was then that the question arose in all its force: *Is Israel still a nation?* If so, how? By virtue of what? To be sure, Jews shared memories, dreams and prayers. But within two or three generations memories fade, dreams falter and prayers unanswered slowly lapse into silence. It was the deepest crisis in Jewish history.

*   *   *

Only against this background can we appreciate the full pathos of the *Sifra*. The question before the sages was not: Where do we find in the Torah the concept that 'all Israel are responsible for one another'? The whole Torah presupposes this concept. But that is because the Torah speaks of Israel as a nation of neighbours and fellow citizens who live and act together and whose actions self-evidently affect one another. Instead the question which faced the sages was: Where do we find that this principle still applies *even when the Jewish people is exiled, dispersed and shorn of power*, when it is no longer bound together by geographical proximity or membership in the same body politic?

There are, in fact, only two passages in the Pentateuch that speak about such an eventuality, namely the two passages of curses which envision Israel defeated and scattered in the land of their enemies.[14] That is why the sages chose the text, 'They will stumble over one another', understanding it to mean, 'They will stumble *because* of one another's sins.' For it was this text, referring to a time when Jews were in exile, that hinted at the profound spiritual truth that even though Jews were shattered politically and scattered geographically, they were still a nation. Even at such a time they are bound by a covenant of mutual responsibility. Jewish fate and destiny are indivisible.

That is how, from the epicentre of tragedy, the sages rescued a vestige of hope. The covenant of Sinai was still in force. The Jewish people were still bound by its terms. They were therefore still a nation – constituted by the responsibility they had undertaken together, first at Sinai, then on the banks of the Jordan at the end of Moses' life, then again in the last days of Joshua, and subsequently during the period of Israel's kings and in the days of Ezra. Bound to God, they were bound to one another. That is what Saadia Gaon meant by his famous remark that 'Our people is a people only in virtue of its Torah.'[15] No other nation had ever constituted itself in such a way. Lacking all the normal prerequisites of nationhood – territory, proximity, sovereignty – Jews remained *even in exile* a people, the world's first global people, a 'virtual' community in the modern sense of a community constituted not in space but in the mind, held together solely by the invisible filaments of collective belonging, shared fate and mutual responsibility.

*   *   *

We now understand why the sages searched for a text where they did, in the passage of the curses. How, though, were they confident of finding it? It is said of Michelangelo that when he carved his statue of David he was conscious not of creating it but of uncovering it. He could already see it there, present in the uncarved rock. None the less, it takes a Michelangelo to see a David in a block of stone. It took a similar giant of the spirit to see, in the shapeless and dispersed remnants of the Jewry, the lineaments of a nation that was still an *am* and an *edah* when to all appearances it was neither of these things. Judaism's Michelangelo was one of its earliest and greatest mystics, Rabbi Shimon bar Yohai.

In physical, empirical and political terms Israel was no longer a nation. It had none of the properties of one. It had neither shared territory nor autonomy. Jews, beginning their journey east to Babylon and west to Europe, were no longer linked by physical proximity or shared citizenship. It was then that the *Mekhilta de-Rabbi Shimon bar Yohai* offered a new definition of Jewish nationhood: '*a kingdom of priests and a holy nation* –

this teaches that they are like a single body and a single soul . . . If one sins, they are all punished . . . If one is injured, they all feel the pain.' It is not too much to say that this affirmation saved the Jewish people.

It offered a mystical definition of nationhood. Jews do not form a nation, says Rabbi Shimon, in any conventional sense, for if that were once true, it is no longer. They are a nation because, in a mystical sense, they are joined in a profound bond of fellow feeling and responsibility. They are like a single body and a single soul. Even if they are not united physically or politically, none the less they are united spiritually. This is not something that can be described or defined within the normal categories of empirical politics. But it is felt by Jews at the deepest levels of emotion. When one Jew suffers, all Jews feel involved. It is as if the Jewish people is a single person. It was this that gave substance to Jewish nationhood when everything else was lost. Without it, Jews in exile might have gone their separate ways as individuals, and there would be no Jewish people today.

More than sixteen centuries later, one of the masters of the Hassidic movement, Rabbi Shneur Zalman of Ladi, defined the concept in the 32nd chapter of his classic text, *Tanya*: 'Therefore all Israelites are called brothers by virtue of the source of their souls in the one God; only their bodies are separated.'[16] Every Jewish soul is, he says, literally a part of God. Just as there can be no divisions within God, so there can be no divisions within the collective Jewish soul. As Jews, we are individuals only as bodies, not as souls. When we live at the level of the body, giving primacy to physical perceptions and desires, there can be conflict between us. But when we live at the level of the soul, there is unity. In such a state the command, 'You shall love your neighbour as yourself' is natural and inevitable, because your neighbour is a part of yourself, or rather, you and your neighbour are both parts of a larger self which is the collective soul of the Jewish people.

This is an essentially mystical vision. It ignores what we can see (the body) and focuses on what we cannot see (the soul). But it had crucial implications for Jewish law. The Talmud rules that if you are about to perform a command and for some reason are unable to make the blessing over it, I may make the blessing for you, even though I have already fulfilled the command.[17] How so? Rashi explains: All Israel are responsible for one another in relation to the fulfilment of the commands. If you do not perform the command, I will carry part of the blame. Your duties are therefore my responsibilities, and that is why I can make a blessing over them.[18] Ritva (Rabbi Yom Tov of Seville), in his commentary, goes further. Since, when it comes to the spiritual realm of the commands, all Israel are like a single person, there is no 'I' and 'You'. There is instead a collective 'We'.[19]

The Torah survived as the law of the Jewish nation because Jews continued to see themselves as a nation, even though they had lost all visible bases of nationhood. They did so because of the essentially mystical vision that even without sovereignty, outside the land of Israel and dispersed throughout the world, they remained 'a single body and a single soul', moved by one another's pain, sharing responsibility for their collective fate. More than any other factor, that belief preserved the Jewish nation through one of the deepest crises of its history, and sustains us today.

*   *   *

In late summer of 1999 I was in Pristina making a television programme about the aftermath of the Kosovo campaign. Outside every church was a NATO tank. At the start of the conflict it had been the Serbian Christians who had attacked mosques. Now they feared reprisals from the returning refugees. The mood was tense. Murders were taking place every night. Revenge was in the air. The most important task was to establish order and a return to civil peace.

I interviewed General Sir Michael Jackson, then head of the NATO forces. To my surprise, he thanked me for what the Jewish community had done: it had taken charge of the city's 23 primary schools. It was, he said, a valuable contribution to the city's welfare. When 800,000 people have become refugees and then return home, the most reassuring sign that life has returned to normal is that the schools open on time. Meeting the head of the Jewish community later that day, I asked him how many Jews were there currently in Pristina. His answer? Eleven.

The story, as I later uncovered it, was fascinating. In the early days of the conflict, the State of Israel had, along with many international aid agencies, sent a field medical team to work with the Kosovan Albanian refugees. Immediately they noticed something others had missed. The aid agencies were concentrating, not unnaturally, on the adults. There was no one working with the children. Traumatized by the conflict and far from home, they were running wild.

The team phoned back to Israel and asked for young volunteers. Virtually every youth group in Israel, from the most secular to the most religious, sent out teams of youth leaders at two-week intervals. They worked with the children, organizing summer camps, sports competitions, drama and music events and everything else they could think of to make their temporary exile feel like a summer holiday. At all levels it was an extraordinary effort. The Kosovan Albanians were Muslims, and for many of the Israeli youth workers it was their first contact and friendship with children of another faith. Their effort won high praise from UNICEF, the United Nations children's organization. It was in the wake of this that 'the Jewish people' – Israel, the American-based 'Joint'[20] and other Jewish agencies – were asked to supervise the return to normality of the school system in Pristina.

That episode taught me many things: the force of *hessed*, acts of kindness; the healing power of kindness extended across the borders of faith; and the way young people can rise to great moral achievements if we set them a challenge. The entire relief effort in Kosovo was a wonderful convergence of many people and agencies, from many faiths and nations. It also showed, though, the practical difference collective responsibility makes to the scope of the moral deed. World Jewry is small, painfully so. But the invisible strands of mutual responsibility mean that even the smallest Jewish community can turn to the Jewish people worldwide for help and achieve things that would be exceptional for a nation many times its size. When a people join hands, becoming even momentarily 'like one body with one soul', they are a formidable force for good.

NOTES

1. *Leviticus Rabbah* 4:6.
2. *Mekhilta de-Rabbi Shimon bar Yohai* to Ex. 19:6.
3. Ibid.
4. *Sifra, Behukotai* 2:7; Babylonian Talmud, *Sanhedrin* 27b; *Shevuot* 39a; *Numbers Rabbah* 10:5; *Song of Songs Rabbah* 7:1; *Yalkut Shimoni, Yitro* 290, 294; *Behukotai* 675.
5. *Sifra, Behukotai* 2:7.
6. *Mekhilta de-Rabbi Ishmael, Yitro* 5.
7. Babylonian Talmud, *Sotah* 37a–b. Emmanuel Levinas analyses this passage in Sean Hand (ed.), *The Levinas Reader* (Oxford: Blackwell, 1989), pp. 211–26.
8. See Yirmiyahu Yovel, *Spinoza and Other Heretics, vol. 1: The Marrano of Reason* (Princeton, NJ: Princeton University Press, 1989).
9. Benedict de Spinoza, *A Theologico-Political Treatise*, trans. R. H. M. Elwes (Mineola, NY: Dover, 2004), p. 48.
10. Ibid., p. 69.
11. Quoted in Gil Graff, *Separation of Church and State: Dina de-Malkhuta Dina in Jewish law, 1750–1848* (University: University of Alabama Press, 1985), pp. 122–3.
12. Babylonian Talmud, *Sanhedrin* 105a. See also Nahmanides, *Commentary* to Lev. 18:25.
13. Babylonian Talmud, *Baba Batra* 60b.
14. Lev. 26:14–46; Deut. 28:15–68.
15. Saadia Gaon, *Emunot ve-Deot* III:7. English translation: Saadia Gaon, *The Book of Beliefs and Opinions*, trans. Samuel Rosenblatt (New Haven: Yale University Press, 1948), p. 158.
16. Shneur Zalman of Ladi, *Tanya* I:32. English version, trans. Nissan Mindel (New York: Kehot, 1989), p. 145.
17. Babylonian Talmud, *Rosh Hashanah* 29a.

18. Rashi, *Commentary* to *Rosh Hashanah* 29a.
19. Ritva, *Commentary* to *Rosh Hashanah* 29a.
20. The American Jewish Joint Distribution Committee, an international Jewish charity which, as I write (2004) has recently sent a trauma team to help the community of Beslan, Ossetia, after the massacre of schoolchildren. In the past few years it has been involved in humanitarian aid in, among others, Bosnia, Macedonia, Rwanda, Sudan, Turkey, Kazakhstan, Uzbekistan and Ukraine, as well as bringing together Israelis and Palestinians in joint welfare and health projects.

Chapter 8

The Kindness of Strangers

Seek the peace of the city to which you have been exiled. Pray to God on its behalf, for in its peace, you will find peace.

(Jeremiah 29:7)

April 2002: another suicide bomb had exploded in Israel, and I had been interviewed for my reactions by the BBC. A few days later I received a letter from a lady in Kent. This is what she wrote:

Having listened to you on the radio today, and hearing your concern for your people, I felt prompted to write you a letter of comfort.

You see, I am a Gentile. I was born in 1943 and [years later] I met a Jewish woman who made a great difference in my life.

I was then in my mid-twenties, the victim of a broken marriage and with a small son to care for. I was seeking employment in South London as a hairdresser to pay for our rooms, and a child-minder.

The unemployment agency sent me to a salon. A large motherly woman greeted me at the interview. Her first words were, 'Are you in trouble, my dear?'

I was given employment in her salon. Then she offered to house us in the rooms above the shop, furnishing them with carpets and furniture from her own home. She thought – then she employed two girls from Leeds to share the flat and so reduce my rent. She also found a very kind child-minder for my son. This Proverbs 31 lady [the famous chapter beginning, 'A woman of worth, who can find?'] also spoke wisdom into my life. I shall always remember her kindness.

On the television news we all saw the dreadful pictures of the bus destroyed in Jerusalem on the eve of the Sabbath. At the sight of the plaited loaf lying in the dust, I felt as if a knife had gone through me as tears ran down my face – for the loaf represents family, unity, the common humanity we all share and which is oh, so fragile.

Please Rabbi Sacks, accept an outstretched hand to you: peace within your borders, comfort for your people, security within your walls. These are my prayers.

Like the story of Stephen Carter, the letter is eloquent testimony to the power of what Tennessee Williams called 'the kindness of strangers'.[1] In Jewish law this kindness has a name. It is called *darkhei shalom*, 'the ways of peace'. That is the idea I explore in this chapter.

The principle of 'the ways of peace' is little understood, yet it has profound implications. It is an important idea, with implications for the way we understand both Jewish law and political theory. It is also an innovative idea, one that emerged from the Jewish experience of exile. It is a concept for our time, an old-new way of thinking about multicultural societies and postmodern liberal democracy.

Darkhei shalom is essentially *hessed* universalized and applied to those who are not members of our faith. This way of putting it already signals that we are dealing with an unexpected development. *Hessed*, we noted in a previous chapter, is covenant love, the intimate and giving relationship between members of the community of faith conceived as an extended family. It is precisely the kind of idea that at first glance *cannot* be universalized. We do not treat all children as if they were ours. We do not treat strangers like friends, or friends like members of the family. *Darkhei shalom* is clearly, then, a radical proposition. On the face of it 'the ways of peace' are self-evident. We could almost summarize them in the words, 'Be kind.' That would be altogether to fail to understand what deserves to be seen as one of the boldest leaps of the rabbinic imagination. To see how, we must first reflect on the concept of peace itself.

*   *   *

The prophets of ancient Israel were the first people in history to conceive of peace as an ideal. They did so in words that have resonated from that day to this, most famously those of Isaiah, carved as an inscription opposite the United Nations building in New York:

> They shall beat their swords into plough-shares,
> Their spears into pruning hooks.
> Nation shall not lift up sword against nation,
> Neither shall they learn war any more. (Is. 2:4)

Isaiah's younger contemporary, Micah, repeated these words and added some of his own:

They shall sit, every man under his vine and under his fig tree,
And none shall make them afraid,
For the mouth of the Lord of the Hosts has spoken. (Mic. 4:4–5)

It is difficult at this distance to sense how revolutionary this was in an age that saw war as inevitable and noble, the arena of virtue and the testing-ground of courage. To the mythological mind, conflict was written into the structure of the cosmos. Storms and floods were clashes of the elements personified as gods. The literature of antiquity told tales of legendary battles and epic heroes. Military virtues were the proof of masculinity and strength. As late as 1914, young men throughout Europe were celebrating the chance of fighting and, if need be, dying in a noble cause. It took years of trench warfare, millions of deaths and the dawning realization that the war itself was pointless, to induce a more sober mood throughout Europe. As the nineteenth-century historian Sir Henry Maine observed, 'War appears to be as old as mankind, but peace is a modern invention.'[2] Against this background Walter Kaufmann is right to say:

> It is hard to do justice to the originality of men who, in the eighth century BCE, untutored by the horrors of two world wars with poison gas and atom bombs, and without the frightening prospect of still more fearful weapons of destruction, insisted that war is evil and must some day be abolished, and that all peoples must learn to dwell together in peace.[3]

What is fascinating is that Judaism pioneered not *one* concept of peace but *two*. The second appeared much later, at around the first or second century CE, after the destruction of the Second Temple. The rabbis gave it the name *darkhei shalom*, 'the ways of peace'. What are they? A series of statements from the Mishnaic period set them out as follows:

> For the sake of peace, the poor of the heathens should not be prevented from gathering gleanings, forgotten sheaves, and corners of the field.
>
> Our masters taught: for the sake of peace, the poor of the heathens should be supported as we support the poor of Israel, the sick of the heathens should be visited as we visit the sick of Israel, and the dead of the heathens should be buried as we bury the dead of Israel.[4]

All of these provisions are ordained because of the principle of 'the ways of peace'.[5] They are positive obligations. Negative duties – things we should not do because they endanger peace – belong to the corollary principle called *eivah*, '[the avoidance of] animosity'.[6]

The difference between the rabbinic and prophetic conceptions is striking. 'The ways of peace' are clearly not peace as Isaiah or Micah envisaged it. At first sight these rabbinic laws lack the grandeur of the prophets: they are small-scale, local, even prosaic. They envisage no transformation of the universe or human sensibility. They seem to be no more than pragmatism, generously conceived. They are attempts to avoid the kind of civil strife from which Jews suffered so often during the long night of exile. For these reasons 'the ways of peace' has not been seen for the innovation it is. I believe this is a mistake. 'The ways of peace' is in its way as original an idea as that of peace itself. We can define it: it is a programme for *peace in an unredeemed world.*

Peace is a paradox. Many religions and cultures praise it and decry conflict and war, yet they engage in war and often find themselves in conflict. In war, even ordinary people become heroes. In pursuit of peace, even heroes are often afraid to take the risk. Those who show courage in the heat of battle are celebrated. Those who take risks for peace are all too often assassinated – among them Lincoln, Gandhi, Martin Luther King, Anwar el-Sadat and Yitzhak Rabin.

The reason is that peace can come to seem to be a kind of betrayal. It involves compromise and settling for less than one would like. It has none of the purity and clarity of war, in which the issues – self-defence, national honour, patriotism, pride – are unambiguous and compelling. War speaks to our most fundamental sense of identity: there is an 'us' and a 'them', there are enemies and friends, and there is no possibility of confusing the two. When enemies shake hands, who is now the 'us' and who the 'them'? Peace involves a profound crisis of identity. The boundaries of self and other, friend and foe, must be redrawn. No wonder, then, that peace is often a mirage: the more we pursue it, the more distant a prospect it becomes.

Usually when a religion speaks of peace, it means 'peace on our terms'. Whatever the language in which it is couched, the argument tends to take this form: 'Our faith speaks of peace; our holy texts praise peace; therefore, if only the world shared our faith and our texts there would be peace.' Tragically, *this path does not and cannot lead to peace* because it is predicated on the conversion of the world – to our religion or ideology conceived as a global truth or universal salvation.

Peace thus conceived is part of the problem, not part of the solution. It does not take into account the irreducible differences between cultures, faiths, ideologies or philosophies of life which make our world, for better or worse, what it is. Indeed, the better could not exist without the worse, for the attempt to impose, within historical time, a single intellectual, cultural or religious order threatens humanity with the loss of the diversity we need – a diversity which, in unredeemed time, is our divinely ordained fate (Gen. 11:7). That is why the prophets were right to envisage peace *not* within historical time but at 'the end of days', and even more so to see this as the work of God, not humankind. The attempt to bring prophetic peace by human action creates not peace but war – what is often called 'holy war'. 'Holy war' is, I believe, unholy war, a desecration of the image of God in the name of God.[7]

What the sages who articulated 'the ways of peace' understood was that *they were not prophets.* They were *heirs* to the prophets, continuers of their tradition, but they did not believe (unlike, say, the Essenes and the sectarians of the Dead Sea scrolls) that they were living at the end of days. They knew that in this not-yet-fully-redeemed world, peace means *living with difference* – with those who have another faith and other texts. That is the fundamental distinction between the prophetic peace of religious unity and the rabbinic peace of religious diversity, with all the compromise, restraint and mutual respect that coexistence requires. The prophets articulated utopian peace; the sages, a *non*-utopian programme for peace in the here-and-now. That is what is fundamental, and original, in the idea of 'the ways of peace'.

*   *   *

Biblical law recognizes the concept of *ger toshav,* 'the resident alien', as an important element in its vision of human, and especially minority, rights (I use the word 'rights' because of its familiarity; in actuality, the Bible speaks of responsibilities rather than rights). The resident alien in biblical times was a Gentile living in a Jewish state. He or she did not convert to Judaism but did, however, recognize universal moral imperatives (called, in a later age, the 'Noahide laws'), basic principles of duty and responsibility. The majority community had duties to such an individual. He or she was to be given economic support in times of need (Lev. 25:35). The resident alien might even – a remarkable provision for its time – own a Jewish slave (25:47). The only 'religious' requirements were that he or she did not engage in idolatry or blasphemy.

The rules of 'the ways of peace' belong to an entirely different social and historical context. The resident alien laws belonged to a Jewish state in biblical times. The situation to which the rabbis spoke was one in which there was no Jewish state. Jews were a minority in a predominantly non-Jewish, and for them pagan, society. By the time these laws were formulated, there were no other monotheisms. Christianity, if it existed at the time (depending on the precise dating of the texts), was still a Jewish sect; Islam had not been born. The 'ways of peace' are set in an early post-biblical environment, and their originality lies in their inclusivity.

Unlike the laws of the resident alien, they do not presuppose acceptance of the Noahide code. They are not confined to neighbours with whom we share basic principles of ethics and belief. The 'ways of peace' apply to idolaters – those opposed to everything we believe. None the less, the sages ruled, we have basic responsibilities to them, not only the negative duty not to harm but the positive duty of welfare. We have to provide them with food when they are hungry, financial support when they are poor. We must visit them when they are sick and comfort them when they are bereaved. That is what the Jewish hairdresser was doing for the woman who wrote me the letter and what Sara Kestenbaum did for Stephen Carter. They were part of the ancient tradition of 'the ways of peace', kindness to strangers.

Where does the idea come from? The rabbis derived it from the verse in the book of Proverbs, 'Its ways are ways of pleasantness, and all its paths are peace' (Prov. 3:17). That is its textual warrant. Historically, however, it was born in the Jewish experience of exile. It emerged because Jews, having in the biblical era lived in their own land, were now dispersed minorities in pagan cultures. Definitive in this context was the letter written 2,600 years ago by the prophet Jeremiah to the exiles in Babylon and Egypt: 'Build houses and settle down, plant vineyards and gardens and eat their fruit. Take wives and have children. Seek the peace of the city to which you have been exiled. Pray to God on its behalf, for in its peace, you will find peace' (Jer. 29:5–7). This was a wise and far-sighted policy and shaped Jewish behaviour from then to the present. Jews were to maintain their identity as Jews but at the same time contribute to the societies to which they belonged – if 'belonging' is not too generous a word to describe the marginal and disfranchised existence to which Jews were often condemned.

Jeremiah was no less a utopian than Isaiah and Micah, but on this occasion his prophecy was pragmatic. Seven centuries later, so was the teaching of the sages. They had seen the failure of two other options. The first was assimilation – specifically Hellenization. This robbed Jews of their identity and led, as in the days of the Seleucids and the Maccabees, to the banning of religious practice. The second was rebellion, in the last years of the Second Temple, and again, 65 years later at the time of the Bar Kochba revolt. These were two of the most disastrous events of Jewish history, leading to defeat, disempowerment and dispersion. Remembering Jeremiah, the sages formulated a third way: to sustain their faith through institutions that (unlike the Temple) could be established anywhere – the synagogue, the school, the house of study and the home. In the meanwhile they would practise what today would be called active citizenship in the countries of their dispersion. They would give to others in need as well as to the members of their own community. 'The ways of peace' were not peace. Israel was in exile. The times were out of joint. But

Diaspora Jewry could none the less create, if not peace, then at least the 'ways' that led to it. They could perform acts of kindness. They could contribute to the common good. Without relinquishing their ultimate hopes of return and the messianic age, they could create at least a fragment of peace in the here-and-now. This was a vision no less noble for its modesty. Sometimes modest ideals change the world more benignly than their more revolutionary counterparts.

No less influential than Jeremiah were two other ethical insights. The first was the command – stated, as the rabbis noted, no fewer than 36 times in the Pentateuch – to love 'the stranger'.[8] To be sure, rabbinic law had given two precise interpretations of the term. 'The stranger', they ruled, meant either the convert or the resident alien. Yet in these biblical texts there are not only laws but a sentiment, a moral sensibility. In the book of Exodus the Israelites are commanded not to afflict the stranger because 'you know *what it feels like* to be a stranger; you were once strangers in the land of Egypt' (Ex. 23:9). The Israelites in Egypt were neither resident aliens nor converts to Egyptian culture, but they knew what it was to be marginal and isolated, to suffer and be treated like pariahs. Jews never lost that memory. Each year on Passover they ate the unleavened 'bread of affliction' and the bitter herbs of slavery. 'The ways of peace' belong to that sensibility. They are an expression of the fact – not halakhic, but psychological – that those who remember suffering can be sensitized, and respond, to the sufferings of others.

The other insight relates to the value of peace itself. We find, throughout the rabbinic literature, a profound wrestling with two conflicting values: truth and peace. The sages recognized, as Greek philosophy did not, that values *can* conflict. They do not coexist harmoniously in a Platonic heaven. Equality and freedom are both values, but if you pursue equality, as in the case of Soviet communism, you sacrifice freedom, and if you pursue freedom, through free market capitalism, you lose equality. A tradition is what it is, not only in virtue of the ideals it espouses, but also *how it resolves conflicts between* those values.

The evidence of the rabbinic literature is that, in most cases, the sages favoured peace over truth. To be sure, they were willing to die for their faith – awesomely so.[9] There are truths more precious than life itself. But the rabbis articulated an ethic heavily weighted toward peace.[10] Heroism, they said, meant conquering oneself, not others.[11] The lights of peace (the Sabbath candles) took precedence over the lights of victory (the Hanukkah candles).[12] God, they noted, was willing to let his name be blotted out, in the ordeal of the *sotah*, the woman suspected of adultery, for the sake of peace between husband and wife.[13] By the third century a rabbi could take it for granted that when a Psalm spoke about a sword it meant not a physical weapon but 'the words of Torah'.[14]

These statements and many others are evidence of the profound transformation in Jewish life and the spiritual response it evoked. Undefeated by the tragedy of the loss of the Second Temple and two failed revolts against Rome, the sages found a way of sustaining their faith without power, sovereignty or national self-determination. *Darkhei shalom* – the pursuit of peace not through conquest but acts of kindness – was one of the results.

*　　　　　*　　　　　*

To understand fully the significance of 'the ways of peace' we need to undertake two explorations, one in Jewish law, the other in contemporary political philosophy. The legal point is intricate but significant. In Jewish law, before performing any religious commandment, we must make a blessing. Its standard form is 'Blessed are you, O Lord our God . . . who has sanctified us with His commandments and has commanded us to . . . ' However, there are exceptions. Most commands require a blessing, but some do not. The medieval Jewish sages searched for a general rule to distinguish one from the other. Various suggestions were made; few were deemed satisfactory. R. Solomon ibn Adret (Rashba) wrote that 'the matter is extremely complicated'.[15] He, like others, doubted whether there was a simple criterion. Maimonides, however, formulated one of breathtaking simplicity: commands between us and God [*bein adam le-Makom*] require a blessing; commands between us and our fellow human beings [*bein adam le-havero*] do not.[16]

Why should this be so? Some offered the suggestion that commands between us and our fellows are not wholly within our control. In the case of charity, for example, the rich man may wish to give but the poor may not wish to accept. It would be wrong to make a blessing over a command that was not wholly within our power.[17] I believe, however, that a different issue is at stake.

There is an obvious difference between the two types of command. In the case of commands between us and God, what matters is the act and the intention with which it was performed. There is a debate in Jewish law as to whether, in general, commands require specific intent (*kavannah*). It is clear, however, that a command between us and God must be directed to God. That is what makes it a religious act as opposed, say, to a custom, an ethnic folkway, or a habit. Intention gives the act the characteristic essential to a religious deed in Judaism, namely that it is a response to a command of God. For an act to be holy, it must be designated and dedicated as holy. In effect, we renounce our own 'devices and desires' and act in response to the divine word. In that minimalist sense, intent is necessary.

An act between us and another human being, however, has a different character. What matters is not the act but its result [in rabbinic terms, not the *peulah* but the *niphal*]. What matters in acts of *tzedakah* or *hessed* is that we help the needy, alleviate the poverty of the poor, ease the distress of the bereaved. The point of the command is its effect on the world, on the other person, not the transaction in the soul between the agent and God. Hence the Talmud makes the radical remark that 'One who gives a sum to charity in order to gain a share in the world to come or save the life of his child is regarded as perfectly righteous.'[18] The doer of the deed in this case has ulterior motives, *but motives are irrelevant to acts the purpose of which is to bring aid to those who are in need.* An intention defines the nature of an act, but here what matters is not the act but its outcome. Kantian or Kierkegaardian purity of will is irrelevant. We are not commanded to give to the poor primarily for the salvation of our souls, but for the sake of the poor.

A command between us and God requires a blessing – because a blessing is, in effect, the declaration of an intention. It is a way of saying, 'I am doing this because I am commanded.' It places the act within the context of holiness. A command between us and other people needs no blessing because it requires no special intent. Someone was in need; we gave. Someone was ill; we visited. Someone was lonely; we invited them home. The religious character of the moment lay not in the act, its intention or the motive for which it was performed, but the comfort given, the help received, the loneliness lifted. In such cases Judaism does not require specific intent. Hence there is no need to make the intent explicit in the form of a benediction. *Far from needing a blessing, the act itself is the blessing.*

It was this line of reasoning that led the nineteenth-century Lithuanian rabbi Isaac Reines to justify his participation in Mizrachi, the religious Zionist movement. He was strongly criticized by those within the Orthodox community who held that by so doing he was associating with transgressors, the non- or even anti-religious Jews who formed the majority within the Zionist fold. Reines rejected the validity of this claim on the grounds that when it comes to rescuing someone from a burning building, we do not examine the religious credentials of those who are giving help. What matters is the rescue itself.

If this is so, we have discovered within Jewish law a principle with far-reaching consequences. It means that good deeds – deeds that make a difference to the lives of our fellow human beings – constitute, as it were, a *universal language.* They are not part of the cluster of behaviour whose character is defined by specifically Jewish beliefs – that God exists, that he communicates with humanity, that he made a covenant with Israel at Mount Sinai, and that as part of that covenant we are bound by certain commands. Commands between us and our fellows address the universal human condition. Tears know no national boundaries. The physical pain of believer and unbeliever are alike. Poverty humiliates, whether its victims are Jewish or not. 'If the wicked oppress the righteous, God takes the side of the oppressed. If the righteous oppress the wicked, God takes the side of the oppressed.'[19]

Our human situation as embodied souls, physical beings, means that we share needs and vulnerabilities. When it comes to acts that address such needs, it is irrelevant who performs them, for whom they are performed, and with what motive or intention. What matters is that they do good, relieve suffering, bring comfort. They redeem human solitude and bring those who suffer back into 'the land of the living'. Commands between us and others address the physical world we share, not the spiritual world which, until the end of days, we do not entirely share.

To put it another way: Judaism is a particularist faith that recognizes the universality of the human condition. I once asked Prince Hassan of Jordan, shortly after the assassination of Israel's prime minister Yitzhak Rabin, whether there was anything that might bring Israelis and Palestinians, Jews and Muslims, together. Was there a bridge over the abyss? He answered, 'Our shared tears, our history of suffering.' That was a wise remark. There are 6,000 languages spoken today, but only one is truly universal: the language of tears. It is to that language and its covenant of human solidarity ('I will be with him in time of trouble' [Ps. 91:15]) that 'the ways of peace' belong.

*　　　　　*　　　　　*

The second, and political, insight we owe to the late Sir Isaiah Berlin, who attributed it in turn to his readings of Machiavelli, Vico, Herder and Herzen. He gave it the name of *pluralism* [20] (the name itself was the creation of an American Jew, Horace Kallen, in the early twentieth century). What he meant by this was that not only individual ideals (like truth and peace) might be incompatible, but that this applied more fundamentally to cultures and civilizations. He attributed this idea to Herder:

> Herder laid it down that every culture possesses its own centre of gravity; each culture has its own points of reference . . . The world was a great garden in which different flowers and plants grew, each in its own way, each with its own claims and rights and past and future. From which it followed that no matter what men had in common . . . there were no universally true answers as valid for one culture as for another.[21]

Long before the phrase entered our public discourse, Berlin diagnosed the clash of civilizations. He wrote:

106

These collisions of values are of the essence of what they are and what we are. If we are told that these contradictions will be solved in some perfect world in which all good things can be harmonised in principle, then we must answer, to those who say this, that the meanings they attach to the names which for us denote the conflicting values, are not ours. We must say that the world in which what we see as incompatible values are not in conflict is a world altogether beyond our ken; that principles which are harmonised in this other world are not the principles with which, in our daily lives, we are acquainted; if they are transformed, it is into conceptions not known to us on earth. But it is on earth that we live, and it is here that we must believe and act.[22]

Any attempt to impose a single vision on the world, or even on a single society, is fundamentally untrue to the human condition and leads to massive and unacceptable loss of liberty. Isaiah Berlin saw this as a radical discovery because it suggested that all great monistic visions, whether philosophical like Plato's, or religious like medieval Christianity and Islam, or secular like fascism and communism – were false and dangerous. The best we could hope for is a modest kind of politics, one in which we do not seek to implement an ideal but in which we grant people maximum freedom to pursue the different and conflicting ideals that constitute the human situation.

What kind of politics would that be like? On this, one of his most important disciples, John Gray, wrote a book, *The Two Faces of Liberalism*, in which he argued that:

Liberalism has always had two faces. From one side toleration is the pursuit of an ideal form of life. From the other it is the search for terms of peace amongst different ways of life. In the former view, liberal institutions are seen as applications of universal principles. In the latter, they are a means to peaceful coexistence. In the first, liberalism is a prescription for a universal regime. In the second, it is a project of coexistence that can be pursued in many regimes.[23]

In recent times, the most famous exponent of the first view was John Rawls; of the second, Isaiah Berlin. Gray calls this second approach, *modus vivendi* liberalism.[24]

What is the difference between Rawlsian liberalism and *modus vivendi* liberalism? Rawlsian liberalism says, in effect, that people may have different religious convictions but they do not bring them into the public square. When you enter the political domain you speak the common language that Rawls calls 'the language of public reason'.[25] This is like the rule adopted by some nineteenth-century German Jews: 'Be a man in the street and a Jew at home.' Religious commitments are private. In the public domain we speak a different, common and essentially secular language, in which our religious differences are filtered out.

There is, however, another conception, an older one, namely that religious convictions or cultural commitments are *not* things you leave behind when you enter the public square. They are part of who and what we are, in the street, the polling booth, even in parliament. If so, then the public square will be an arena of real and intractable conflict. Whether we speak of voluntary euthanasia, stem cell research, cloning, animal welfare, environmental ethics or any other of the myriad issues that concern us, public debate will disclose substantive conflicts for which there is no neutral decision procedure, and the best we can hope for is not that we will agree but that we will get along. We will establish, not a consensus but a *modus vivendi*, a way of living peaceably together.

This was the kind of politics Sir Isaiah believed in. He was convinced that we could never create an ideal society in which all our multiple visions of the good were simultaneously realized. His favourite quotation in this context was the sentence he attributed to Professor R. G. Collingwood's translation of a line by Immanuel Kant, 'Out of the crooked timber of humanity, no straight thing was ever made.' I add, as a footnote, that Kant himself was here quoting the Bible: 'That which is crooked cannot be made straight' (Eccl. 1:15).

To be sure, Isaiah Berlin's view of humanity conflicts with one of Judaism's greatest ideas, the *Messianic Age*. We *do* believe that one day there will be a perfect world; but if Berlin was right, there cannot be. One should, though, not exaggerate the conflict. The Jewish answer to the question, 'Has the Messiah yet arrived?' is always 'Not yet.' (A friend of ours calls his plumber Messiah: he awaits him daily but he never comes.) In any case, the third-century rabbinic sage Samuel believed that 'The only difference between our time and messianic time is that the Jewish people will no longer be under the dominion of other nations.'[26] According to Samuel there will be no miraculous transformation of human nature; it is merely that Jews will return to their land. Ultimately Judaism does believe, as Berlin did not, in the power of human beings to transcend violence and war. That is the prophetic hope. But in the meantime, like Berlin, the sages believed in an undramatic yet generous politics of co-existence.

Darkhei shalom is a strong form of *modus vivendi* liberalism, a set of principles of how to live graciously with people whose beliefs and way of life are incompatible with ours. Despite profound differences, we must engage in common citizenship, contributing to the welfare of other communities as well as our own. That is the political significance of rabbinic, as opposed to prophetic, peace. The prophets envisaged peace as it would come to pass in what Francis Fukuyama, following Hegel, called the 'end of history'. The rabbis constructed a template of peace tailored to the crooked timber of humanity. That is why it speaks directly to our situation in the religiously and culturally plural liberal democracies of the West.

By chance, or providence, I had the opportunity to join with others in putting a programme of *darkhei shalom* into action. In 2002 Queen Elizabeth celebrated her golden jubilee as queen, and I wondered what gesture might be appropriate from the Jewish community, or faith communities in general, as a way of expressing our gratitude and paying tribute. I recalled a conversation a few years earlier between Prince Charles, the Archbishop of Canterbury and myself in which we discussed ways of improving community relations and strengthening the sense of citizenship among young people. The idea emerged that we might ask each of the faith communities in Britain to encourage their members to do an act of kindness to someone who was *not a member of their faith* – to reach out a hand of friendship across the boundaries.

We revived the idea, and the Prince of Wales gave it his backing. The programme – called 'Respect' – was launched in England in the spring of 2002, and later in the year in Scotland. All nine of the major religious groupings in Britain participated – Christian, Jewish, Muslim, Hindu, Sikh, Buddhist, Jain, Zoroastrian and Bahai. It was 'the ways of peace' in action. What it expressed is that civic peace demands more than tolerance, a live-and-let-live attitude to those not like us. *Darkhei shalom* is an active mandate not a passive one, doing good to others and thereby showing that the threads of our common humanity, with their variegated colours, are part of the social fabric we weave together. At a time of tension between resurgent ethnic and religious minorities, it is an idea whose time has come again.

*　　　　　*　　　　　*

I began with a story of kindness across the boundaries of faith. I end with another, from a different age. A young woman, not Jewish, had married a Jewish man, an Israeli who, together with his family, had left to find work in the Diaspora. He had then died, as had his brother and father, leaving the two sisters-in-law and their Jewish mother-in-law alone. The elder woman decided to return to her home in Israel. The two daughters-in-law offered to accompany her, but she refused. Israel was her home, not theirs. There, they would find themselves strangers, knowing no one. Better that they remained where they were and remarried. One agreed, but the other persisted. I will go with you, she said, and make Israel my home, for you have become like a mother to me and I will not let you go alone.

So they went. The neighbours who had known the older woman years before could hardly recognize her. Time and grief had done their work. She was not the woman they had known. She and her daughter-in-law were in a dire situation. They had no work, little money, few possessions. But there was a distant relative who might help. She sent her daughter-in-law to see him. Remembering the family connection, he gave her food and work, but the young woman intrigued him. She was obviously not Jewish by birth but by adoption, and had left everything behind out of faithfulness to her mother-in-law. Quietly he told the people who worked for him to give her special attention. One night they were alone and he asked her to marry him. It is an old and lovely story, and eventually found its way into the Hebrew Bible. The young woman was called Ruth, her mother-in-law Naomi, and the man Boaz. Not only did she give her name to a biblical book, but she also added a word to the English language, no longer used though its opposite – 'ruthless' – still is. The word 'ruth' meant kindness.

At one stage, early in their encounter, Ruth asks Boaz a question: 'Why have I found such favour in your eyes that you recognize me [*lehakireni*] – a foreigner [*nokhriah*]?' (Ruth 2:10). The Hebrew contains an extraordinary play on words, untranslatable into English. There are certain rare words, known as contronyms, which have two meanings, one the opposite of the other (the English word 'cleave' is an example: it means both 'to split' and 'to join'). In Hebrew the root *n-k-r* is a contronym. It means 'to recognize' – to grant rights and privileges. It also means 'to be a stranger', someone others do not recognize. Ruth uses it in both senses in the same sentence. 'I am a stranger; why have you treated me like a friend?' A single Hebrew word spans the spectrum of human interaction between recognition and estrangement, compassion and indifference. The question posed by the book of Ruth is: do we, or do we not, recognize our common humanity across cultural and religious divides? Ruth's story is about people whose kindness transcends difference. If one were to give it a subtitle, it would surely be 'the kindness of strangers'. The marriage to which that kindness led had consequences. From it, seven generations later, King David was born. From it, one day, the Messiah will come.

NOTES

1. In his play *A Streetcar Named Desire*, Blanche says that she 'depends on the kindness of strangers'. Tennessee Williams, *A Streetcar Named Desire* (New York: Limited Editions Club, 1982).
2. See Michael Howard, *The Invention of Peace* (London: Profile, 2000).

3. Walter Kaufmann, *The Faith of a Heretic* (New York: Anchor, 1963), p. 205.
4. Mishnah, *Shevi'it* 4:3, 5:9, *Gittin* 5:9, *Tosefta*, *Gittin* 3:13–14, *Avodah Zarah* 1:3; Babylonian Talmud, *Gittin* 59a–61a.
5. For a summary of rules under this heading, see *Talmudic Encyclopaedia*, vol. 7 (Jerusalem: Talmudic Encyclopaedia Publications, 1956), pp. 716–24.
6. For these rules, see *Talmudic Encyclopaedia*, vol. 1 (Jerusalem: Talmudic Encyclopaedia Publications, 1951), pp. 228–30.
7. Despite what is often said by critics of Judaism, it contains no concept of holy war – that is to say, a war designed to propagate the faith, convert populations, or establish religious truth by military or political dominance. Judaism contains the concept of an obligatory war (*milhemet mitzvah*), but this is limited to national self-defence.
8. See, e.g., Ex. 22:20, 23:9, Lev. 19:34, Deut. 10:18–19.
9. Thus, in one midrashic passage (*Mekhilta, Ba-hodesh* 6) a sage speaks, as if it were an unexceptional fact, of 'those who dwell in the land of Israel and risk their lives for the sake of the commandments. "Why are you being led out to be decapitated?" "Because I circumcised my son." "Why are you being led out to be burned?" "Because I read the Torah." "Why are you being led out to be crucified?" "Because I ate unleavened bread"' (English version: Jacob Z. Lauterbach, *Mekilta de-Rabbi Ishmael* [Philadelphia: Jewish Publication Society, 1933], vol. 2, p. 247). Another passage refers to Gentiles asking Jews, 'Why are you so ready to die for him [God] and so ready to let yourselves be killed for him?' (*Mekhilta, Shirata* 3; English version, ibid., p. 26). There is no doubt that, at several historical junctures, non-Jews found the willingness of Jews to die – or commit collective suicide – for their faith awesome, even uncanny.
10. See, e.g., *Sifre, Bamidbar* 42; *Genesis Rabbah* 8.
11. Mishnah, *Avot* 4:1.
12. Babylonian Talmud, *Shabbat* 23b.
13. Babylonian Talmud, *Shabbat* 116a.
14. Babylonian Talmud, *Shabbat* 63a.
15. *Responsa Rashba* 1:18.
16. Maimonides, *Mishneh Torah, Berakhot* 11:2 according to the interpretation of Kesef Mishneh ad loc. For a different explanation than the one I give below in the text, see Nahum Rabinovitch, *Yad Peshutah to Sefer Ahavah* (Jerusalem: Horeb, 1984), pp. 1179–81.
17. For these rules, see *Talmudic Encyclopaedia*, vol. 4 (Jerusalem: Talmudic Encyclopaedia Publications, 1952), pp. 519–20.
18. Babylonian Talmud, *Pesahim* 8a.
19. *Leviticus Rabbah* 27:5.
20. 'My intellectual path', in Isaiah Berlin, *The Power of Ideas* (London: Chatto and Windus, 2000), pp. 1–23. On Berlin's pluralism, see John Gray, *Isaiah Berlin* (London: HarperCollins, 1995), pp. 38–75.
21. Ibid., p. 9.

22. 'The Pursuit of the Ideal', in Isaiah Berlin, *The Crooked Timber of Humanity* (London: Fontana, 1991), p. 13.
23. John Gray, *The Two Faces of Liberalism* (New York: New Press, 2000), p. 2.
24. The term comes from John Rawls himself. See John Rawls, *Political Liberalism* (New York: Columbia University Press, 1993).
25. Ibid., pp. 212–54.
26. Babylonian Talmud, *Berakhot* 34b.

Chapter 9

Responsibility for Society

The love for people must be alive in the heart and soul, a love for all people and a love for all nations, expressing itself in a desire for their spiritual and material advancement . . . One cannot reach the exalted position of being able to recite the verse from the morning prayer, 'Praise the Lord, invoke His name, declare His works among the nations' (1 Chron. 16:8), without experiencing the deep, inner love stirring one to a solicitousness for all nations, to improve their material state and to promote their happiness.

(Rabbi Abraham Isaac Kook)[1]

The late Ansell Harris was one of Anglo-Jewry's more unforgettable characters. Obstinate, single-minded, impossible to argue with and equally impossible not to admire, I thought of him as a latter-day Amos, his life a commentary to the words 'Let justice well up as waters, and righteousness as a mighty stream' (Amos 5:24). It was something he learned from his parents, who had set up a refuge for immigrant children fleeing Nazi Germany. Throughout his adult life that memory drove him to seek out suffering and offer its victims practical help.

He became honorary treasurer of Oxfam, and in the last decade of his life devoted his energies to UK Jewish Aid and International Development, whose role is to provide medical, educational, social and financial help to people in distress regardless of their religion or ethnicity. Through it he was instrumental in bringing humanitarian aid to Bosnia, Kosovo, Albania and Macedonia. He set up a water-filtration plant in Mozambique, a mobile ophthalmic clinic in Zimbabwe, and a student exchange for Tibetan exiles. His energy was prodigious, his moral passion inexhaustible.

Ansell never tired of reminding us that as Jews we have a responsibility to work across the borders of faith and be a blessing to humanity as a whole, seeking neither recognition nor reward. At the memorial service

113

held in his honour, one of the speakers was Lord Bhatia, a Muslim whom Ansell had come to know through his work for Oxfam. It was clear from the tone of his tribute that the two men shared a moral vision and had been close friends. In the course of his remarks, Lord Bhatia told an amusing story. Ansell, he said, loved music, but only on the condition that he chose it himself. He hated background music in public places.

On one of their trips to India, he tried to get the airport staff to turn off the music coming over the public address system. He failed. He tried it again on the plane, and again he failed. Arriving at the hotel, he heard more music in the lobby and stormed up to the receptionist, insisting that it be turned off. This time he succeeded. 'I have no doubt, Ansell, that you are now in heaven with the Lord and his choir of angels', said Lord Bhatia, 'But whatever you do, don't ask God to turn the music off!'

What held them together, one a passionate Jew, the other a no less committed Muslim? The short answer is that they cared for something larger than their respective faith communities. They cared for humanity. When they saw disease, poverty and despair, they didn't stop to ask who was suffering; they acted. They knew that tears are a universal language, and help a universal command. They saw faith not as a secluded castle but as a window onto a wider world. They saw God's image in the face of a stranger, and heard his call in the cry of a starving child.

*   *   *

There are certain questions that are not asked within a particular culture, simply because the circumstances that give rise to it never occurred. Throughout history, Jews took it as axiomatic that they were responsible for one another. The question they did *not* ask was: to what extent are we responsible for the wider society and the world?

As we saw in the previous chapter, this does not mean that Jews did not contribute to the common good. The opposite is the case: whenever they could, they did so out of all proportion to their numbers. But that was under the rubric of 'the ways of peace', not collective responsibility. It is one thing to give, to do acts of kindness to strangers and play a part in furthering the economy, the arts, sciences and welfare. It is another thing to hold that we bear responsibility for the position a society takes in relation, say, to abortion, euthanasia, the breakdown of the family, the criminal justice system or the consumerization of society. Does Judaism hold that collective responsibility extends beyond the boundaries of the community of faith?

The question was not asked because it never arose. For eighteen centuries of Diaspora history, Jews had no civil rights. They had no vote. Until the nineteenth century, they were not admitted to universities, the professions, parliaments, local government or offices of state. Even after emancipation, in the nineteenth and early twentieth centuries, they entered the public domain as citizens rather than as Jews. Public culture was either Christian or secular, and there was no point of entry for, or interest in, a Jewish voice.

Even today the primary concern of most Jews as Jews is to defend Jewish interests rather than articulate Judaic principle. How could it be otherwise? What concerned Jews was the freedom to practise their faith, not a desire to convert others to it. Judaism admits converts but does not seek them – not because it is exclusive but because it does not believe that you have to be Jewish to achieve salvation, a place in 'the world to come'. What interest could a non-Jewish public have in the Sabbath, Jewish dietary laws, Jewish marriage and divorce, circumcision or any other particularistic Jewish practice? Jews were and are a minority in every country except Israel, and have lived with that situation for millennia. They have no desire to impose their views on the majority. Their interests coincide with the basic principles of liberal democracy: minimum government interference with private religious practice and a public policy that is, as far as possible, neutral or inclusive on controversial moral issues.

In any case, collective responsibility in Judaism is associated with the Sinai covenant. It was there in the days of Moses that the Israelites accepted the terms of their vocation as 'a kingdom of priests and a holy nation'. Covenant-making is a highly distinctive form of politics, predicated on active interpersonal responsibility. Other forms of politics do not assume that responsibility is shared by all. On the contrary: rulers rule, the rest obey. Even representative democracy limits the exercise of public responsibility to one vote in the course of several years, referendums excepted. It is by no means clear that a secular moral theory would hold all citizens responsible for the actions of a government, even if they voted for it, still less if they voted against. It may therefore be that collective responsibility is a special feature of the biblical covenant, not a universal principle of societies as such.

In fact, the secular philosophical literature displays a parallel lacuna. Much has been written in the course of history on other forms of responsibility. Does a king derive his authority from the people or from God? To whom is he answerable? Do the people exist to serve the state or does the state exist to serve the people? What are the 'natural' or 'inalienable' rights of the person and what may be ceded, by way of social contract, to the state? What are the moral limits of power? These are staple themes of political philosophy. On collective responsibility – an ethical rather than political question – the literature is sparse.

Examining the little that has been written, one is struck by its extremism. On the one hand there are passages in which responsibility is stretched to the point of incoherence. In Dostoevsky's *The Brothers Karamazov* the following remarkable passage appears, in which Father

Zossima is reporting a conversation between his younger brother and his mother:

> 'And let me tell you this, too, Mother: everyone of us is responsible for everyone else in every way, and I most of all.' Mother could not help smiling at that. She wept and smiled at the same time. 'How are you', she said, 'most of all responsible for everyone? There are murderers and robbers in the world, and what terrible sin have you committed that you should accuse yourself before everyone else?' 'Mother, my dearest heart', he said (he had begun using such caressing, such unexpected words just then), 'my dearest heart, my joy, you must realize that everyone is really responsible for everyone and everything.'[2]

This is offered as a Christian view, but one can find such passages in the work of a secular existentialist such as Jean-Paul Sartre who speaks, in *Being and Nothingness*, of 'absolute responsibility': 'The essential consequence of our earlier remarks is that man, being condemned to be free, carries the weight of the whole world on his shoulders, he is responsible for the world and for himself as a way of being.'[3] This is responsibility stretched beyond the limits of sense. That one can be responsible for events one could not affect, or even know about, is either mystical or non-sensical.[4] At the other extreme is the libertarian individualism associated with the name of John Stuart Mill. Mill, in his famous 1859 essay *On Liberty*, argued that there is 'one very simple principle' limiting the scope of social intervention in the lives of individuals:

> That principle is that the sole end for which mankind are warranted, individually or collectively, in interfering with the liberty of action of any of their number, is self-protection. That the only purpose for which power can be rightfully exercised over any member of a civilised community, against his will, is to prevent harm to others. His own good, either physical or moral, is not a sufficient warrant.[5]

This is a perfectly legitimate position, and it is an interesting question as to whether a Jewish argument could be constructed on similar lines.[6] What marks the transition from liberalism to libertarianism, however, is the attempt to translate this from a political statement to an ethical one – to say, in other words, that not only the *state* but also *society* and the individuals who comprise it have no right to pass adverse judgement on the behaviour of others, using moral influence rather than political power. Mill himself did not draw this conclusion. In fact he explicitly opposed it:

It would be a great misunderstanding of this doctrine to suppose that it is one of selfish indifference, which pretends that human beings have no business with each other's conduct in life, and that they should not concern themselves about the well-doing or well being of one another, unless their own interest is involved. Instead of any diminution, there is need of a great increase of disinterested exertion to promote the good of others.[7]

Despite these remarks, the history of postmodern ethical thought in the West has been precisely 'a great misunderstanding of this doctrine' – namely, that it is wrong in principle ('judgementalism') to pass adverse public comment on any form of behaviour freely chosen by individuals. Forgetting who first said these words, we have reached the conclusion that we are no longer 'my brother's keeper'.

With some notable exceptions,[8] secular thought sheds little light on the question of the collective moral responsibility of citizens for society or humanity for the global community. In this chapter I want to explore this question from a Jewish perspective. Despite the paucity of sources, there are enough to construct an answer, although it will not be one shared by all.

*   *   *

The first is the biblical story of Jonah, sent by God to deliver a call to repentance to the inhabitants of Nineveh. Not surprisingly, Jonah flees. What does he have to do with these strangers? Besides which, Nineveh was part of Assyria, Israel's enemies, the very people who would later attack, conquer and send to oblivion the northern kingdom, the 'lost Ten Tribes'. From Jonah's point of view, either they would respond to his call or they would not. If they did, they would be saved, and thus free to commit evil some other time. If they did not, Jonah would merely be the bringer of bad news, and would doubtless be blamed if it transpired. There seemed to be no logic, no happy outcome, to his mission.

In a famous scene, God brings about a storm that threatens the ship on which he is fleeing, and sends him back. Jonah proclaims his message – 'In forty days, Nineveh will be destroyed' (Jonah 3:4), a mere five words in biblical Hebrew – the people repent and disaster is averted. Jonah has been made to look a fool (he said the town would be destroyed; it was not) and prays to die. God, in another famous scene involving a vine that grows overnight and gives Jonah shade, delivers a lesson:

> You are concerned about this vine, though you did not tend it or make it grow. It sprang up overnight and died overnight. But

117

Nineveh has more than a hundred and twenty thousand people who cannot tell their right hand from their left, and many cattle as well. Should I not be concerned about that great city? (Jonah 4:10–11)

God's 'tender mercies are on all His works' (Ps. 145:9). Neither justice nor repentance, sin nor restitution, has ethnic or religious boundaries. The people of Nineveh are God's creatures no less than others. That is what the book of Jonah is about.

Historians have sometimes suggested that universalism is a late development in biblical history. It is not so, and the conclusion can only be reached by those who read the Hebrew Bible through a tendentious view of human evolution, seeing particularism as primitive, universalism as advanced, and the two (parochial versus cosmopolitan) as opposed. In fact, the Hebrew Bible sees particularism and universalism as two essential facets of identity. On the one hand we are human, sharing our basic fate with all humanity; on the other, we have particular ways of being human, and there is no other way of doing so. Our particularity *is* our universality. Only by being what we uniquely are, can we respect other people for what they uniquely are.

Isaiah famously spoke of Israel as a 'light to the nations' (Is. 42:6, 49:6). Jeremiah was charged with being a 'prophet to the nations' (Jer. 1:5). Amos delivered oracles about peoples other than his own, as did other prophets. Five times in the book of Genesis the patriarchs are told 'through you all the families of the earth shall be blessed'.[9] Zephaniah anticipates the day when 'I will purify the lips of the peoples, that all of them may call on the name of the Lord, and serve Him shoulder to shoulder' (Zeph. 3:9). Zekhariah foresees a time when 'The Lord will be king over the whole earth; on that day He will be one and His name one' (Zekh. 14:9). Malachi, last of the prophets, says, 'From the rising to the setting of the sun, My name is great among the nations' (Mal. 1:11). The Hebrew Bible is particular, not parochial. It could not be otherwise. The God of Israel is the God of all humanity, whether or not he is recognized as such.

The inference I draw from the Bible as a whole is that the moral demands on humanity are universal. John Barton, writing on Amos's oracles to the nations, concludes that for the prophet, 'All the nations of the world are bound by certain moral laws and are accountable for their conduct.'[10] Israel is particular for two reasons: first its vocation as a *holy* nation, second its unique mutuality (what the French revolutionaries called 'fraternity') as a covenantal people. As we will see, some medieval Jewish authorities did draw practical conclusions, especially from the case of Jonah. But the biblical sources are not sufficient to prove that we are responsible for cultures and communities not our own, for an obvious reason: the moral principle that 'ought implies can'. We are responsible only if we could have achieved something but did not. Jonah aside, what impact could Israel have had in the ancient world? No other nation shared its monotheism. The Greeks, noting their refusal to offer sacrifices to idols, called them atheists. To be sure, in Genesis we see Joseph saving Egypt from famine. But beyond that, until recently, the idea that a civilization might heed a moral voice from the outside would have been absurd.

Moving to the twelfth century, Maimonides makes an interesting observation in his law code, the *Mishneh Torah*. It concerns a difficult episode in the 34th chapter of Genesis. Shehem, a prince of the tribe that bore his name, had fallen in love with Jacob's daughter Dina, and had raped and abducted her. Dina's brothers Simeon and Levi conceive of a plan to rescue her and avenge the crime. They tell Shehem and the men of the town that they are willing to let their sister marry the prince on condition that they undergo circumcision. They agree and have the operation performed. On the third day, as they are weak because of the operation, Simeon and Levi rescue Dina, killing all the men of the town.

Jacob is shocked by this act of violence and remembers it to his dying day. Instead of blessing the two brothers, he curses them: 'Simeon and Levi are brothers – their swords are weapons of violence . . . Cursed be their anger, so fierce, and their fury, so cruel!' (Gen. 49:5–7). At the time, however, Jacob and his sons have an angry conversation that breaks off mid-way:

> Then Jacob said to Simeon and Levi: 'You have brought trouble on me by making me a stench to the Canaanites and Perizzites, the people in this land. We are few in number, and if they join forces against me and attack me, I and my household will be destroyed.'
>
> But they replied, 'Should he have treated our sister like a prostitute?' (Gen. 34:30–1)

Two giants of medieval Jewry, Maimonides and Nahmanides, differed in their assessment of this exchange. Maimonides says, 'Therefore the people of Shehem deserved destruction, because they witnessed Shehem committing an act of abduction and rape and did nothing to bring him to justice.'[11] Maimonides assumes that all societies are bound by mutual responsibility. They are obliged to establish a system of justice, and if they fail to do so they are collectively guilty for the wrong committed in their midst.

Nahmanides disagrees.[12] To be sure, he gives an even wider definition than Maimonides of the universal obligation to institute justice, but if Gentiles fail to do this they are not liable to collective punishment. The proof lies, he argues, in the biblical text itself. Jacob condemned Simeon and Levi. He would not have done so had there been a moral justification for what they did. The universal requirement of justice imposes on all societies the obligation to establish laws and a judiciary, but the members of a society are not collectively responsible for the crimes others commit.

One way of understanding their disagreement is to relate it to the scope of the covenant with humanity after the Flood. At Sinai, the children of Israel pledged themselves to the principle of collective responsibility: 'All Israel are sureties for one another.' Was this unique to that event, or was it true of the earlier Noahide covenant as well? Nahmanides assumes the former, Maimonides the latter. For Nahmanides, the universal rules established after the Flood bind humanity to keep the law, but not necessarily to ensure that *others* do so. Maimonides thought otherwise, maintaining that collective responsibility is a universal feature of moral and political life.[13]

The next authority to touch on the issue was the Spanish rabbi and moralist Rabbenu Jonah ben Abraham Gerondi (c. 1200–63). In his ethical treatise, *The Gates of Repentance*, he writes:

'You shall surely rebuke your neighbour, and not bear sin because of him' (Lev. 19:17). We have hereby been exhorted not to bear sin through the sins of our neighbours by failing to rebuke them. If one man sins, the whole congregation is punished when his sin becomes known, if they do not reprove him with the rod of correction, as it is written, 'Did not Akhan the son of Zerah commit a trespass concerning the devoted thing, and wrath fell upon all the congregation of Israel and that man perished not alone in his transgression' (Josh. 22:20) . . . And even Gentiles said, '. . . that we may know for whose cause this evil is upon us' (Jonah 1:7). How much more, then, should Jews, who are responsible for each other, govern themselves after this fashion.[14]

Rabbenu Jonah is talking about Jewish, not general responsibility, but he invokes as a proof-text the passage in the book of Jonah when a storm threatens the ship, and the (Gentile) sailors believe that they are being punished for the sins of someone on board. They cast lots to discover who it is, and the lot falls on Jonah. They assume that they are being collectively punished – as were the Israelites in Joshua's time when, because of the sin of one of them, Akhan son of Zerah, they were defeated in their battle with Ai. In both cases, the identity of the wrongdoer is established by casting lots, and the guilt of the community is lifted by bringing the wrongdoer to justice. R. Jonah takes it for granted, like Maimonides, that there is collective responsibility beyond the covenant of Israel.

A similar idea appears in the *Sefer Hassidim*, a compendium of moral instruction compiled by the northern European Jewish pietists in the thirteenth century. This states that 'If one sees a Gentile committing a transgression, if one can protest then one should, since the Holy One, blessed be He, sent Jonah to Nineveh to cause them to repent.'[15] Here, Jonah's mission is taken as evidence of a more general responsibility on the part of Jews to ensure, when they can, that those around them are faithful to the Noahide laws.

A more philosophical approach is to be found in the work of the fifteenth-century Spanish–Jewish philosopher and exegete Isaac Arama.[16] Reflecting on the harshness of the punishment of Sodom in comparison with other biblical episodes, he draws on Aristotelian ethics to make a distinction between countries where the inhabitants do wrong, and those in which the law itself condones wrongdoing. Where crimes are committed by individuals, they alone bear the guilt, but where the law itself permits their behaviour, or where judges turn a blind eye to it, wrongs are 'transformed from the sins of individuals to the sins of the community as a whole'. Both Arama's example, Sodom, and his source, Aristotle, lie outside a specifically Jewish frame of reference, and it appears that he regarded this as a moral fact about society as such. Laws – even those made by a monarch – involve the tacit consent of the people. It is therefore no excuse to say, 'I did no wrong; the sin belongs to someone else.' Merely being part of a society and failing to protest its wrongdoing renders one liable for part of the guilt – the guilt of the *bystander*, one who could have acted but did not.

In the early twentieth century, two outstanding rabbis, Ben-Zion Uziel (1880–1953) and Abraham Isaac Kook (1865–1935), respectively Sephardi and Ashkenazi Chief Rabbis of pre-state Israel, delivered strong statements on the universality of Jewish moral concern:

> The settlement of the world [*yishuvo shel olam*] in its many ramifications is a precondition and vital need for our attaining our proper way in life . . . Each country and each nation which respects itself, does not and cannot be satisfied with its narrow boundaries and limited domains. Rather, they desire to bring in all that is good and beautiful, that is helpful and glorious to their national [cultural] treasure. And they wish to give the maximum flow of their own blessings to the heritage of humanity as a whole. Each [self-respecting nation] desires to establish a link of love and friendship among all nations, for the enrichment of the human storehouse of intellectual and ethical ideas and for the uncovering of the secrets of nature. Happy is the country and happy the nation that can give an account of what it has taken in from others, and more importantly, of what it has given to the heritage of all humanity. Woe to the country and nation that encloses itself within its own four cubits

and limits itself to its own narrow boundaries, lacking anything of its own to contribute, and lacking the tools to receive from others.[17]

Rabbi Uziel could not be more explicit: there is a global project, 'the settlement of the world', to which every nation should contribute, and from which each should draw. Cultural exclusivism is a sign not of strength but of weakness, not of confidence but fear. Rabbi Kook put it equally strongly:

The highest position in the love of people must be taken by the love of man, and it must extend to all men, despite all differences of opinion, religion and faith, despite all distinctions of race and climate . . . We must know that the point of life, light and holiness never moved from the divine image bestowed on humanity in general, and on every people and tongue, each according to its significance, and that this holy kernel will elevate all. Because of this point of life we wish for the total elevation that will affect the world, the light of justice and righteousness . . . the perfection of all that is created, and man and all his faculties first.[18]

Most strikingly, the principle was taken up by the late Lubavitcher Rebbe, R. Menahem Mendel Schneersohn. He campaigned to encourage Jews to exert their influence to persuade people in general to keep the Noahide laws. Basing his position on Maimonides' ruling[19] that when Jews hold power they must ensure that Gentiles adhere to these laws, he argued that power was not a precondition; even influence was an opportunity. In the past, Jews had generally kept themselves to themselves, not intervening in wider social debates. But that was due to circumstance, not principle. Times had changed, and with them our responsibilities. Wherever one could influence others in a moral direction, one should.

This is, in fact, stated as a general principle in the Talmud:

Whoever can forbid his household [to commit a sin] but does not, is seized for [the sins of] his household. [If he can forbid] his fellow citizens [but does not] he is seized for [the sins of] his fellow citizens. [If he can forbid] the whole world [but does not] he is seized for [the sins of] the whole world. Rav Pappa observed, 'And the members of the Exilarch's [household – the Exilarch was the head of Babylonian Jewry] are seized for the whole world.' This is as Rabbi Hanina said: Why is it written, *The Lord will enter into judgement with the elders of His people, and the princes thereof* (Is. 3:14)? If the princes sinned, how did the elders sin? The answer is that the elders sinned because they did not forbid the princes.[20]

We bear responsibility for whatever we could have prevented but did not. Maimonides codifies this (admittedly in a Jewish context) as law.[21] Where it is certain that one will fail, then there is no obligation to try. As the Talmud says: 'Just as one has a duty to say what will be heeded, so one has a duty *not* to say what will *not* be heeded.'[22] But if there is even a remote possibility, one must register a protest. God says this explicitly to the prophet Ezekiel: 'Son of man . . . The people to whom I am sending you are obstinate and stubborn. Say to them, "This is what the sovereign Lord says." And whether they listen or fail to listen – for they are a rebellious house – they will know that a prophet has been among them' (Ezek. 2:3–5). We may not be silent in the face of wrongdoing or injustice. We must use whatever influence we have. If we succeed, we have made a difference. If we fail, we have honoured our obligation by doing what we could. The philosopher Karl Jaspers came to a similar conclusion in his *The Question of German Guilt*:

> There exists a solidarity among men as human beings that makes each co-responsible for every wrong and every injustice in the world, especially for crimes committed in his presence or with his knowledge. If I fail to do whatever I can to prevent them, I too am guilty. If I was present at the murder of others without risking my life to prevent it, I feel guilty in a way not adequately conceivable either legally, politically or morally. That I live after such a thing has happened weighs upon me as indelible guilt.[23]

He calls this *metaphysical* as opposed to *moral* guilt, restricting the latter to wrongs I myself committed. My view is that it does not need metaphysics. It flows from such imperatives as 'Do not stand still when your neighbour's life is in danger' (Lev. 19:16) and from such precedents as Moses' intervention when he sees shepherds molesting Jethro's daughters (Ex. 2:16–19). There is a duty to intervene to prevent wrong when we can, regardless of who commits it and against whom it is committed, sometimes by physical action, at others by argument, reason and persuasion. Its simplest expression was formulated by Holocaust historian Yehudah Bauer: *Thou shalt not be a bystander.*

*   *   *

This is not the place to discuss the precise parameters of what Judaism calls the Noahide covenant, the basic norms and responsibilities of human conduct.[24] In any case, R. Nissim Gaon (c. 990–1062), in his preface to the Talmud, states that 'all commands that flow from reason and human understanding have obligated humanity since God first created man on earth'.[25] This is as close as Judaism comes to natural law and to John Rawls' 'language of public reason'.

I find the distinction, fundamental to Judaism, between the universal requirements of human decency and the particular code of a religious tradition, helpful, even essential in a multicultural society. There is the common ground of the common good, and there are the semi-private domains of our diverse religious traditions. We are responsible to society for the former, to our own community for the latter. That is, I believe, as it should be. No one should seek to impose his or her religious convictions on society, but we should seek to bring the insights of our respective faiths to the public conversation about the principles for which we stand and the values we share. That would involve, for the religious groups within society, a shift from the *politics of interests* to the *politics of principle*. It is when our horizons extend beyond our own faith communities that our separate journeys converge and we become joint builders of a more gracious world.

There is something at stake here of great contemporary relevance. I have argued elsewhere[26] that there is a distinctive political philosophy to be found in the Hebrew Bible. The whole thrust of modern political thought from the seventeenth century onward (Hobbes, Locke, Rousseau) has focused on the *social contract*: that agreement, tacit or explicit, by which individuals transfer some of their rights to a central body (king, parliament, legislature) in return for which it protects them from enemies without and lawlessness within. On this view, politics is a matter of collective self-interest. However, the early theorists of social contract were able to take one thing for granted, namely the existence of a shared culture – Christianity – by which people made sense of their moral obligations. The battle in the seventeenth century was merely over which *form* of Christianity should prevail. *Politics* might be the arena of self-interest, but it was counterbalanced by an ethical tradition that spoke a different language altogether, that of altruism and service-to-others.

That can no longer be taken for granted. Postmodern societies are marked by their *lack* of moral consensus. They contain people of radically different faiths. Secular culture, meanwhile, has largely abandoned the project of morality as a society-wide enterprise. It has become instead the exercise of autonomy: morality as private and personal choice (the Bible sees this as anarchy: 'In those days Israel had no king; everyone did as he saw fit' [Judges 21:25]). It is hard to see how society can survive in the long term under such conditions. Morality is the history of humanity's attempts to construct a common life on the basis of shared codes, conventions and convictions. Without shared moral discourse, the public square is reduced to a quasi-economic exchange: the provision of services in return for taxes. That is too fragile a basis on which to build a viable nation, let alone a gracious world. It leaves it entirely open to question, for example, why people who feel they are not getting a fair deal should abide by the political process at all. Why not simply reject society if you feel that it is rejecting you? That would plunge us back into the 'state of nature' – the war of all against all, civil unrest – that provoked the crisis of modernity in the first place.

Faced with such a situation, there is much to be said for revisiting an alternative view of politics. What is striking about the Hebrew Bible is that it is based on *two* processes, not one: the social *contract* that creates a *state*, and the social *covenant* that creates a *society*. Israel enacted its social contract in the days of Samuel, when it voted for a monarchy (1 Sam. 8). It entered its social covenant several centuries earlier, at Mount Sinai, when it accepted the sovereignty of God and the authority of his commandments. Israel was not yet a *state*: it had not even entered its land. But from that moment on, it was a *society*, bound precisely by the principle of shared responsibility we analysed in Chapter 7. America underwent a similar process. First came its equivalent of covenant: the Declaration of Independence of 1776. Only later did it formulate its social contract: the Constitution of 1787. The message of the Bible for the politics of the contemporary West is that it is not enough to have a state. You also need a society – meaning, that *common belonging* that comes from a sense that we are neighbours as well as strangers; that we have duties to one another, to the heritage of the past and to the hopes of generations not yet born; that society is not a *hotel* where we receive services in exchange for money, but a *home* to which we feel attached and whose history is (literally or adoptively) our own. That requires covenantal, not just contractual, politics.[27]

So too does globalization. Why *should* we feel morally implicated in the problems of ethnic conflict, mass poverty, famine relief, AIDS, and actual or attempted genocide – when these are happening far away to people we have never met, with whom we have little in common, and whose consequences will touch us only tangentially, if at all? Yet we *do* feel implicated. There *is* a covenant of human solidarity. John Donne said it memorably long ago: 'All mankind is of one author, and is one volume . . . No man is an island, entire of itself . . . any man's death diminishes me, because I am involved in mankind; and therefore never send to know for whom the bell tolls; it tolls for thee.'[28]

*　　　　　*　　　　　*

The concept of the covenant with Noah is genuinely helpful here. It tells us that, prior to our particular commitments to this faith or that, this culture, nation, civilization or that, we are human beings, cast together in a fate which grows more interconnected with every passing century, each passing year. We have a duty, not just to ourselves, our families and friends, but also to the ever-widening concentric circles – community, society, humanity – of which we are a part. We are responsible for what we could do, but did not, to alleviate the human condition. To be sure, these responsibilities are not open-ended: we can't do it all. We have limited time, energy and resources, and those with whom we are most closely bound in a web of obligations have a right to expect that we will give them priority. It is morally wrong – as Dickens so memorably showed in his portrait of Mrs Jellyby in *Bleak House* – to try and save the world while neglecting our own children. But what applies to a community applies to society, and ultimately to the world: we are worth what we are willing to share. Each of us has a contribution to make, and 'whether we do much or we do little, what matters is that our heart is turned to heaven'.[29]

The same applies to faith. There is all the difference in the world between the attempt to impose your faith on others and the willingness to share it with others. Our faiths are different. Judaism is not Christianity; Christianity is not Islam; the Abrahamic monotheisms are different from Eastern mysticisms on the one hand, scientific humanism on the other. Yet when we bring our respective heritages of wisdom to the public domain, we have no need to wish to convert others. Instead, we are tacitly saying: if this speaks to you, then please take it as our gift. Indeed, it is yours already, for wisdom (unlike revelation) belongs to us all. The willingness non-coercively to share our several traditions of moral insight is, in a religiously plural culture, an essential part of the democratic conversation, indeed of societal beatitude.

And yes, it can lead to paradoxical results. Shortly after the attack on the World Trade Center on 11 September 2001 I received the following e-mail from a stranger:

Dear Dr Sacks,

I hope that you read this personally.

I am an American and a Christian and I work in San Jose, California. The events of September 11th traumatized me, as they did many around the world. The thought of death is scary but I was more frightened at the realization of abused, hungry, lonely and ill people, in every country, that I have forgotten. I am sorry I did that.

In the scary, sleepless nights that followed, I reflected on my life's purpose – how well I knew it as a child – and how I could recapture and live it. I knew I could only achieve that if I devoted myself once more to God and live the way he would want me to live. I prayed often but was apprehensive about going to church. I thought of you and your lectures and turned to *Faith in the Future* for help.

126

I found strength and understanding in what I read, especially that God has faith in us. This was a new concept to me. It made me take responsibility for my faith and it filled me with joy to think of faith as reciprocal.

I also understood the call to remember. Since I've read that, I have spent much time remembering my life and society and also the lives of others and their societies. I've remembered why I've made certain decisions in my life, like studying political sociology at university, and why. 'Why' was to understand the Holocaust so that it never happened again. I made peace initiatives my career because of it, yet as my life got more comfortable, my passions lessened. Only through remembering have I come to realize that my skills and my time are needed to accomplish the goal I set out to achieve.

Finally, I took on board the importance of loving the stranger once again. I used to do that naturally, but I don't anymore. Now, I've reached out to many. I've started with my husband, family and colleagues and I'm now doing it again with the stranger (although there is much to be done).

So, why did I write to you? Well, forgive me for sounding melodramatic, but if I died that night, I would have died knowing my Lord again and remembering him. That is a great gift you've given. You reached out to the stranger, and that stranger was me.

Should I be thankful or perplexed that I, a Jew, helped a Christian rediscover her faith? I, for one, thanked God for the privilege of bringing his word to another person, for though our faiths are different, profoundly so, I believe that all prayers that come from the heart converge in God's infinity, where all persons are loved if they themselves love.

NOTES

1. Abraham Isaac Kook, 'The Moral Principles' (*Middot ha-Rayah*). English version in Abraham Isaac Kook, *The Lights of Penitence, Lights of Holiness, The Moral Principles, Essays, Letters and Poems*, trans. Ben Zion Bokser (London: SPCK, 1979), p. 136.
2. Quoted in Jonathan Glover, *Causing Death and Saving Lives* (London: Penguin, 1977), p. 204.
3. Jean-Paul Sartre, *Being and Nothingness*, trans. Hazel Barnes (New York: Washington Square Press, 1966), p. 707.
4. That is precisely the point of the distinction made by Rabbi Judah the Prince (Chapter 7 above) between publicly known and 'secret' offences.

5. John Stuart Mill, *Utilitarianism, On Liberty and Considerations on Representative Government*, ed. H. B. Acton (London: Dent, 1984), p. 78.
6. See, for example, Nahum Rabinovitch, *Darkah shel Torah* (Jerusalem: Maaliot, 1998) pp. 3–102.
7. Mill, *Utilitarianism*, p. 144.
8. See, for example, Karl Jaspers, *The Question of German Guilt* (1947), trans. E. B. Ashton (New York: Capricorn, 1961); Hans Jonas, *The Imperative of Responsibility* (Chicago: University of Chicago Press, 1984); Larry May, *Sharing Responsibility* (Chicago: University of Chicago Press, 1992); Richard Swinburne, *Responsibility and Atonement* (Oxford: Clarendon Press, 1989). On the move from liberalism to libertarianism, see Jonathan Sacks, *The Politics of Hope*, second ed. (London: Vintage, 2000).
9. Genesis 12:3; 18:18; 22:18; 26:4; 28:14.
10. John Barton, *Amos's Oracles Against the Nations* (Cambridge: Cambridge University Press, 1980), p. 48.
11. *Mishneh Torah, Melakhim* 9:14.
12. Nahmanides, *Commentary* to Gen. 34:13.
13. There was, of course, one difference between the covenant with Noah and the covenant at Sinai. The latter was accepted by the people; the former was imposed by God. Neither Noah nor his descendants were asked for their consent. Perhaps at issue between Maimonides and Nahmanides is whether collective responsibility *requires* consent.
14. Jonah ben Abraham Gerondi, *The Gates of Repentance* III:72.
15. *Sefer Hassidim* 1124; Reuben Margoliot (ed.) (Jerusalem: Mossad haRav Kook, 1978), p. 562.
16. *Akedat Yitzhak*, Genesis, Gate 20 (Jerusalem, 1978), pp. 161–3.
17. Benzion Uziel, *Hegyonei Uziel*, vol. 2, pp. 109, 127. I am indebted to Marc Angel, *Loving Truth and Peace: the grand religious worldview of Rabbi Benzion Uziel* (Northvale, NJ: Jason Aronson, 1999), pp. 50–2, for these references.
18. *Musar Avikha* 96, 98. Quoted in Yoel Ben Nun, 'Nationalism, Humanity and *Knesset Yisrael*', in Benjamin Ish-Shalom and Shalom Rosenberg (eds.), *The World of Rav Kook's Thought* (Jerusalem: Avi Chai Foundation, 1991), p. 212.
19. *Mishneh Torah, Melakhim* 8:10.
20. Babylonian Talmud, *Shabbat* 54b.
21. *Mishneh Torah, De'ot* 6:7. The subject is a large one. See Jonathan Sacks, *Rabbinic Conceptions of Responsibility for Others*, PhD Thesis, University of London, 1981.
22. Babylonian Talmud, *Yevamot* 65b.
23. Jaspers, *The Question of German Guilt*, p. 36.
24. See David Novak, *The Image of the Non-Jew in Judaism: an historical and constructive study of the Noahide Laws* (New York: E. Mellen Press, 1983); *Natural Law in Judaism* (New York: Cambridge University Press, 1998). For my own statement of a global ethic, see Jonathan Sacks, *The Dignity of Difference* (London: Continuum, 2002).
25. Ran, *Commentary, Berakhot*, introduction.

26. Sacks, *The Politics of Hope*.
27. The late Daniel Elazar wrote many scholarly books on covenantal politics. See especially his *Kinship & Consent: the Jewish political tradition and its contemporary uses*, second ed. (New Brunswick, NJ: Transaction, 1997); *Covenant & Polity in Biblical Israel* (New Brunswick, NJ: Transaction, 1995); *Covenant and Civil Society: the constitutional matrix of modern democracy* (New Brunswick, NJ: Transaction, 1998); and also the insightful discussion in Philip Selznick, *The Moral Commonwealth* (Berkeley: University of California Press, 1992).
28. John Donne, 'Devotions upon Emergent Occasions, meditation XVII', in John Hayward (ed.), *John Donne: complete poetry and selected prose* (London: Nonesuch, 1930), pp. 537–9.
29. Babylonian Talmud, *Menahot* 110a.

Part 2

The Theology of Responsibility

Chapter 10

The Birth of
Responsibility

Responsibility: A detachable burden easily shifted to the shoulders of God, Fate, Fortune, Luck or one's neighbour. In the days of astrology it was customary to unload it upon a star.

(Ambrose Bierce)[1]

Where did it come from, this Jewish passion to change the world, and which, directly or indirectly, *did* change the world? For in the course of time, the vision of the prophets inspired other traditions which, though they parted company with Judaism, were influenced by its passion for social justice and redemption – among them, Christianity (especially the Puritanism that led to both the English and the American revolutions), Islam, and the secular–messianic utopia of Karl Marx.

Ideas do not appear from nowhere, nor are all thoughts possible within every configuration of culture. The world of myth was profoundly conservative. Indeed, throughout most of history, religions and civilizations have tended to reinforce, rather than challenge, the status quo. They have taught acceptance, not protest; continuity, not revolution. Their governing assumption has been that the world is as it is because that is the nature of things. Hierarchical societies mirror the order of the heavens. Nations are organisms, unfolding like plants. There is nothing in nature to make us think we can rise above nature and its inexorable laws of birth, growth, decay and death. In the struggle for survival, the strong win, the weak die, power rules and fate is blind. From where, then, do the thoughts arise that we can change the world and humanize it, making it less random and cruel and creating within its deserts, oases of justice and gardens of grace?

The key idea is *transcendence:* that God is to be found not within nature but beyond it. At a stroke, this relativized all human institutions. Nothing in society is as it is because it could not be otherwise. God is free: therefore the human person, created in his image, is also free. Hierarchy, inequality, the corruptions of power, the exploitation of the weak, imperial conquest and the enslavement of peoples are not justified merely because they exist. For the first time a gap is opened up between 'is' and 'ought'. Not everything that is, is good. Not all that is done, is right. We can imagine a world different from the way it is now and has been in the past; and because we can imagine it, we can decide to act in such a way as to begin to bring it about. When God is conceived of as *both* beyond the natural universe *and* endowing humanity with his most distinctive attribute, creativity, a momentous human freedom is born. For the first time, religion becomes a world-transforming rather than world-accepting force.

With freedom is born responsibility. If we are *not* free – if what we do is the result of natural laws, inexorable forces beyond our control – then we are not responsible. I may be unfortunate, but I am not guilty, for things I could not help doing. Freedom, choice, moral agency, accountability, merit, guilt, retributive justice, atonement and forgiveness are interlocking concepts that were born together, and have their genesis in the Hebrew Bible. Without it, the moral landscape of the West would not be what it became.

In this and the following four chapters, I take up the story where I left it at the end of Chapter 2, with the assertion that 'The Bible is God's call to human responsibility'. I do so because ideas do not exist in a void. They have a history and an ecology. One of the occupational hazards of philosophy in the Platonic mode is to believe that ideas come from a realm of disembodied space called pure reason. In the case of the ethics, it isn't so. There is more than one kind of ethical life, and reason does not decide between them. There is the civic ethic – whose highest virtue is readiness to die for one's city – which flourished in classical Greece. There is the ethic of duty, strongly associated with hierarchical societies. There is the ethic of honour, common in militaristic societies with codes of chivalry. And there is the ethics of responsibility, with its emphasis on love of God and humanity, and on the categorical dignity of the individual as such, regardless of status or power.[2] Because this last is so strange, and so much at risk, I want to tell the story, as best I can, of how it arose and the radical ideas it involves. That story is told in the Hebrew Bible, which is, as I will show, an extended essay on human responsibility.

On the face of it, this is a strange claim to make. Surely, of all religions, Judaism emphasizes the work of God, not humans. It was God who took the Israelites out of Egypt, led them through the wilderness, divided the Red Sea, gave them water from the rock and manna from heaven, God who acts and to whom we pray. Biblical faith is usually thought of as belief in the saving acts of heaven, not heaven's belief in the saving power of humankind. How then can I say that it is God's call to us to accept responsibility and become, with him, co-authors of the script of history, his partners in the work of creation? A close reading of the Pentateuch will, however, show us that responsibility is not merely consistent with its message. It is, in fact, its greatest overarching theme.

*   *   *

The Bible begins with four stories: Adam and Eve, Cain and Abel, Noah and the Flood, and the Tower of Babel. What are they *about?* Why are they there? The story that dominates the Bible – God's covenant with the children of Israel and its tempestuous history – does not begin until Genesis 12 with God's call to Abraham to leave land, home and his father's house. What then is the function of the first eleven chapters? To what *genre* do they belong? They are more than history. They represent a search for meaning in history. They are, in fact, a philosophical drama in four acts, a sustained and tightly constructed exploration of the concept of responsibility.

Act I is set in the Garden of Eden: Adam, Eve and paradise. Around the first couple lies the rich profusion of the created world. One thing alone is forbidden, the fruit of the tree of knowledge of good and evil. This is a notional constraint, a warning at the beginning of human time that not everything is permitted. There are boundaries, transgression of which is evil. Hence the appearance for the first time of the word *ra*, 'evil', in a creation account dominated by the word 'good'. Needless to say, it is to this tree that they are drawn. 'Stolen water', says Proverbs (9:17), 'tastes sweet'. They eat; their 'eyes are opened'; they feel shame. What is fascinating is their reaction:

> Then the man and his wife heard the sound of the Lord God as He was walking in the garden in the cool of the day, and they hid from the Lord God among the trees of the garden. But the Lord God called to the man: 'Where are you?'
>
> He answered, 'I heard you in the garden, and I was afraid because I was naked, so I hid'.
>
> And He said, 'Who told you that you were naked? Have you eaten from the tree that I commanded you not to eat from?'
>
> The man said, 'The woman you put here with me – she gave me some of the fruit from the tree, and I ate it'. (Gen. 3:8–12)

The first human instinct is denial. The man blames the woman. By implication he blames God as well. It was, after all, he who made her, he who decided that 'It is not good for man to be alone'. We hear for the first time a proposition that has undergone many transformations but always with the same conclusion: 'I am not responsible. I am not to blame.' The fault may lie in our stars, our socioeconomic class, early childhood traumas, the configuration of our genes or the several other varieties of determinism, each of which denies the freedom of human action. Adam is guilty of what Jean-Paul Sartre called bad faith, the self-deception that we are objects not subjects, acted on by forces outside our control.[3] Not to be outdone, the woman repeats the strategy: 'Then the Lord God said to the woman, "What is this you have done?" The woman said, "The serpent deceived me and I ate"' (Gen. 3:13). She too declares herself innocent, the victim not the perpetrator, the deceived not the self-deceived. The Bible describes this as 'hiding'. When Adam and Eve hide themselves among the trees, they are acting out a psychological state: shame seeking concealment.

Something highly significant is taking place in this narrative. Before the woman had been formed, God had told the man: 'You are free to eat from any tree in the garden; but you must not eat from the tree of the knowledge of good and evil, for when you eat of it you will surely die' (Gen. 2:16–17).[4] Only on the most superficial reading is this about a tree, or sexual knowledge. It is about the birth of the ethical life. For the monotheistic mind, the world is not what it was in myth: a place of magic and mystery, spirits and demons, gods and demigods, hostile powers and ever-present dangers. Man and God confront one another from immeasurable distance but also in unprecedented immediacy. God is more than a power. He is a voice: conscience. There is unparalleled drama in this stark confrontation between the lone God and the lonely first man. It represents the birth of the individual in Western civilization.[5]

In myth, both human beings and the gods are part of nature. The gods are often seen as forces of nature: the sun, the storm, the sea, the earth. In nature, there is no freedom. There are clashes, battles, struggles for dominance. The strong win, the weak lose, but the laws of nature govern all. That is not only an ancient view. It is shared by many modern theories also: sociobiology, evolutionary psychology, physicalist theories of the brain and so on. Freedom, on this view, is an illusion. We are part of nature, and thus subject to universal laws of cause and effect. We like to think that we are masters of our fate, but we are not. We are concatenations of chemicals, part of the dance of genetic mutation and natural selection, whose ringmasters are the blind watchmaker and the selfish gene.[6] This is, of course, a parody, but the point is real. Adam and Eve represent the conscious birth of freedom.

They do so because they are made in the image of a God who transcends nature, who creates the world out of no compulsion but as a free act of love. He gives humanity his greatest gift – that of freedom itself. Unique among created beings, *Homo sapiens* is capable of being creative. We have language, imagination, the ability to recall the distant past and, especially, use the future tense. We can frame alternatives and choose between them. But *freedom has limits*. That is the point of the command about the tree. Without limits, freedom for the strong means slavery for the weak. Freedom for the rich means misery for the poor. These limits have nothing to do with nature. The limits of nature are about power: they are about what we *can* do. The limits God places on humankind are about ethics: what we *may* do. The birth of the moral imperative – command, prohibition, 'Thou shalt not' – occurs at the moment *Homo sapiens* is first capable of understanding that with freedom comes responsibility.

The story of Adam and Eve is not primitive science. It is an elegant statement of the first principle of ethics, which is that freedom generates a new kind of law. Scientific laws describe, moral laws prescribe. Scientific laws predict what *will* happen, moral laws tell us what *ought to* happen. Only a free agent can understand a moral law, and only a free agent can break one. This, the Bible intimates, is never without consequences – for which we are responsible. That is the knowledge conveyed by the fruit of the tree. To break a law is to taste forbidden fruit and know that one has strayed into the territory called 'evil', however harmless the first steps are.

This is what Adam and Eve simultaneously experience and deny. The first beings to discover freedom, they are also the first to feel what Erich Fromm called 'the fear of freedom'.[7] Freedom *is* fearful, precisely because it involves responsibility. It is comforting and comfortable to live under someone else's tutelage and power; to be able to say, 'It wasn't my fault'; to look elsewhere for deliverance. The knowledge that there are laws you can break, and for whose breach you bear the guilt, *is* the exile from Eden, the loss of childhood and innocence; and that is never without pain. Hence the depth and originality of the story is not that Adam and Eve sinned (sin is rarely original) but its insight into the psychodynamics of self-deception. Their first instinct is to deny that they were acting freely at all. They deny *personal* responsibility.

*   *   *

With the second act, the human drama descends into tragedy. Two human children, Cain and Abel, have been born, and with them, sibling rivalry – one of Genesis' recurring themes. They both bring offerings to God. Abel's is accepted; Cain's is not. Why his was not accepted will become clear in the course of the narrative. Cain is indignant. He 'was very angry and his face was downcast'. God, reading his thoughts, responds: 'Then the Lord said to Cain, "Why are you angry? Why is your face downcast? If you do what is right, will you not be accepted? But if you do not do what is right, sin is crouching at your door. It desires to have you, but you must master it"' (Gen. 4:6–7). This is a speech that connects precisely with the previous act. Adam and Eve denied personal responsibility. God tells Cain that such denial will not be accepted. Besides which, it is not true. Yes, there is temptation and what the sages called the 'evil inclination'. Those who act under its sway may claim to be powerless to resist, but they are wrong. Sin is not irresistible: 'It desires to have you, but you must master it.' God closes this route of escape. For Cain there can be no denial of freedom or personal responsibility. None the less, Cain kills Abel.

> Then the Lord said to Cain, 'Where is your brother Abel?'
> 'I don't know', he replied. 'Am I my brother's keeper?'
> The Lord said, 'What have you done? Listen! Your brother's blood cries out to Me from the ground'. (Gen. 4:9)

Cain does not deny personal responsibility. He does not say, 'I could not help it. The blame lies elsewhere.' He denies something different, namely *moral* responsibility. He acted, and acted freely, but he sees no reason why he should be held to account for what he did. He is not his brother's keeper.

Adam claimed that *his will was powerless before the world* as it acted on him in the form of his wife. Cain believes the opposite, that *the world is powerless before his will*. We are entitled to do what we choose to do, and conscience does not impose constraints. The great exponent of this view in modern times was Nietzsche, who objected to religious morality, which he rightly held to be the great opponent of the will to power. 'We deny God', he wrote; 'in denying God, we deny accountability: only by doing *that* do we redeem the world.'[8] After the Holocaust, those words have a chilling ring. Hitler called conscience a Jewish invention.

Nietzsche was only an extreme example of an intellectual tendency that dominated post-Enlightenment moral thinking: the idea that ethical principles, since they cannot be inferred from nature, have their origin in human choice. Kant called this 'autonomy'. Whatever is heteronomous, imposed from outside, is not an ethical imperative, he said. If we obey a law because we seek reward or fear punishment, we are not acting morally, merely prudentially or pragmatically. To be moral is to be one's own legislator. We do not submit to an ethical power higher than ourselves for there is no such power.[9] When Byron sought a prototype for the rebellion of reason against submission to authority, he found it in Cain.

Cain thinks of religion in a way that is both ancient and very modern. It is there to serve us. We are not here to serve it. In mythic cultures, religious ritual is a way of placating, appeasing or manipulating the gods – getting them to do, in other words, what we want them to do. The idea that someone might offer a sacrifice to God and hear the answer 'No' is deeply shocking to Cain – and that is why his sacrifice is rejected. Cain has performed all the right moves, only to discover that God is not a force to be cajoled or a power to be placated. God sees the heart, and refuses to be manipulated.

Cain responds by killing his brother. Why? Erich Fromm suggests that sadistic violence has its origin in feelings of aloneness and powerlessness:

> All the different forms of sadism which we can observe go back to one essential impulse, namely, to have complete mastery over another person, to make of him a helpless object of our will, to become the absolute ruler over him, to become his God, to do with him as one pleases. To humiliate him, to enslave him, are means to this end and the most radical aim is to make him suffer, since there is no greater power over another person than that of inflicting pain on him, to force him to undergo suffering without his being able to defend himself. The pleasure in the complete domination over another person (or other animate objects) is the very essence of the sadistic drive.[10]

Having failed to impose his will on God, Cain inflicts it on Abel in the most ultimate form, by murdering him. Cain does not fear freedom. On the contrary, he relishes it. What he fears is *someone else's* freedom: the freedom of God to say 'No'. He takes his revenge by denying Abel the freedom to be. That is what is wrong with the will to power. I purchase my freedom at the cost of yours. Why should I accept constraints on my behaviour? Why should I not do as I wish? The answer is, of course, that this cannot but result in conflict, bloodshed and tragedy. That, ultimately, is why morality exists, whatever we take to be its source. Only if my freedom respects yours can we create a non-tragic human world.

The power of the story of Cain lies in its candid acknowledgement, at the dawn of human time, of the connection between religion and violence. The first murder was occasioned by the first act of worship. According to René Girard, the greatest theoretician of 'violence and the sacred', religion is born in the attempt to deflect violence away from the group by practising it on a surrogate victim, the 'scapegoat'. Primitive societies are riven by vendettas. A member of one family kills a member of another. Relatives of the victim take revenge, and a cycle of retaliation begins to which there is no natural end. The only way the group as a whole can experience catharsis is by killing a substitute, animal or human, from outside the group.[11] The Cain narrative is, in a way, more profound, because it tells us that violent conflict can exist not only between different members of a group but within a single human mind as well. Cain takes out on Abel the violence he feels towards God. It is a story of great psychological candour.

Cain denies neither his deed nor the freedom with which it was performed. What he denies is accountability: 'Am I my brother's keeper?'

For him, there is no 'I ought' to countermand 'I want' or 'I will' – no voice beyond choice, no authority beyond emotion and desire. Cain refuses the terms of morality itself, its otherness, its givenness, its unyielding insistence that there is something to which the will itself is subject, a reality by whose constraints we are bound and which we did not choose. Cain denies, not personal, but *moral* responsibility.

*　　　　　*　　　　　*

Act III brings us to Noah and the Flood. The case of Noah is one of the strangest in the Bible. We are introduced to him in terms of unrivalled praise. He is 'righteous, perfect in his generations; Noah walked with God.' Yet the last glimpse we have of him is unforgettable and tragic:

> Noah, a man of the soil, began the planting of vineyards. He drank some of the wine, became drunk, and lay naked inside his tent. When Ham father of Canaan saw his father naked he told his two brothers outside, so Shem and Japheth took a cloak, put it on their shoulders and walked backwards, and so covered their father's naked body. Their faces were turned the other way so that they did not see their father naked. (Gen. 9:20–3)

Noah, the hero of humanity, has become Noah, the embarrassment to his children. Adam and Eve ate from the tree of knowledge; Noah drank from the fruit of the vine, the tree of oblivion, of not-knowing. Adam and Eve were naked and ashamed. Noah is naked and unashamed. It is his two sons who are ashamed to look on him.

The moral ambiguity of Noah is already subtly signalled in the announcement of his birth. Lamech, his father, calls him Noah, saying 'this one will bring us relief [*yenachamenu*] from our work and from the hard labour that has come upon us because of the Lord's curse upon the ground' (Gen. 5:29). There is something not quite right here. The root *n-ch-m* does not yield the name Noah but *Menachem*.[12] The name Noah comes from the word that means 'to rest'. Complex resonances are being set up. Noah is the man who rested when he should have acted, for when disaster threatens the world he saves himself and his family; no one else. The biblical text also contains a wordplay lost in translation. Noah's Hebrew name, the two letters *n-ch*, is an exact reversal of the word *ch-n*, 'grace, favour', a key word in the story: 'Noah found *favour* in the eyes of the Lord'. Noah's grace is ambivalent, his life a reversal. Most significantly, the word used by Lamech at Noah's birth, *n-ch-m*, reappears later in the story with the opposite meaning to that which Lamech intended: 'When the Lord saw that man had done much evil on earth and that his thoughts and inclinations were always evil, He regretted [*vayinachem*] that He had made man on earth and He was grieved to His very heart' (Gen. 6:6). *N-ch-m* turns out to be a contronym.[13] It means 'relief' but also 'regret', comfort but also discomfort. Noah does bring relief from man's work, but it is the release found in death. Not only did Noah fail to lift 'the Lord's curse upon the ground' but lived through the worst curse of all. Noah's greatness was also his weakness. Noah ('rest') stood still. By contrast, Abraham begins his service of God by moving, leaving home and travelling to a distant land. Noah's gift was that, living through a time of widespread evil, he was not affected by it. He was unmoved. But he was also unable to grow. The Jewish sages heard in the phrase 'righteous in his generations' a subtle criticism. Relative to his generation, he was righteous, but in absolute terms he was not.[14]

What was Noah's failure, according to the classic commentators? Told that there would be a flood and that he should build an ark, he busied himself in the labour. The text goes out of its way to emphasize his obedience, stating no less than three times that Noah did 'exactly as God had commanded him'. Throughout the whole of the narrative – the warning of the deluge, the building of the ark, the gathering of the animals, the beginning of the rain – Noah says nothing. The silence, in contrast with the dialogues Adam and Cain have with God, is unmistakable.

Noah's failure is that, righteous in himself, he has no impact on his contemporaries. He does not engage with them, rebuke them or urge them to mend their ways. Nor does he pray for them, questioning the justice of the Flood, as Abraham was later to do for the people of the cities of the plain. Jewish tradition judged him unfavourably. Noah, the sages said, walked *with* God, whereas Abraham walked *ahead* of God. ('Walk ahead of Me', says God to Abraham, 'and be wholehearted'.) In Jewish folklore Noah became a *tzaddik im peltz*, 'a righteous man in a fur coat'. There are two ways of keeping warm on a cold night: buying a fur coat or lighting a fire. Buy a coat and you keep yourself warm. Light a fire and you keep others warm also. Noah, the righteous man, fails to exercise *collective responsibility*.

You cannot survive while the rest of the world drowns, and still survive. After the Holocaust, the phenomenon was given a name: survivor guilt. Noah is the first intimation in the Bible that individual righteousness is not always enough. You may not be silent while others suffer. 'Do not stand idly by the blood of your brother', the Bible later commands (Lev. 19:16). 'How can I stand and watch disaster befall my people?' pleads Esther to the king (Esth. 8:6). To be moral is to live with and for others, sharing their responsibility, participating in their suffering, protesting their wrongs, arguing their cause.

The moral enterprise is essentially social. Maimonides notes that the individual is prior to society. One could imagine, he says, a completely isolated individual, alone on a desert island, in communion with God.

Such an individual would have no need of moral virtue and no possibility of exercising it. But once we are in society we are cast, with or against our will, into the moral situation. Accepting Aristotle's definition of man as a social animal, he says that laws – rules of right and wrong – are essential because of the differences between human beings and their need to cooperate if they are to form communities. Law, though not part of nature, 'enters into what is natural'.[15]

Noah, who saves himself and his family by building an ark against a flood of rain, is the opposite of Joseph who saves an entire region by building storehouses against a lack of rain. Noah's ark contrasts with the ark in which Moses is saved as a child (the Hebrew word *tevah* is the same in both stories). Moses, who three times in his early years intervenes when he sees injustice, is the antitype of Noah. These resonances are not accidental. They are part of the Pentateuch's tightly structured moral narrative. Noah exemplifies the truth that responsibility extends beyond the self. 'It is not good for man to be alone.' We are part of society, sharing its rewards when it does well, its guilt when it does wrong. Noah fails the test of *collective responsibility*. One who saves only himself, even himself he does not save.

*　　　　　*　　　　　*

Act IV, the Tower of Babel, is a text of extraordinary compactness. The story takes a mere nine verses, and is packed with wordplay and literary allusion, mostly lost in translation. Two of the key words, for example, are 'brick', the first man-made building material, and 'confuse', God's act of confounding the language of the builders so that the project is never completed. The two Hebrew words are mirror images of one another: the Hebrew for 'brick' is *l-v-n*, for 'confuse' is *n-v-l*. The reversal of letters mirrors God's inversion of the builders' plans. They wanted to build the city so that they 'would not be scattered over the face of the earth', but the result was that they were 'scattered over the face of the earth'. They sought 'to make a name for ourselves' and they succeeded, but the name they made, Babel, became a symbol not of creation but confusion.

Wordplay is essential, also, to understanding what their sin was, which is not stated explicitly in the text. The narrative begins and ends with a phrase containing the word *ha-aretz*, 'the earth'. It begins, 'The whole *earth* had one language' and ends, 'From there the Lord scattered them over the face of the whole *earth*'. Within this frame, there is continuous phonemic play on the words *sham*, 'there', *shem*, 'name', and *shamayim*, 'heaven'. *Sham* and *shem* together appear seven times. The word *shamayim*, 'heaven', appears at the key point of the narrative: 'Let us build a city with a tower that reaches heaven'.[16] Babel is a story about the relationship between heaven and earth. Specifically it echoes the first verse in the Bible: 'In the beginning God created the heavens and the earth'. Babel is what happens when human beings, in full exercise of their creative powers, attempt to build cosmopolis, the city as man-made-universe in which they, not God, rule.[17] Once again, Nietzsche comes to mind: his madman who announces the 'death of God' adds, 'Must we not ourselves become gods simply to seem worthy of it?'[18]

One of the key words of the first chapter of Genesis is the root *b-d-l*, 'to distinguish, separate, impose and respect order'. It occurs five times in the course of the chapter. The universe that God creates is a place of carefully calibrated harmony, each object and life-form in its appropriate domain. One word is repeated at each stage: 'good' (it appears seven times in the chapter). At the end of creation, immediately prior to the Sabbath, God 'saw all that He had made, and behold it was *very* good', meaning: each thing was good in itself, and *very* good in relation to all else.[19] The goodness of the world in Genesis 1 is ontological and ecological. It depends on respect for boundaries – in a word, *order*.

The opposite of order is Babel – 'confusion'. The builders of the Tower defy the principle stated in the book of Psalms: 'The heavens are the heavens of the Lord; the earth He has given to the children of mankind' (Ps. 115:16). The Hebrew word *averah*, like its English equivalent, 'transgression', means 'straying across a boundary, entering forbidden territory'. A sin is an act in the wrong place, a failure to honour the boundaries and constraints that form the deep structure of the universe. It is a failure to engage in *havdalah*, the cognitive act of knowing the difference between one thing and another and what belongs where. In a ceremony of great beauty, Jews start the week, as the Sabbath ends, with a ceremony known as *havdalah*. God invites us, his 'partners in the work of creation', to begin each seven-day cycle as he did, by *making distinctions*. Aspiring to make their home in heaven, the builders of Babel failed to honour the distinction between man and God.

Their punishment precisely fits the crime. By creating disorder, they inherit disorder, an inability to communicate with one another and thus engage in the collaborative activity on which all human achievement depends. By dishonouring language – God creates the world with words, because words create order, classifying and labelling distinctions – their language is dishonoured. They believe that their tower will reach heaven (the actual ziggurat at Babylon, to which the story refers, was a seven-storey structure some 300 feet high).[20] In a pointed touch of irony the text says that God had to 'come down' to see it. To the builders, it looked tall. To God it seemed insignificant. There is humour here: God laughs at man's hubris. By aspiring to reach heaven by technological prowess rather than moral conduct, the builders of Babel discovered that not only do we fail to reach heaven; we lose our compact nature, our unity, on earth.

Babel is a profound commentary on the human desire to take the place of God. The word 'responsibility' comes from the word 'response'. It implies the existence of an other who has legitimate claims on my conduct, for, or to, whom I am accountable. The Hebrew equivalent, *achrayut*, derives from the word *acher*, meaning 'an other'. Responsibility is intrinsically relational. The ethical is never private. In biblical terms it is a matter of covenant between two parties, God and humanity, both of whom enter into certain undertakings toward the other. H. Richard Niebuhr defines the biblical ethic of responsibility as the principle: 'God is acting in all actions upon you. So respond to all actions upon you as to respond to his action.'[21]

Babel represents the failure of *ontological* responsibility, the idea that we are accountable to something or someone beyond ourselves. Fired by their technological breakthrough, the discovery of man-made building materials that made tall, multi-storeyed buildings possible, the men on the plain of Shinar attempted to construct a self-sufficient universe (an artificial holy mountain) in which man is accountable only to himself. There is no Other beyond nature to whom we are answerable and by whom we are judged. Writing of a later city-state, the Athens of Socrates and Plato, Lord Acton described the inevitable self-destruction that follows in the wake of such an undertaking:

> [T]hey became the only people of antiquity that grew great by democratic institutions. But the possession of unlimited power, which corrodes the conscience, hardens the heart, and confounds the understanding of monarchs, exercised its demoralising influence on the illustrious democracy of Athens. It is bad to be oppressed by a minority, but it is worse to be oppressed by a majority . . . The philosophy that was then in the ascendant taught them that there is no law superior to that of the State – the lawgiver is above the law. It followed that the sovereign people had a right to do whatever was within its power, and was bound by no rule of right or wrong but its own judgment of expediency.[22]

The result was that 'the emancipated people of Athens became a tyrant'. Responsibility is *response*-ability: accountability to an authority beyond us, in the here-and-now. The alternative, from Babel to Nazi Germany and Soviet communism, is a story of human blood shed on the altar dedicated to the greater glory of humankind.

*   *   *

The first eleven chapters of Genesis are not a mere series of historical narratives. They are a highly structured exploration of responsibility. They begin with two stories about individuals, Adam and Eve, then Cain, followed by two stories about societies, the generation of the Flood and the builders of Babel. The first and last – the tree of knowledge, the tower – are about the failure to honour boundaries: between permitted and forbidden, heaven and earth. The inner two are about violence, individual then collective. They constitute a developmental psychology of the moral sense. First we discover *personal* responsibility, our freedom to choose. Then we acquire *moral* responsibility, the knowledge that choice has limits; not everything we can do, may we do. Later we learn *collective* responsibility: we are part of a family, a community and society and we have a share in its innocence or guilt. Later still, we realize that society itself is subject to a higher law: there are moral limits to power.

All of this is a prelude to the appearance of Abraham, who does not emerge in a vacuum. His life is a culmination of all that has gone before. The first words of God – 'Leave your land, your birthplace and your father's house' – are a call to *personal* responsibility. Abraham is commanded to relinquish everything that leads human beings to see their acts as not their own. The call to Abraham is a counter-commentary to the three great determinisms of the modern world. Karl Marx held that behaviour is determined by structures of power in society, among them the ownership of land. Therefore God said to Abraham, 'Leave your land.' Spinoza believed the human conduct is given by the instincts we acquire at birth (genetic determinism). Therefore God said, 'Leave your place of birth.' Freud held that we are shaped by early experiences in childhood. Therefore God said, 'Leave your father's house.' Abraham is the refutation of determinism. There are structures of power, but we can stand outside them. There are genetic influences on our behaviour, but we can master them. We are shaped by our parents, but we can go beyond them. Abraham's journey is as much psychological as geographical. Like the Israelites in Moses' day, he is travelling to freedom.

Abraham exercises *moral* responsibility by entering into battle, in Genesis 14, to rescue (not his brother, but his brother's son) Lot. He *is* his brother's keeper. He scales the heights of *collective* responsibility when he prays for the inhabitants of Sodom even though he knows, or suspects, that for the most part they are wicked. He reaches *ontological* responsibility in the trial of the binding of Isaac, by recognizing the primacy of the divine word over human emotion and aspiration. In each case Abraham *responds*, and in so doing points the way beyond the failures of previous generations.

It is now clear why the biblical story does not begin with Abraham. Responsibility is not a given of the human situation. On the contrary, it is all too easy to deny it. It wasn't my fault (Adam). I don't see why I shouldn't do what I wish, not what I ought (Cain). I am responsible for myself, not others (Noah). We are answerable to no one but ourselves (Babel). The journey to responsibility is long, and there are many temptations to stop short of the final destination. But in the end, there is no real alternative if we are to live our full humanity. Adam loses paradise. Cain is condemned to wander. Noah declines into drunkenness. Babel is left unbuilt. Responsibility is the condition of our freedom, and we cannot abdicate it without losing much else besides.

But the story does not end there. In the next chapter I want to show how the theme continues throughout the rest of the Pentateuch. Why does it continue? If Abraham is a culmination, what more is there to say? The answer is that humanity is not comprised of individuals alone. We cannot live alone, nor can we create alone. We are social animals. That is why God's covenant with Abraham must be succeeded by another and more extensive order. Only a nation can build a society, and only a society can bring the divine presence into the public square: its economy and politics, its shared life and collective history. Genesis is about individuals. In the first chapter of Exodus, we encounter for the first time in connection with Abraham's children the word *am*, 'a people'. The question to which the rest of the Pentateuch is an answer is: How does a people, a nation, acquire responsibility?

NOTES

1. Ambrose Bierce, *The Devil's Dictionary* (London: Folio Society, 2003).
2. See Harry Redner, *Ethical Life: the past and present of ethical cultures* (Lanham, MD: Rowman and Littlefield, 2001).
3. Jean-Paul Sartre, *Being and Nothingness*, trans. Hazel E. Barnes (London: Methuen, 1957), chapter 2, part 2. For a summary of Sartre's argument see Mary Warnock, *Ethics Since 1900* (London: Oxford University Press, 1960), pp. 162–96.
4. According to one view in Judaism, that the existence of death preceded that of sin, the verse may refer to knowledge: 'You will become aware that you will die; you will be conscious of your own mortality.'
5. See the interesting comments of Charles Taylor, *Sources of the Self* (Cambridge: Cambridge University Press, 1992), pp. 211–47.
6. For a sophisticated recent discussion, see Daniel Dennett, *Freedom Evolves* (New York: Viking, 2003).
7. Erich Fromm, *The Fear of Freedom* (London: Routledge, 2001).
8. F. Nietzsche, *Twilight of the Idols* (London: Penguin, 1969), p. 54.
9. H. J. Paton, *The Moral Law: Kant's Groundwork of the Metaphysic of Morals* (London: Hutchinson, 1981).
10. Fromm, *The Fear of Freedom*, p. 135.
11. René Girard, *Violence and the Sacred* (Baltimore: Johns Hopkins University Press, 1978); *The Scapegoat* (Baltimore: Johns Hopkins University Press, 1986); *Things Hidden Since the Foundation of the World* (London: Athlone, 1987).

12. See Rashi, *Commentary* to Gen. 5:29.

13. On contronyms, see Bill Bryson, *Mother Tongue* (London: Penguin, 1991), p. 63.

14. See Rashi, *Commentary* to Gen. 9:1.

15. Maimonides, *The Guide for the Perplexed*, II:40, III: 54.

16. For further analysis of the rich literary structure of the passage, see J. P. Fokkelman, *Narrative Art in Genesis* (Sheffield: JSOT, 1991).

17. See Stephen Toulmin, *Cosmopolis: the hidden agenda of modernity* (New York: Free Press, 1990).

18. Quoted in Donald Cupitt, *The Sea of Faith* (London: BBC, 1984), pp. 207–8.

19. Samson Raphael Hirsch, *Commentary* to Gen. 1:31. English edition, trans. Isaac Levy (Gateshead: Judaica Press, 1982), pp. 37–40.

20. Nahum Sarna, *Understanding Genesis* (New York: Schocken, 1970), p. 70.

21. H. Richard Niebuhr, *The Responsible Self* (London: Harper and Row, 1978), p. 126.

22. Lord Acton, *Essays in the History of Liberty*, ed. J. Rufus Fears (Indianapolis: Liberty Classics, 1985), pp. 13–14.

Chapter 11

Divine Initiative, Human Initiative

The highest reward for man's toil is not what he gets for it, but what he becomes by it.

(John Ruskin)

There is a memorable scene in the life of Moses. The prophet has been wrestling with God and with the people after the episode of the Golden Calf. A mere 40 days after the greatest epiphany in history – the revelation at Mount Sinai – the people become anxious at the absence of Moses, who has ascended the mountain to receive further revelation and has not yet come down. Leaderless, they persuade Aaron to make a substitute. They give him their ornaments, and from them a golden calf is made. God informs Moses, who comes down, sees the calf and the people cavorting around it. It is a shocking moment: reading the text, we feel it still. Moses acts decisively. He smashes the tablets on which God has inscribed the commandments, burns the calf, grinds it to dust and castigates the people. He then returns up the mountain to pray to God for forgiveness. God grants his request, and as a sign, bids Moses to hew a second set of tablets. Moses descends (tradition ascribes this moment to Yom Kippur, the annual Day of Atonement), but something in him has changed:

> When Moses came down from Mount Sinai with the two tablets of the Testimony in his hands, he was not aware that his face was radiant because he had spoken with the Lord. When Aaron and all the Israelites saw Moses, his face was radiant, and they were afraid to come near him. (Ex. 34:29–30)

It was the mistranslation of this passage – reading *keren* as 'horn' rather than 'ray' or 'radiant' – that was responsible for the horns Michelangelo gave Moses in his great statue of the prophet. What is intriguing, however,

148

is the fact that Moses did *not* radiate when he brought down the first tablets, but on the second occasion he did. In fact, the fate of the second tablets was altogether different from the first. The first were 'the work of God; the writing was the writing of God, engraved on the tablets' (Ex. 32:16). The second tablets were hewn by Moses himself, though the writing was done by God. Despite their greater sanctity, the first tablets did not last – as if, like a meteorite, they disintegrated on entering earth's atmosphere. There are some things too holy to survive. Wholly divine, they are too sacred to be fully integrated into the life of human beings. The second tablets were the result of a partnership between Moses and God – and they did survive. Moses himself was changed as the result of his participation. His face shone. After the first tablets, where he was merely the passive recipient of God's gift, he was still the same Moses. After the second, he was different. *We are changed, not by what we receive, but what we do.*

This one detail sheds light on the entire structure of the Mosaic books. Recall the Marxist critique: religion makes us passive, not active; dependent, not independent. It leads us to accept the world, not change it. On the face of it, this rings true. The Hebrew Bible is about the saving acts of God, not humans. It is about miraculous interventions on the part of heaven into events on earth. It is God who liberates the Israelites from Egypt, not Moses, who is a mere emissary. The Pentateuch seems to be about divine power, not the human capacity for self- and social transformation. The message would seem to be: pray, don't act; wait patiently, don't take the initiative. If God wills it, it will happen; if he doesn't, it won't. The force that shapes history is beyond the reach of humankind.

In fact, I argue in this chapter, the reverse is the case. There is a movement in the Bible, traceable along many axes, from divine initiative to human endeavour, from the supernatural to the natural, from a *controlling* to an *empowering* presence of God. Unless we understand this, we will misread the entire structure of the biblical message. God begins the work, but he asks us to complete it.

The most helpful concepts here are two terms drawn from Jewish mysticism. The kabbalists spoke of two kinds of religious experience: *itaruta de-leylah*, 'an awakening from above', and *itaruta de-letata*, 'an awakening from below'. The former is an act initiated by God, the latter, one set in motion by human beings. An awakening from above is the kind of event to which we give the name 'miracle'. The plagues in Egypt, the division of the Red Sea, manna from heaven and water from a rock were like this. They are described in the Bible as supernatural events, breaking through the causal nexus of the universe. Each was an intrusion of God into the natural order. A miracle is a moment when the veil behind which God is hidden is lifted and we see a signal of transcendence. Yet an awakening from above, for all its glory, has limited impact on human beings. Three

149

days after the division of the Red Sea, the Israelites were already complaining about the bitterness of the water they had to drink. Forty days after Sinai, they made the Golden Calf. *An awakening from above changes nature, but it does not change human nature.*[1] It calls for nothing on the part of man other than to be still and patient, to wait, hope and receive.

An awakening from below lacks the drama of an awakening from above. It is not miraculous. It does not change the order of nature. We do not count it as one of God's wondrous deeds. But its impact is greater, its effect deeper and longer-lasting. It changes us. If an awakening from above is God's gesture of reaching down to humankind, an awakening from below is a human gesture of reaching up toward heaven. When that happens, the horizons of human possibility are enlarged. We are what we do, and what human beings have done once, they can do again. The first tablets, made entirely by God, were an awakening from above. The second, hewn by Moses, involved an awakening from below. That is why Moses was transformed, and why, only after the second tablets, did his face shine.

The Bible is replete with other examples of the same movement, the same shift of responsibility. One occurs at the division of the Red Sea, the moment at which the Israelites pass from the domain of Pharaoh to that of God. Immediately before and after the crossing, the Israelites are faced with battle, but the difference between the two is total. In the first, they see the assembled Egyptian forces, their chariots and heavily armed warriors, and are terrified. They say, 'It would have been better for us to serve the Egyptians than to die here in the desert.' Moses tells them, in effect, *Do nothing:* 'Do not be afraid. Stand firm and see the deliverance the Lord will bring you today. The Egyptians you see today you will never see again. The Lord will fight for you. You have only to keep still' (Ex. 14:13).

The second confrontation, shortly after the crossing, is with the Amalekites. This, however, is a battle the Israelites have to fight themselves:

> As long as Moses held up his hands, the Israelites were winning, but whenever he lowered his hands, the Amalekites were winning. When Moses' hands grew tired, they took a stone and placed it under him and he sat on it. Aaron and Hur held his hands up, one on one side, one on the other, so that his hands remained steady until sunset. (Ex. 17:11–12)

If there is a hint here of miracle, it is a different kind than the division of the sea. So long as the Israelites looked up, they prevailed. When they looked down, they started to lose. This is divine assistance of a new kind, working *through* human beings, not independently of them. No longer is

God fighting Israel's battles on its behalf, it is God giving them the strength to fight and win on their own. The crossing of the sea is, in the fullest sense, a *rite de passage*. After it the Israelites learn to act with, rather than merely rely on, God.

The same transition occurs before and after the revelation at Mount Sinai. Beforehand, the Israelites do nothing other than prepare themselves for the supreme encounter. They purify themselves. They abstain from sexual relations. A boundary is set around the mountain. God appears with overwhelming presence. 'When the people saw the thunder and lightning and heard the ram's horn and saw the mountain in smoke, they trembled with fear and stood at a distance. They said to Moses, "Speak to us yourself and we will listen. But do not have God speak to us or we will die"' (Ex. 20:16). The unmediated presence of God is awesome, literally unbearable. The infinite threatens to obliterate the finite.

After the Golden Calf, however, the rest of the book of Exodus is devoted to an exhaustively detailed account of the construction of the sanctuary, at the end of which we read that 'The cloud covered the Tent of Meeting and the glory of the Lord filled the Tabernacle.' There is a precise parallel between the sanctuary and Mount Sinai. Like the mountain, the sanctuary was divided into three domains of ascending sanctity:

Sinai	**Sanctuary**
Foot of the mountain – people and altar	Outer Court
Up the mountain slope – priests and elders	Holy Place
Top of the mountain – Moses	Holy of Holies

A similar parallel exists between the appearance of God at Sinai when the covenant was confirmed (Exodus 24) and his appearance at the dedication of the Tabernacle (see page 152).

The parallels are deliberate.[2] They tell us that the sanctuary was a portable equivalent of Sinai, a permanent abode for the divine presence as the Israelites journeyed through the desert. There was, though, one significant difference. The sanctuary was *a place they had constructed themselves* – just as Moses had himself hewed the second tablets. The presence of God was the result of the fact that the people had themselves created the space he would inhabit. They had contributed their donations, given of their possessions, time and skill, and thereby acquired the dignity that comes with the act of construction and creation.

There is another parallel. The key words used in describing the making of the sanctuary are the same as those used in Genesis 1, the creation of the universe. The implication is radical and unmistakable: *Creating the universe, God made a home for human beings. Making the sanctuary, human beings made a home for God.* Just as in creation, the metaphysical

Exodus 24:15–18	Completion of the Tabernacle
Moses goes up the mountain and the cloud covers it	The cloud covered the Tent of Meeting
The presence of God dwelled on Mount Sinai	The presence of God filled the Tabernacle (Ex. 30:34)
And the cloud covered it for six days	Moses could not come into the Tent of Meeting for the cloud dwelled on it (Ex. 40:35)
He called to Moses on the seventh day from the cloud	He called to Moses . . . and God spoke to him from the Tent of Meeting (Lev. 1:1)
And the appearance of the Glory of God was that of a consuming fire upon the Mount	The glory of God appeared to the entire nation (Lev. 9:23). Fire went out from before God and consumed upon the altar
Beheld by the children of Israel	And the nation beheld and rejoiced (Lev. 9:24)
Moses went into the cloud and ascended the Mount	Moses and Aaron came into the Tent of Meeting (Lev. 9:23)

drama lay in God making a space for the finite, so in the construction of the sanctuary it lay in human beings making a space for the Infinite. Sinai was the awakening from above, the sanctuary, the awakening from below. What we make, rather than what others make for us, leads to transformation. Even after Sinai the people were still capable of making a golden calf. After the sanctuary, not for several centuries did they make an idol again.

*　　　　　　*　　　　　　*

We see the same movement from divine to human initiative if we examine the several covenants between God and humanity throughout the Hebrew Bible. The first is made with Noah after the Flood, and through him with all humankind. This is a unilateral act on the part of God. Noah makes a thanksgiving offering after leaving the ark. Then we read:

> The Lord smelled the pleasing aroma [of Noah's sacrifice] and said in His heart, 'Never again will I curse the ground because of man, even though every inclination of his heart is evil from childhood. And never again will I destroy all living creatures, as I have done. As long as the earth endures, seedtime and harvest, cold and heat, summer and winter, day and night will never cease.' (Gen. 8:21–2)

God neither asks for nor seeks a response from Noah. To be sure, the covenant carries with it a set of laws, chief of which is the prohibition against murder:

> Whoever sheds the blood of man
> By man shall his blood be shed;
> For in the image of God has God made man. (Gen. 9:6)

But in this, the first covenant, the human partner is entirely passive. It is a covenant because it has reciprocal obligations: self-restraint on the part of God, matched by self-restraint on the part of man. But Noah has no part in the act of covenant-making. No assent is required, no act needed to warrant the gift of grace.

The second covenant, this time with Abraham, demands a specific act, circumcision: 'When Abram was ninety-nine years old, the Lord appeared to him and said . . . "As for Me, this is my covenant with You: You will be the father of many nations. No longer will you be called Abram; your name will be Abraham, for I have made you a father of many nations"' (Gen. 17:1–5). Abraham, however, must do something in return as a covenantal sign: 'This is My covenant with you and your descendants after you, the covenant you are to keep: every male among you shall be circumcised' (Gen. 17:10). Besides this, Abraham has already done much to warrant a special relationship with God. He has left his home, his family and his birthplace and begun a journey at God's express command. He knows that he must live a life apart while being a blessing to those around him. Abraham is a far more active figure than Noah, a man willing to argue with heaven on the one hand, and obey it on the other, even at the seeming cost of sacrificing his child. God has begun to invite a greater degree of human participation.

The third covenant, the one that defines Israel's destiny as a nation, takes place at Mount Sinai. No less fascinating than the revelation itself is the scene that takes place beforehand:

> Then Moses went up to God, and the Lord called to him from the mountain and said: 'This is what you are to say to the house of Jacob and what you are to tell the people of Israel: "You yourselves have seen what I did to Egypt, and how I carried you on eagles' wings and brought you to Myself. Now if you will obey Me fully and keep My covenant, then out of all the nations you will be My treasured possession. Although all the earth is Mine, you will be for Me a kingdom of priests and a holy nation." These are the words you are to speak to the Israelites.'
>
> So Moses went back and summoned the elders of the people and

set before them all the words the Lord had commanded him to speak. The people responded together, 'We will do everything the Lord has said.' So Moses brought their answer back to the Lord. (Ex. 19:3–8)

God's self-revelation at Sinai depends on the prior assent of the people. A far-reaching principle is here articulated for the first time: *There is no legitimate government without the consent of the governed, even if the governor is creator of heaven and earth.* It is this proposition – restated in the American Declaration of Independence – that properly marks the birth of the concept of a free society.[3] God is not a transcendental equivalent of a Pharaoh. The commonwealth he invites the Israelites to join him in creating is not one where power rules, even the power of heaven itself. The nation is born in freedom in the sense that the people must freely consent to the terms of the covenant if it is to be a genuine 'constitution of liberty'. Only after the people have signalled their agreement ('We will do everything the Lord has said') can the revelation proceed.

To be sure, there is a view in the Talmud that questions whether a people entirely under the protection of God could be said to be free in their assent: 'The Holy One, blessed be He, suspended the mountain over them like a cask, and said to them, "If you accept the Torah, it will be well. If not, here will be your burial."'[4] Immediately thereafter, however, the Talmud records the remark of R. Aha bar Jacob, that 'If so, this is a fundamental objection to the Torah.' The answer it provides is that 'None the less, the Israelites reaffirmed the covenant in the days of Ahasuerus, as it is written, "They [the Jews] confirmed and took upon themselves" (Esth. 9:27) – meaning, they confirmed what they had taken upon themselves before.'[5] Even on this view, in other words, the sages were unwilling to grant the validity of a covenant without the free consent of the people, even if that meant giving a later date to its ratification. Here, reciprocity reaches its summit. The free God desires the free worship of a free people. One difference between the God of the Bible and the gods of myth is that the Creator of all does not seek to impose his authority by force.

This is the first, not the last, covenant ceremony in Israel's national history, but it is the fulcrum of the biblical narrative. From then on, all other ceremonies will be ratifications of the covenant at Sinai – Moses on the banks of the Jordan (Deut. 29), Joshua at the end of his life (Josh. 24) and the covenant renewal ceremonies during the reigns of Asa (2 Chron. 15), Joash (2 Kings 11) and Josiah (2 Kings 23; 2 Chron. 34). Each of these occurs on the basis of human initiative, as does the last, the *amanah* or binding agreement made in the days of Ezra in the aftermath of the Babylonian exile and return (Neh. 8–10).[6] Thus covenant-making, the act binding heaven and earth in mutual obligation, follows the same dynamic we have observed elsewhere. Divine initiative gradually gives way to human initiative.

A similar shift appears in the threefold division of the books of the Bible itself. The Hebrew canon has three divisions: Torah (the Pentateuch or Mosaic books), *Nevi'im* (the prophetic literature) and *Ketuvim* ('Writings'). Each has a different sanctity and authority. Torah is the basic source of Jewish law and faith. The prophetic literature is roughly co-extensive with the Israelites' experience as a people in its land, from the days of Joshua to the Second Temple. *Ketuvim*, which contains such varied works as the liturgical Psalms, the wisdom literature of Proverbs, Ecclesiastes and Job, and later histories such as Ezra–Nehemiah and Chronicles, is of a lesser sanctity still. The difference is that in Torah, God speaks *to* human beings; in the prophetic works, God speaks *through* human beings; in the Writings, human beings speak to God.

Insofar, then, as we can speak of an overarching theme in the Hebrew Bible, it is the story of the transfer of initiative from heaven to earth, from God to humankind, from caring father to wayward but slowly maturing child. In the early stages, barely out of the womb of slavery, the Israelites were often petulant and ungrateful. As the centuries pass, they became – whether in the return of Ezra and Nehemiah or in that paradigm of Diaspora life, the book of Esther – astonishingly faithful, as they were to remain for most of the post-biblical era, from the fall of the Second Temple to the nineteenth century. Ironically, when the Israelites were surrounded by God's miracles, they complained. During the long centuries of 'the hiding of God's face' they became, on the contrary, obstinate in holding fast to the covenant. They became the faithful people, 'God's witnesses' on earth. The implication is simple: passive dependence on God inhibits religious maturity. Just as, in Jewish law, a child is bound by the command to honour its parents only when he or she is no longer a child (12 for a girl, 13 for a boy), so Israel only learned to honour God when it accepted responsibility.

*   *   *

What is happening here? The greatest possible theological mistake is to read the Bible as if it were written by Plato. For Plato, God and truth are beyond time. God is the unmoved mover, disengaged from the flux of history, beyond emotion and passion, neither interested in nor cognisant of the affairs of humankind. History is mere distraction, 'noise'. Truth is timeless, unchanging, eternal. That is not the story we read in the Hebrew Bible.

Instead, we see God fashioning a universe, shaping humans with his own hands and breathing into them the breath of life. He is engaged with his people and their journey through time. He hears their prayers, knows their suffering, is deeply wounded by their infidelity yet loves them with an unshakeable love. There are some things that are eternal, not least God as he is in himself. But that is not what the Bible is about. It is a book, not of metaphysics but of history. Insofar as God relates to humanity, he enters time, for it is only in and through time that the human story is told. God's covenants are eternal, but his relationship with humanity is historical, because it takes time for God's message to penetrate and be internalized by the human mind. We stumble and fall, take false turnings and blind alleys, but we learn and thereby grow. The journey from Egypt to the Promised Land was a distance of days, but it took 40 years. In one sense we are on that journey still, for humanity has not yet reached its destination, the world of peace known as the Messianic Age. The biblical imagination is not *logical* but *chronological*. It tells the story of truth as it is realized in time.

It is to Jean Piaget (1896–1980) more than any other individual that we owe our modern understanding of the developmental nature of childhood.[7] The question he asked was, how does knowledge grow? The discovery he made was that every child goes through a series of cognitive developments, always in the same order though not necessarily at the same pace. Just as a child will not walk and talk until it is ready, so it will not be able to handle certain intellectual tasks until it has reached the appropriate phase in its growth. There is a series of stages through which it must pass before it matures, and there are no short cuts. Time is of its essence.

The Hebrew Bible is closer to Piaget than to Plato. Truth is not something we discover at one time. That is how things are for God, but not for us. For Judaism, truth – as understood and internalized by humanity – is a developmental process. That is why so much of the Bible is narrative and so many of its books are works of history. The prophets of ancient Israel were the first to see meaning in history, to see memory as a religious duty, and time itself as the narrative of humans in search of God, God in search of humans. Hence the single most important metaphor of the Hebrew Bible: God is a parent and we are his children. The prophets never tire of this analogy:

Do you thus requite the Lord,
You foolish and senseless people?
Is He not your Father, who created you . . . ? (Deut. 32:6)

When Israel was a child, I loved him,
And out of Egypt I called My son . . .
It was I who taught Ephraim to walk,
Taking them by the arms,
But they did not realize it was I who healed them. (Hos. 11:1, 3)

I thought you would call Me Father,
And not turn away from following Me. (Jer. 3:19)

These are deeply felt sentiments and reflect the character of time as it functions in the Bible: time as linear rather than cyclical, an arena of growth and development rather than eternal recurrence. In the beginning, God tended the people, newly released from slavery, as if they were children. He rescued them from their oppressors, led them safely through the sea, gave them food and drink and protected them against their enemies. But like a responsible parent, he wanted them to mature, to learn to fight their own battles and to become responsible agents themselves. The history of Israel recapitulates the development of the individual. At first, a child is almost totally dependent on its parents for food and safety. But as the years pass, a parent must gradually let the child do things for itself or it will never grow into an adult. This can be painful. At first a child cannot walk without falling, or choose without making mistakes. Yet in the fullness of time, if parenthood is successful, the child appropriates the values of its parents and makes them its own.

The movement from the 'awakening from above' to the 'awakening from below' is the basic structure of biblical time. Little by little as the story unfolds, God's miracles become fewer and the deeds of human beings become more prominent. Biblical truth, a truth that cannot emerge at once but only through the experience of formative events, is *a movement from acts done by God for the sake of human beings, to acts done by human beings for the sake of God.*

Nowhere is this more sharply expressed than in the rabbinic understanding of the dual Torah: the Written Law and the Oral Law. According to tradition, the first tablets represented the Written Law. The second were accompanied by the Oral tradition as well. According to the third-century sage R. Yohanan, 'God made a covenant with Israel only on the basis of the Oral Law, as it is said [of the second tablets], "Then the Lord said to Moses: Write down these words, for in accordance [*al pi*, literally, 'by the mouth of'] these words, I have made a covenant with you and with Israel."'[8]

The audacity with which the sages understood the concept of the Oral Law is unparalleled. The written word is divine, they believed, but its interpretation is human. God empowers his sages to make authoritative decisions on the meaning of the biblical text. They described God debating matters of Jewish law with the angels in the academy on high, and relying on human beings to clinch the argument. Here, for example, is the Talmudic account of the death of one of the sages, Rabbah bar Nahmani:

In the academy on high, they were debating an instance in the laws concerning leprosy. The Holy One ruled 'Clean' while the rest of the academy on high maintained, 'Unclean.' Finally they asked, 'Who is to decide the matter?' They answered, 'Rabbah bar Nahmani, who said, "I am unique in understanding the laws of leprosy and the laws of tents in which there is a corpse."' They sent the angel of death [to bring him to heaven] but the angel was unable to touch him, because his mouth did not stop studying even for an instant. Then a wind blew up and made a rustling noise in the reeds. Imagining it to be a legion of horsemen, he said, 'Let me die at the hand of the angel of death, rather than be delivered into the hands of the government.' As he was dying, he declared, 'Clean, clean.' A divine voice cried out, 'Happy are you, Rabbah bar Nahmani, whose body is pure and whose soul has departed with [the word] "clean".' In Pumbeditha [Rabbah's town] a tablet fell from heaven upon which was written, 'Rabbah bar Nahmani has been summoned to the Academy on High.'[9]

Most famous of the Talmudic episodes is the one in which, in the course of an argument with his fellow sages, R. Eliezer ben Hyrcanus invokes the authority of heaven, which endorses his view ('A heavenly voice was heard, saying, Why do you dispute the view of R. Eliezer, seeing that the law is always in accord with his opinion?'). At this, R. Joshua, one of the disputants, 'stood up and protested, *It is not in heaven* [Deut. 30:12]', meaning: we pay no attention to a divine voice, because at Mount Sinai, God himself had declared, *After the majority must one incline* [Ex. 23:2]. The sages outvoted R. Eliezer despite the fact that he had been supported by heaven itself. The denouement comes when Rabbi Nathan meets the prophet Elijah – seen by the sages as an intermediary between heaven and earth – and asks him what God said at the moment when the heavenly voice was outvoted: 'ELIJAH: He laughed [with joy] and said, "My sons have defeated Me, My sons have defeated Me."'[10]

It is impossible to understand the depth of these passages without recalling the historical background against which they are set. The Second Temple had been destroyed. Jerusalem lay in ruins. Israel was in Roman hands, and the regime had been brutal in suppressing Jewish life. There were now no priests or sacrifices, kings or prophets, and – with the failure of the Bar Kochba rebellion – no hope of an imminent recovery of Jewish independence. It was the greatest crisis in Jewish history. Yet out of it the sages rescued a momentous dignity. They had nothing left except the Torah, yet out of it they fashioned a vehicle strong enough to sustain Jewish life in exile for almost 2,000 years. The Torah became, in Heine's telling phrase, the 'portable homeland of the Jew'.[11]

In the Written Torah God had given Israel his word, but in the Oral Torah he had given Israel the authority to *interpret* his word. In this idea, never far from the surface of rabbinic consciousness, the drama of biblical Judaism moved to its penultimate phase. The father had empowered his children. They had internalized his word and made it theirs. The full weight of prophetic Judaism is contained and transcended in the words of Elijah to R. Nathan: 'My sons have defeated Me; My sons have defeated Me.' At the very moment that Jewry lost its place in the arena of history it found, in the house of study, the dignity of mind and spirit that allowed the Jewish people to survive the humiliation of powerlessness and dispersion. Thus was hope rescued from tragedy.

*　　　　　*　　　　　*

I find this whole narrative – for it *is* a single unbroken narrative from Genesis to today – profoundly moving. It speaks of the tense, conflictual, but always transfiguring love of a parent for a child and a child for its parent. It begins with God ever-present, intervening to protect his fledgling nation, 'teaching them to walk' as Hosea says, and seeing them so often fall. It had moments of profound crisis when it seemed as if Israel's adolescent rebellion had broken all bounds and bonds. But God's covenant of love is unbreakable, for he has given his word and will not retract it. In and through this word, endlessly studied, interpreted, argued over, commented on, codified and then debated again, the relationship developed and the child finally became an adult. By making the divine word their own through endless study, Jews eventually fulfilled Jeremiah's famous prophecy:

'The time is coming', declares the Lord,
'When I will make a new covenant with the house of Israel
And the house of Judah.
It will not be like the covenant I made with their forefathers
When I took them by the hand to lead them out of Egypt,
Because they broke My covenant,
Though I was their master', declares the Lord.
'This is the covenant I will make with the house of Israel after that time',
declares the Lord.
'I will put My law in their minds
and write it on their hearts.
I will be their God
And they will be My people.' (Jer. 31:31–3)

Internalizing God's word, the sages completed the transformation, begun in the Bible, of the human experience of the divine from a God who intervenes in history to protect a defenceless people to a God who speaks within the heart of a people, giving it the strength to construct its own defences. God has not changed, but the people have. God is now no longer encountered as a warrior but as a teacher. He is not the force relieving Israel of responsibility, but the guide who shows them how to exercise responsibility. There was only one human being to whom the sages attached an honour approaching that of God himself – namely a teacher. For it is as parent and teacher – parent *as* teacher – that God eventually brings Israel to maturity. This is the God who smiles when his children accept the challenge and says, 'My children have defeated Me!' God wants his children to grow, and slowly, over the course of many centuries, effaces himself that they may do so. Jewish history begins in miracles, but culminates in human responsibility. What changes us is not what is done for us by God, but what we do in response to his call.

NOTES

1. See Maimonides, *The Guide for the Perplexed*, III:32.
2. See Joshua Berman, *The Temple: its symbolism and meaning then and now* (Northvale, NJ: Jason Aronson, 1995).
3. For more on this subject, see Jonathan Sacks, *The Politics of Hope*, second ed. (London: Vintage, 2000), pp. 55–146; *Radical Then, Radical Now* (London: HarperCollins, 2000), pp. 105–72.
4. Babylonian Talmud, *Shabbat* 88a.
5. Ibid.
6. There is a large theological literature on the concept of covenant. See, for example, Delbert Hillers, *Covenant: the history of a biblical idea* (Baltimore: Johns Hopkins University Press, 1969). There is, however, a clear difference between Jewish and Christian understandings, both of the idea, and of the way it plays out in historical time as seen through the eyes of faith. The Jewish understanding of covenant, both in the biblical and in the post-biblical literature, emphasizes mutuality and divine empowerment as opposed to the fallen condition of humanity and its dependence on divine grace. Jon D. Levenson has significant things to say on the difference between Jewish and Christian readings of the biblical text, in his *The Hebrew Bible, the Old Testament, and Historical Criticism: Jews and Christians in biblical studies* (Westminster: John Knox Press, 1993).
7. See Jean Piaget, *The Language and Thought of the Child*, trans. Marjorie Gabain (London: Routledge, 2001).
8. Babylonian Talmud, *Gittin* 60b.
9. Babylonian Talmud, *Baba Metzia* 86a.

10. Babylonian Talmud, *Baba Metzia* 59a–b.
11. Heinrich Heine, *Confessions*, 1854. The translation in F. Ewen, *Poetry and Prose of Heinrich Heine* (New York: Citadel Press, 1948), p. 663, is: 'The Jews . . . trudged around with it through the Middle Ages as with a portable fatherland'.

Chapter 12

The Holy and the Good

> Is not this the kind of fasting I have chosen:
> to loose the chains of injustice
> and untie the cords of the yoke,
> to set the oppressed free
> and break every yoke?
> Is it not to share your food with the hungry
> and to provide the poor wanderer with shelter –
> when you see the naked, to clothe him,
> and not to turn away from your own flesh and blood?
>
> (Isaiah 58:5–7)

But does religion really make a difference to the moral life? Do you have to believe in God to be good? Was Dostoevsky right when he said, 'If God does not exist, all is permitted'?[1] I have told the story of the birth of a particular conception of God, humanity and moral responsibility. Is it, though, the only way of arriving at these ideas? And once we have reached them, do we still need the religious narrative that gave them life? Is it like the foundation of a building, without which the superstructure crumbles, or is it more like scaffolding we can remove once the house is complete?

The connection between ethics and the religious life, despite the vast literature it has generated, is seldom addressed with the subtlety it deserves. All too often, it is treated superficially, as if 'ethics' and 'religion' were simple concepts instead of what they actually are: terms bringing together vastly different phenomena. Philosophers have tended to search for Yes/No answers, as if these questions could be treated independently of time, place and context. Anthropologists have been wiser, knowing that it is impossible to separate the moral life from the totality of a culture or civilization. The very words 'ethics' and 'religion' are abstractions that date from European Enlightenment: the Hebrew Bible – which is certainly about both – has no word for either. If we oversimplify, we may arrive at answers that are simple, lucid and wrong.

I want to begin by clearing out of the way the three most obvious challenges to the concept of religious ethics, namely that you don't have to be religious to be good; you don't need revelation to tell you what is good; and that to be moral you have to do what is right because it is right, not because God commands you to. To the first – that you can be good without being religious – the simple answer is: *of course*. Who ever thought otherwise? The Bible is full of examples. Rahab, who saves the lives of Joshua's spies when they come to Jericho, is a Canaanite prostitute (Josh. 2). Yael, the heroine who comes to Israel's rescue against an invading army, is a Kenite (Judges 4). Ruth, whose name became a synonym for compassion (sadly, the word is no longer in use; only its negation, 'ruthless', remains) was a Moabite (Ruth 1). The most striking example is Pharaoh's daughter, who rescues Moses as a baby, gives him his name and protects him during childhood by adopting him as her own (Ex. 2). These women were all outsiders to ancient Israelite monotheism, but they were heroines of the moral life.

There is nothing inherently 'religious' about the moral sense. The Bible takes it for granted that human beings know the basic difference between good and evil. Without this, the story of Cain would be unintelligible. God had not yet pronounced the words 'Thou shalt not murder', yet Cain is deemed guilty. So are the inhabitants of Sodom when they attempt to submit Lot's guests to homosexual rape (Gen. 19). In his oracles against the nations, Amos accuses Israel's neighbours of cruelty and faithlessness, yet he nowhere implies that they have had a divine revelation, their equivalent, say, of the Ten Commandments. As John Barton points out, Amos assumes a common moral code, a kind of natural law, that is self-evident to all regardless of their religious convictions.[2] As the eleventh-century scholar Rabbi Nissim ben Jacob ibn Shahin pointed out, 'All commandments that are rational and amenable to human understanding have been binding on everyone since the day God created man on earth'.[3] You don't have to be religious to know that murder, cruelty, theft and violent crime are wrong.

The second challenge was famously set out by Plato in his dialogue Euthyphro. 'Is something right', he asked, 'because the gods command it, or do they command it because it is right?'[4] This creates a dilemma. If something is right only because the gods command it, then what if they command murder, or theft, or some other moral outrage? Morality would be nothing more than obeying the arbitrary will of the gods, and could lead to evil rather than good. If, on the other hand, the gods command something *because* it is right, then it is right before and independently of the gods' command. If the gods tell us to honour our parents because it is right to do so, then we did not need the gods to tell us. It remains right whether or not they said anything on the subject.

Plato's dilemma is elegant because it forces us to make a choice between two invidious possibilities: religion is either opposed to ethics or superfluous to it. In fact, however, Plato's dilemma belongs to a particular time and place, Athens in the fourth century BCE. The culture of Plato's day was mythic and polytheistic. The gods fought and committed appalling crimes. Kronos castrates his father Uranus, only to be murdered by his son Zeus in turn. Greek myth is amoral or pre-moral, and what Plato represents is one of the earliest attempts to think morally by breaking free from the mythological past. Looking back with the hindsight of history, we can see that for Plato, to be moral was to liberate yourself from the world of myth – much as Abraham, in Jewish tradition, could only arrive at truth by breaking his father's idols. In their different ways, Abraham and Plato were both iconoclasts.

In Judaism, the Euthyphro dilemma does not exist.[5] God commands the good because it is good. Without this assumption, Abraham's challenge over the fate of Sodom – 'Shall not the Judge of all the earth do justice?' – would be incomprehensible. God and humans are equally answerable to the claims of justice. But the good is what God commands because God-the-lawgiver is also God-the-creator-and-redeemer. Morality mirrors the deep structure of the universe that God made and called good. Plato's challenge arises because the Greek gods were not creators. Matter was eternal. The gods had no special authority except for the fact that they were held to be powerful. Plato was therefore correct to challenge the popular cults of his day by, in effect, drawing a principled distinction between might and right. The gods may be strong, but that is no reason to invest them with moral authority. For the Bible, however, God who teaches us how to act in the world is also the maker of the world in which we act. This means that in monotheism, morality means going with, not against, the grain of the cosmos and history. God himself empowers his prophets to challenge kings – even himself – in the name of justice or mercy. To be sure, there are occasions – most famously, the binding of Isaac – in which God seems to demand pure obedience; but this itself suggests that the story may be more subtle than it seems.[6] Taken as a whole, Judaism embodies divine faith in the moral capacity and literacy of humankind.

The third challenge is Kantian. Kant held that morality, to be moral, must be autonomous. It must flow from our own convictions and self-legislation. Heteronomy – obedience to the voice from outside – is not morality. To obey someone else's command, even God's, out of fear of punishment or expectation of reward may be pragmatic or prudential but it is not moral.[7] Judaism does not disagree. As Maimonides wrote:

Let a person not say, 'I will observe the precepts of the Torah and occupy myself with its wisdom in order that I may obtain all the blessings written in the Torah, or to attain life in the world to come . . .' It is not right to serve God after this fashion for whoever does so, serves Him out of fear. This is not the standard set by the prophets and sages . . .

Whoever serves God out of love, occupies himself with the study of the teachings and the fulfilment of commandments and walks in the paths of wisdom, impelled by no external motive whatsoever, moved neither by fear of calamity nor by the desire to obtain material benefits – such a person does what is truly right because it is truly right, and ultimately, happiness comes to him as a result of his conduct.[8]

What is flawed about the Kantian approach is that it sees heteronomy and autonomy as opposites rather than what, in fact, they are: two different stages in moral development. We begin, as children, by obeying other people's orders. But we do not end there. Moral growth is that process by which external commands are internalized through habituation and study. That is precisely what Judaism assumes. We begin by obeying commands because they are commands. We end by making them our own.[9]

Of course, I simplify. Generations of study and a library of literature has been dedicated to these questions. They fail, however, to touch on the real issue, namely: what difference does religion make to the moral life *even if* we concede that you don't have to be religious to be moral?

*   *   *

The first difference is hope. The sociologist Peter Berger called hope a signal of transcendence.[10] There are no logical grounds to believe that tomorrow will be better than today. The alternative – the tragic sense of life – is equally coherent and consistent with the facts of human history. Nonetheless, Judaism is a religion of hope. Even after the early narratives of failure – Adam, Cain, the generation of the Flood, the Tower of Babel – God does not give up, and because of that, neither do we. I find it astonishing that after all the catastrophes of the past, even after the Holocaust itself, Jews did not despair.

Where does hope come from? Unlike pleasure, pain, aggression and fear, hope is not a mere feeling, something we share with non-human forms of life. Nor does it exist in every possible culture. It comes from a specific set of beliefs: that the universe is not blind to our dreams, deaf to our prayers; that we are not alone; that we are here because someone willed us to be and that our very existence is testament to the creative force of love. We are not wrong to strive for justice; nor are we without help in our strivings. There is nothing written into the structure of the universe that dictates that hate, violence, war and bloodshed are constitutive features of the human situation. Nor are these views plucked from the void. The history of Israel begins with the liberation of an enslaved people from an enslaving power. It exists in virtue of a covenant between the people and God in which both sides pledge themselves to mutual loyalty and to the task of constructing a society and set of communities in which the human person as such – regardless of rank, power or privilege – is honoured as the bearer of the divine image.

There is, to repeat, no logical basis for hope. The human story – the same facts, the same dramatis personae, the same sequence of events – can be told many ways. The Hebrew Bible could be turned into Greek tragedy *without changing a single word*. All it would take would be to end its first book, not after Genesis 50, but after Exodus 1. All the hopes of the patriarchs for a land would be seen to end in slavery in Egypt. The Pentateuch would end, not with Deuteronomy, but with the book of Judges and its closing sentence: 'In those days there was no king in Israel; everyone did what was right in their own eyes' (Judges 21:25). Instead of creating the just society, Israel would be seen to have failed and been reduced to anarchy.

Hope and tragedy do not differ about facts but about interpretation and expectation. But they make a moral difference. Those who hope, strive. Those who are disillusioned, accept. In that respect, they are self-fulfilling prophecies. A morality of hope lives in the belief that we can change the world for the better, and without certain theological beliefs it is hard to see where hope could come from, if not from optimism. Optimism and hope are not the same. Optimism is the belief that the world is changing for the better; hope is the belief that, together, we can *make* the world better. Optimism is a passive virtue, hope an active one. It needs no courage to be an optimist, but it takes a great deal of courage to hope. The Hebrew Bible is not an optimistic book. It is, however, one of the great literatures of hope.

*   *   *

The second difference is that the existence of God *changes the moral equation* even on the assumption, which I make throughout this book, that God empowers us to be his partners in the work of healing a fractured world. There is a children's puzzle: You come across three people who have earned, in the course of a day, seventeen gold coins. Because of their differential contributions to the success of the enterprise, they have agreed in advance that A will receive a half of the takings, B a third, C a ninth. Try as they may, they cannot make the division work. What do you do? The answer is that you take one gold coin from your pocket, add it to those already there – making eighteen – give A nine, B six, C two, put the remaining coin back in your pocket and move on.

God alters the equation without himself being changed. Divine ownership of the world means that the worldly goods we enjoy, we do not own, we merely hold on trust. Hence the concept of *tzedakah*, charity-as-justice, becomes possible in a way it would not if there were absolute human ownership. Divine ownership of the land ('The land shall not be sold in perpetuity, for the land is Mine: you are strangers and temporary residents with Me' [Lev. 25:23]) means that all the redistributive measures of the Pentateuch – the forgotten sheaf, the corners of the field, the tithe given to the poor, the return of ancestral lands to their original owners in the Jubilee – are written into the structure of covenantal society. The fact that human beings are made in the image of God means that life belongs to him, not us. Hence infanticide, murder, suicide, active euthanasia and most forms of abortion are forbidden. These equations are fragile without the existence of a transcendent source of moral authority.

The existence of a covenant with God means that all human sovereignty is delegated, conditional and constitutional. This gives rise to the principles of crimes against humanity and justified civil disobedience. If there is a conflict between the laws of humans and the law of God, the latter takes priority. This is the greatest single safeguard against tyranny, totalitarianism and the rule of might over right. It is also the principle that brought into being one of the great moral institutions of humankind: the prophet, the world's first social critic. The man or woman who 'speaks truth to power' does so on the specific mandate of God himself. Plato wanted to ban poets from his ideal republic because they were subversive of the established order. The Israelite prophets took as their mission to be subversive of the established order, whenever they saw the corruptions of power.

The existence of God solves problems that are otherwise intractable. One is the leap beyond solipsism and egoism. How do I know that there are other minds? Why should I consider other people's interests as well as my own? Why shouldn't I act only on the basis of self-interest? After all, I feel only my own pains and pleasures. I am not even sure of anyone else's, let alone feeling bound to factor them into my behaviour. Monotheism solves this problem because it represents *the reality of otherness.* God, who knows me better than I know myself, knows others also. He cares for *me* because he cares for *us* and therefore cares for those who are not me. God is the bridge that spans the metaphysical abyss between self and other, me and you. Just as I acknowledge my brothers because I know I have a father, and I know they stand in the same relationship to him as I do, so the parenthood of God turns humanity into a single extended family with all the mutual obligations that entails.

Another problem – raised by Jean-Jacques Rousseau and Friedrich Hayek – is that of time- and interest-horizons as they affect societies. It is difficult to persuade people to think in terms of the common good as against private gain, and to forgo short-term gain for the sake of consequences in the distant future. Rousseau was scathing on the point:

> Perspectives which are general and goals remote are alike beyond the range of the common herd; it is difficult for the individual, who has no taste for any scheme of government but that which serves his private interest, to appreciate the advantages to be derived from the lasting austerities which good laws impose.[11]

Rousseau therefore believed that religion was essential to good government, not necessarily because it was true, but because it lifted ethics and politics beyond self-interest and immediate advantage.

Hayek spoke of the 'fatal conceit' that leads people to believe that 'man is able to shape the world around him according to his wishes'.[12] This brings disaster in its wake, because of the law of unintended consequences. Things never turn out as we expect them to. By the time we realize it, it is often too late to repair the damage. Religious restraints, he believed, represent the rules that work over time. The proof lies in the fact that they, and the civilizations to which they gave rise, have survived. The 'extended order' (his term for modern society) is preserved not by conscious planning but by respecting institutions and traditions, 'many of which men tend to dislike, whose significance they usually fail to understand, whose validity they cannot prove'.

What is interesting about Rousseau and Hayek is that though they were not religious (Hayek called himself a 'professed agnostic'), they recognized that the monotheistic imagination transforms human horizons. The God of all and of eternity makes us think of all and of eternity. Faith is the great counterforce to self-interest and short-term gain. So, like a catalyst, God transforms the human situation without himself being transformed. Like the gold coin, his existence solves problems otherwise insoluble.

*　　　　　*　　　　　*

The third difference, though, is the most significant. Philosophy has tended – not always, but often – to present ethics as the problem of What and Why: what should we do, and why should we do it? Interesting though these are, they are not the major issue in the history of humankind. The real question is: what does it take to make people moral given all the distractions, temptations and alternatives that our complex natures constantly throw in our path? If ethics were as simple as it is portrayed in some textbooks – empathy, sympathy, the disinterested spectator, doing your duty, obeying universal rules or acting so as to maximize beneficial consequences – then how is it that for most of history corruption, injustice, deceit, exploitation, violence and war have been real and present dangers? If ethics is so easy, how does it turn out to be so hard?

The short answer is that there is nothing inevitable about human virtue. Marx, Darwin, Freud, René Girard and others remind us that there are other forces at work: conflicts of interest, competition for scarce resources, latent hostilities and potential aggression. The moral sense is a flickering flame in a strong wind: hard to light, easy to extinguish. A philosophical treatise on ethics bears the same relationship to the ethical life as a medical textbook does to being healthy. Health is less a matter of what we know than of how we live – what we eat, how we exercise, how we handle stress – and unless we develop healthful habits, practised daily, all the medical knowledge in the world will not save us from ourselves.

The fundamental task of ethics is not only to know the good but to make it part of our lives. The Bible is less a philosophical treatise on the nature of the good than a choreography of human action: commands, judgements, statutes, rituals, observances and prayers. To be sure, Judaism is about knowledge of the good. It is a religion of study and ethical reflection. But it is also, and intensively, about practice: about what we eat, how we conduct every aspect of our lives, and how we structure our time. The life of the commands is an ongoing exercise in character formation, a sustained seminar in Judaism's 'habits of the heart'. We become ethical not just by what we know, but also by what we do.

Hence the great commandments. On the Sabbath, we do no work, nor are we permitted to employ others to work. All relationships of hierarchy and dominance are temporarily suspended, one day in seven. During the six weekdays, we think of ourselves as creators. On the seventh, we become aware that we are also creations – part of the natural order, whose integrity we are bidden to respect. The Sabbath is thus the most compelling tutorial in human dignity, environmental consciousness, and the principle that there are moral limits to economic exchange and commercial exploitation. It is one of the great antidotes to consumerization and commodification. We spend time with our family at home, and with the community in the synagogue. The Sabbath thus becomes a weekly renewal of the bonds of civil society. The nineteenth-century writer Ahad Ha-am once said that 'More than the Jewish people have kept the Sabbath, the Sabbath has kept the Jewish people.' He was right. Even in the depths of poverty and persecution, for one day in seven every Jew was a person of leisure, a guest at God's banquet, a free and equal citizen in the commonwealth of heaven.

The Jewish festivals, by re-enacting the great events of the Jewish past, turn history into memory – and memory is one of the great guardians of conscience. Every year, on Pesach, Jews eat the unleavened bread of affliction and taste the bitter herbs of slavery, to remind us that liberty needs constant vigilance and to identify with the plight of those who are still slaves. On Sukkot (Tabernacles), we leave the comfort of our homes to live in shacks, with only leaves as a roof, not only to remember our ancestors' wilderness years, but also to know what it feels like to be homeless. These festivals are more powerful than any conventional learning experience. It is one thing to know that there are people who are poor, unfree, unhoused; it is another thing altogether to experience, from the inside, the pain and the cold. The fact that many Jews worked with and for Gandhi, Martin Luther King and Nelson Mandela was not coincidental. The biblical narrative – exile and exodus, slavery and redemption – is engraved into the minds of successive generations of children because they not only learned it: they lived it, symbolically, in the course of each Jewish year.

Judaism has strict laws about sex and marriage: modesty in dress, the separation of the sexes in prayer, the avoidance of intimacy during the period of menstruation, the use of the *mikvah* (ritual bath) and so on. These rules invest Jewish marriage with sanctity and the Jewish home with immense strength, whatever the sexual mores of the wider society. We tend to forget that marriage is a social institution, not just a private contract between two individuals, and it needs social support. Non-Jews are sometimes surprised, knowing how strong Jewish families often are, to discover that in Judaism for at least the past 2,000 years, divorce laws have been exceptionally liberal. It is not the difficulty of divorce that gives marriage its power within Judaism, but the intricate and often very beautiful rules, customs and traditions with which it is surrounded.

Even the apparently non-rational laws known within Judaism as 'statutes' – commands like the prohibition against eating milk with meat, wearing clothes of mixed wool and linen, and not sowing a field with diverse kinds of seed – have a clear logic in terms of respecting the boundaries of nature, the ecology of creation. Read Leviticus 19, in which many of these laws are set out, and you discover that is also the chapter that contains the great commands, 'Love your neighbour as yourself' and 'Love the stranger.' Its stark and powerful opening is 'Be holy, for I the Lord your God am holy.' The holy and the good are different categories, but their artful interweaving in Leviticus 19 shows that they belong to a single vision, the 'priestly' cosmos of Genesis 1, with its emphasis on order, separation and harmonious balance. An orderly universe is a moral universe, in which each creation has its place and each is given its due.

Far too little attention has been paid to the role of ritual in the moral life – in fact, I can't recall a single book on the philosophy of ethics that mentions it. Yet it makes a difference – sometimes all the difference – by turning abstract rules into living practices that, in turn, shape ethical character. The fact that each day I must pray, give money to charity and make a blessing over all I eat and drink; that once a week, however busy I am, I must stop and spend time with my family and community; that once a year, during the High Holy Days, I must atone for my sins and apologize to those I have offended: these things transform life. Would I apologize to those I had wronged if there were not a set time of the year for it, and were it not a sacred duty? Without prayer, would I consciously recall, each day, that there are those to whom I am accountable – God, humanity, my ancestors who prayed the same prayers and entrusted their hopes to me? I don't know. All I can say is that ritual is to ethics what physical exercise is to health. Medical knowledge alone will not make me healthy. That requires daily discipline, a ritual – and religion is the matrix of ritual.

*   *   *

There can be religion without ethics, and ethics without religion. There can be pious individuals who are cruel or insensitive, and atheists who are environmentally conscious, socially committed, and vastly generous with their money and time. Yet taken as a whole and over time, when religion and ethics are separated, they both suffer. There is a rare form of cerebral lesion in which the right and left hemispheres of the brain are both intact, but the connection between them is damaged. The result is dysfunction of the personality. That is what happens when the good and the holy lose their intimate connection. Without the constraints of ethics, religion can become a force for evil as well as good. People have undertaken pogroms, persecutions, murders and holy wars in the name of God. Contrariwise, without religion, in the long run ethics tends to lose touch with reverence, respect, responsibility and restraint. That is not to say that individuals will not act nobly or courageously: they will. Nor is it to say that the effect will be immediate: it will not. Cultures can live for generations on the accumulated moral capital of earlier religious habits. None the less, Tolstoy was not wrong when he said:

> The instructions of a secular morality that is not based on religious doctrines are exactly like what a person ignorant of music might do, if he were made a conductor and started to wave his hands in front of musicians well rehearsed in what they are performing. By virtue of its own momentum, and from what previous conductors had taught the musicians, the music might continue for a while, but

obviously the gesticulations made with a stick by a person who knows nothing about music would be useless and eventually confuse the musicians and throw the orchestra off course.[13]

The call of the prophets was not, 'Be religious', nor was it, 'Be ethical.' It was, 'Be religious *by being* ethical.' Hence Jeremiah:

Hear the word of the Lord, O king of Judah, you who sit on David's throne . . . This is what the Lord says: Do what is just and right. Rescue from the hand of his oppressor the one who has been robbed. Do no wrong or violence to the stranger, the fatherless or the widow, and do not shed innocent blood in this place. (Jer. 22:2–3)

This is Amos on religious worship without social responsibility:

Away with the noise of your songs!
I will not listen to the music of your harps.
But let justice roll on like a river,
Righteousness like a never-failing stream! (Amos 5:23–4)

And, most passionately, Isaiah:

'The multitude of your sacrifices – what are they to Me?' says the
    Lord . . .
'When you spread out your hands in prayer, I will hide My eyes
    from you;
Even if you offer many prayers, I will not listen.
Your hands are full of blood.
Wash and make yourselves clean. Take your evil deeds out of My
    sight!
Stop doing wrong. Learn to do right!
Seek justice, encourage the oppressed,
Defend the cause of the fatherless, plead the case of the
    widow . . .' (Is. 1:11–17)

The prophetic works are full of such sentiments. Their message was that the holy must lead to the good, and the good always lead back to the holy. There is nothing intrinsically religious about feeding the hungry, giving shelter to the homeless or healing the sick. Yet there is something inherently religious about the faith that gives these acts the particular coloration they have had in the West for the past 2,000 years. Social responsibility as covenantal, peace, justice and freedom as religious ideals and personal dignity as rooted in the image of God – these are not ideas that were born fully formed from the matrix of human imagination. They have a history that began in ancient Israel, and we who are moved by that vision are still charged with realizing it, living the life, telling the story, observing the commands and celebrating the festivals through which our most redemptive energies are born and renewed.

The link between monotheism and the moral life is that a universe seen as the home of many gods or none is an arena of conflicting forces in which the strong prevail, the weak suffer, the manipulative exploit the vulnerable, and might is sovereign over right. A world without a Judge is one in which there is no reason to expect justice. The human condition becomes a tragic script in which ideals prove to be illusions, revolution a mere change of places in the seats of power, and the ship of hope destined to be wrecked by the cold iceberg of reality.

The holy and the good are not the same but they are linked in a cyclical process of engagement and withdrawal. Our prayers, texts and rituals hold before us a vision of how the world might be. Our work, service to the community and social life take us into the world as it is, where we make a difference by mending some of its imperfections, righting wrongs, curing ills, healing wounds. The juxtaposition of the two creates moral energy, and when they are disconnected, the energy fails. The holy is where we enter the ideal; the good is how we make it real. Long ago, alone at night, Jacob dreamed a dream of a ladder connecting heaven and earth, and of angels ascending and descending. Life is that ladder, for earth cannot be mended without a glimpse of heaven, nor heaven live for humankind without a home on earth.

NOTES

1. I have not been able to track down this statement, widely attributed to Dostoevsky, in his writings. It may be that it is a popular summary of the position of Ivan Karamazov in the early chapters of Dostoevsky's novel, *The Brothers Karamazov*. At one point, Ivan says: 'If there is no immortality, there is no virtue.'
2. John Barton, *Amos's Oracles Against the Nations* (Cambridge: Cambridge University Press, 1980).
3. R. Nissim ben Jacob, *Commentary to Babylonian Talmud, Berakhot*, introduction.
4. *The Dialogues of Plato*, trans. Benjamin Jowett (London: Sphere, 1970), pp. 35–56. Jowett translates the relevant passage (p. 46): 'The point which I should first wish to understand is whether the pious or holy is beloved by the gods because it is holy, or holy because it is beloved of the gods.'

5. Needless to say, I am here stating my own position. There are other voices within the Jewish tradition. For two recent treatments of the subject, see Avi Sagi and Daniel Statman, *Religion and Morality* (Amsterdam: Rodopi, 1995); Michael J. Harris, *Divine Command Ethics* (London: Routledge Curzon, 2003).

6. I address this subject in my forthcoming book, *Making Space*.

7. Kant, *Groundwork of the Metaphysic of Morals*, part II, in H. J. Paton, *The Moral Law: Kant's Groundwork of the Metaphysic of Morals* (London: Hutchinson, 1981), pp. 71–106.

8. Maimonides, *Laws of Repentance*, 10:3.

9. Babylonian Talmud, *Kiddushin* 32b.

10. Peter Berger, *A Rumour of Angels* (New York: Anchor, 1969), pp. 55–86.

11. Jean-Jacques Rousseau, *The Social Contract*, II, 7 (London: Penguin, 1968), p. 86.

12. F. A. Hayek, *The Fatal Conceit* (London: Routledge, 1990), p. 27.

13. Tolstoy, *A Confession and Other Religious Writings*, trans. Jane Kentish (London: Penguin, 1987), p. 150.

Chapter 13

The Monotheistic Imagination

The human being is not one thing among other things. Things determine each other. Man, however, determines himself. Rather, he decides whether or not he lets himself be determined, be it by drives and instincts that push him, or the reasons and meanings that pull him.

(Viktor Frankl)[1]

Monotheism makes a difference to what we believe and do, but does it make a difference to the kind of person we become? Does the way we see the totality of things affect our reactions to what happens to us in our lives? Is there such a thing as the monotheistic personality? The question intrigues me because of my fascination with Jewish history. What gave a people the capacity to survive every catastrophe and begin again? What creates resilience in the human mind? From Plato to Freud, thinkers have traced a connection between ontology and psychology, the objective world 'out there' and the subjective world 'in here'. Many saw the soul as a microcosm of external reality. If the way we see the external world changes, so too should the human personality. The religious imagination is the most fundamental way of organizing our thoughts about the universe and our place within it – and in the history of thought there has been no greater single revolution than the one by which all the forces that seem to create conflict and chaos were located within a single creative will. It is therefore worth asking, however speculative our answer, what difference monotheism might make to the human personality.

Towards the end of his *God: A Biography*, the Jesuit scholar Jack Miles proposes a highly original thought-experiment. What would the Bible look like if written as a polytheistic text – if, instead of a single God, each aspect of the divine personality were seen as a separate deity? The following gives a flavour of the result:

In the beginning, the god Eloh created the physical world. Then Eloh and his brother Yah set about creating the human race. Eloh, calm and benign, proposed to Yah that they create humankind 'in our image'. For Eloh, the human creature was to be the crown and culmination of creation. Yah, however, was reluctant to have humankind 'be like one of us'. He claimed the actual making for himself, and he chose to make humankind from the dust, though impulsively he breathed his own spirit into his creature. Eloh had sought a male-and-female human race from the outset. Yah, whose action always seemed to precede his understanding, at first made only the male but gradually realized that a companion was required . . .

The reptilian goddess Mot then lured the woman into disobeying Yah, and the woman in turn misled her husband into joining her in sin. Yah, enraged, humiliated Mot, requiring her henceforth to crawl, snakelike, on her belly, but the punishment he imposed on her was less severe than what he imposed on the man and woman . . .[2]

And so on. What is happening in this transformation? This is Miles' comment:

Retold in this way, the course of events, playing roughly the role that the course of events would play in a well-populated Greek myth, is more important than any one actor. As each of the several gods mentioned is reduced to a signature trait or two, the narrative acquires, notwithstanding the turbulence of the action, a certain underlying calm: What will be will be.[3]

Events take on an air of inevitability. The complexity lies in the plot, not the characters. All conflict has been externalized.

The Hebrew Bible, Miles argues, represents a radically different type of narrative. The human characters, all the more so God himself, are complex. There is nothing predictable about their responses to situations. God can react with justice or mercy, punishment or forgiveness, anger or acceptance. At one time he can send a warning through the prophets of impending disaster; at another he can convey to the same prophet a message of surpassing hope. The unfolding of events has become suddenly uncertain, dependent as it is not on the blind clash of opposed forces but on emotion, attitude, choice, will. In short, though Miles does not put it this way, mythic time has given way to historical time, time as the arena of free agents responding to one another in freedom. Just as in a genuine conversation, so in a biblical narrative, you do not know, *cannot* know, how it will end.

That, says Miles, is why the Hebrew Bible is more like Shakespeare's *Hamlet* than Greek tragedy:

> The classic Greek tragedies are all versions of the same tragedy. All present the human condition as a contest between the personal and the impersonal with the impersonal inevitably victorious . . . Hamlet is another kind of tragedy . . . The contest is unlike that between doomed, noble Oedipus and an iron chain of events. It is, instead, a conflict within Hamlet's own character between 'the native hue of resolution' and 'the pale cast of thought'.[4]

Miles alerts us to a fact of immense consequence. Monotheism relocates conflict from 'out there' to 'in here', transferring it from an objective fact about the world to an internal contest within the mind. This changes our view of God, and fate, and history. But it changes, also, our view of the soul, the self, the human personality. It is surely no coincidence that the struggle between Jacob and Esau, which begins in the womb and brings their relationship to the brink of violence, is resolved only when Jacob wrestles alone at night with an unnamed adversary – according to some commentators, a portrayal of inner, psychological struggle.[5] The next day, Jacob and Esau meet after a separation of 22 years, and instead of fighting, they embrace, and part as friends. If we can wrestle with ourselves, the Bible seems to suggest, we need not fight as enemies. Conflict, internalized, can be resolved.

One consequence is the birth of hope as a human emotion. I have had occasion in the past to note the strange fact that, despite the appalling catastrophes that have struck them many times in history, Jews never coined a word that meant 'tragedy' in the Greek sense. When Hebrew was revived as a spoken language in the nineteenth century, they simply borrowed the word, Hebraizing it into *tragediah*. Tragedy tells the story of human beings, with their aspirations and ambitions, in a world governed by *ananke*, blind fate. To be human is to wish, to plan, to dream. But our dreams are destined to crash against the rocks of a reality fundamentally indifferent to our existence. They are *hubris*, and are always punished by *nemesis*. Oedipus and the other great figures of Greek drama fail to defeat the forces of fate, as they were bound to do. Tragedy is a consequence of the emotional void between humanity and the gods. Zeus, like other ancient deities, had no special affection for human beings. They disturbed his peace. They threatened to steal his secret knowledge. The gods of polytheistic cultures tended to be at best mildly irritated by, at worst actively hostile to, human beings.

A tragic universe is a place where bad things happen for no particular reason; where there is no ultimate justice and no expectation of it; where we learn to accept, with Stoic courage, the random cruelties of circumstance. As Jean Anouilh wrote:

In tragedy nothing is in doubt and everyone's destiny is known. That makes for tranquillity. There is a sort of fellow-feeling among characters in a tragedy: he who kills is as innocent as he who gets killed: it's all a matter of what part you are playing. Tragedy is restful; and the reason is that hope, that foul, deceitful thing, has no part in it.[6]

There is no tragedy in this sense in Judaism. That is not because there are no disasters, crises, catastrophes. Manifestly there are. Jewish history has all too often been written in tears. Nor is it because in a Jewish story there is always a happy ending. On the contrary: Genesis ends with Jacob's children in exile in Egypt, the promise of the land still unfulfilled. Deuteronomy closes with Moses unable to cross the Jordan, seeing the land only from afar. Biblical stories lack what Frank Kermode calls 'the sense of an ending'.[7] Like life itself, they are open-ended. But there is always hope, grounded hope, justified not by optimism, innocence or a 'Whiggish theory' that sees history as constant progress, but by the terms of the covenant between heaven and earth. *Judaism is the principled rejection of tragedy in the name of hope* – precisely because there is no inexorable fate. Nor does hope stand alone. It belongs to a world in which not only God but also human beings, his image, are free, masters of their fate, responsible for their destiny.

At the end of his life Moses sets out, in the series of speeches known as the book of Deuteronomy, his vision of the future. It is a work that opens up vast temporal horizons. The Israelites have not yet entered the land, but already he sees beyond war and conquest, settlement and ease, to decay, moral drift and eventual exile, and beyond that to return. Against this huge backdrop of time, he returns time and again to the idea of choice: 'This day, I call heaven and earth as witnesses against you that I have set before you life and death, the blessing and the curse; therefore choose life, so that you and your children may live' (Deut. 30:19).

The Pentateuch ends as it began, with choice, freedom and responsibility. In the beginning it was the choice of individuals – Adam and Eve, then Cain – now it is the choice of the nation as a whole. The God of freedom summons humanity to freedom: responsible, law-governed, self-restrained, the liberty that honours the liberty of others, but never less than freedom. That is the principle from which the Hebrew Bible never deviates.

One feature of this worldview is essential, however alien it may be to the contemporary mind: its doctrine of reward and punishment. This is one of Deuteronomy's constant themes. 'If you carefully observe these commands, then . . .'; 'But if you go astray, then . . .' There is here an equation of suffering and guilt that nowadays we would resist – especially Jews, especially after the Holocaust. Not all suffering, surely, is deserved.

Not all those who die do so because of their sins. Much of Judaism is a protest against such an idea: the book of Job is its classic expression. Yet the Bible is surely pointing to something that has played a large part in the monotheistic imagination.

Two ideas rescue the biblical idea of justice from tragedy. The first is *repentance*. Whatever wrong we have done, we can redeem, either by restitution or remorse, preferably both. The second is *forgiveness*. God does not condemn us for the evil we do if we openly and candidly admit the evil we have done. David sins. Confronted by the prophet Nathan he acknowledges his sin, and is forgiven (2 Sam. 12:1–13). Repentance expresses the freedom of the sinner, forgiveness the freedom of the sinned-against. Between them they constitute the biblical refutation of tragedy. No evil decree cannot be rescinded. There is no inexorable fate. That is the difference between a Greek oracle and a biblical prophet. An oracle predicts; a prophet warns. If a prediction comes to pass, it has succeeded. If a prophecy comes to pass, it has failed. That is why the prophets were agents of hope. The future they foresaw was neither inescapable nor final. For every sin there was atonement, for every exile a return.

The result was a *penitential culture*: an entropy-defying containment of energy, as if Judaism were a system designed against 'the expense of spirit in a waste of shame'.[8] Entropy is the law that says: all systems lose energy over time. Penitence conserves energy by turning suffering into a new impetus to do good. Every national catastrophe in Israel's history led to a return to first principles, a renewal of the covenant. Because, in monotheism, all evil as well as good comes from a single source, there was no way that the Jewish people could blame an alien force for their troubles. The fault lay not in their stars but in themselves. *A penitential culture is the opposite of a blame culture.* Given the terms of their theology, the Israelites could not see themselves as hapless victims of a hostile power. They could not give themselves over to self-pity, anger, resentment or rage. Given the terms of the covenant and the theology that lies behind it, they could not but see themselves as the sole cause of their troubles; therefore they had it within themselves to put things right.

Odd though it might seem, there is something profoundly liberating about the idea of penitence. It lies in the fact that when we suffer, there are two questions we can ask. The first is, 'Why did this happen to me?' The second is, 'What then shall I do?' So different are these questions that they generate two distinct types of culture. The first focuses on the past, the second on the future. When I ask, 'Why did this happen?' I see myself as an object. When I ask, 'What then shall I do?' I see myself as a subject. The first is passive, the second active. In the first I search for someone or something to blame. In the second, I accept responsibility. When I do that, a profound human dignity is born.

Rabbi Joseph Soloveitchik put it eloquently:

Man is born as an object, dies like an object, but possesses the ability to live like a subject, like a creator, an innovator, who can impress his own individual seal upon his life and can extricate himself from a mechanical type of existence and enter into a creative, active mode of being. Man's task in the world, according to Judaism, is to transform fate into destiny; a passive existence into an active existence; an existence of compulsion, perplexity, and muteness into an existence replete with a powerful will, with resourcefulness, daring, and imagination . . . When the man of destiny suffers he says to himself: 'Evil exists, and I will neither deny it nor camouflage it with vain intellectual gymnastics. I am concerned about evil from a halakhic standpoint, like a person who wishes to know the deed which he shall do. I ask one simple question: What must the sufferer do so that he may live through his suffering.'[9]

'When sufferings come upon a person, they should examine their deeds and return in repentance.'[10] That is the instinctive response of the Talmudic sages as it was of the prophets. Suffering is less a punishment for sins than a call to return. That is what happens when the doctrine of divine justice is allied to Judaism's relentless focus on the future. A penitential culture is one in which the instinctive response to suffering is to say: 'Dear God, I accuse no one but myself. Forgive me. Accept my broken heart. Then give me the strength to change.'

I am struck by how little anger there is in the literature of medieval Jewry, the age of blood libels and accusations of Jewish guilt from ritual desecration to the plague, the era of massacres, expulsions, forced conversions, inquisitions, burnings at the stake, ghettoes and pogroms. In the *kinot*, laments, Jews wrote after these events, there is prayer, pleading, anguish; but of hate, rage and the desire for revenge, little.[12] When, in 2003, a group of Orthodox Jews travelling back in a bus from prayers at the Western Wall were struck by a suicide-bomber, leaving 23 dead and many others injured, secular Israelis were awed by the dignity of their grief. In the tightly knit community of Meah Shearim (an ultra-Orthodox district of Jerusalem), there were no expressions of anger, but an intense, quiet, collective rededication to study, prayer and good deeds. There is something inspiring in a worldview that has such power to turn negative energies into a renewed commitment to the good.

I recall once undergoing a medical check-up. The doctor instructed me to run on a treadmill. As I was doing so, I asked him what he was testing: how fast I could run, or for how long? 'Neither', he replied. 'What I want to test is how long it takes, when you have finished, for your pulse to return to normal.' That was when I learned that health is measured by the ability to recover.

Several students of Jewish history – Nietzsche was one, Sigmund Freud another – have been fascinated by the capacity of the people of the covenant to recover from catastrophe. What was it about Judaism that led Jews, in circumstances that should rationally have led to despair, not merely to survive, but to respond with a new burst of creativity? For that, historically, is what happened. The division of the kingdom after Solomon led to the flowering of prophecy. The destruction of the First Temple and the Babylonian exile reinvigorated the study of Torah. Responding to the destruction of the Second Temple, the sages created the vast rabbinic literature: Mishnah, Midrash and the two Talmuds. The encounter with Karaites and, later, Christianity gave impetus to Jewish bible commentary; with Islam, to Jewish philosophy. The Crusades led to new forms of North European Jewish pietism. The Spanish expulsion evoked the mysticism of Safed. The Holocaust, in human terms the worst tragedy of all, led to the single greatest affirmation of the collective Jewish will to survive: birth of the State of Israel.

The health of a culture has as much to do with mental as with physical strength. Like Nietzsche and Freud, I am fascinated by people and groups with the capacity to recover, who having suffered the slings and arrows of outrageous fortune are not defeated by them but fight back, strengthened and renewed. I am convinced that they share an attitude, a cognitive stance, that enables them to face fate without fear. The ability to defeat tragedy is not mysterious. It is a matter of ideas, patterns of explanation, the kinds of story we tell about what has happened to us, the 'script' by which we understand our lives.

I believe it stems from the rejection of the blame culture. Jews survived, recovered, turned tragedy into creativity, because they refused to see themselves as victims. The biblical worldview, with its endless insistence on freedom and responsibility, left no room for self-pity or a tendency to blame others for their plight. I am awestruck by the fact that, after the Holocaust, many of the great rabbinic figures hardly spoke about it, even those who had been through the concentration camps themselves. Surely they mourned inwardly and wept for the injustice and the murdered generations, but outwardly they sought to affirm life, not remember death. They built schools, not museums; communities, not memorials; they encouraged their followers to marry and have children, not to grieve. Perhaps they remembered the fate of Lot's wife who, turning to look back at the destruction, was turned into a pillar of salt. The Jewish calendar has its days of grief, but Judaism as a whole is not a religion of grief. If it had been, it would not have survived, nor would it have been true to itself as an expression of faith in life. Judaism is not a victim culture. The people I learned this from were often Holocaust survivors.

*   *   *

Postmodern secular culture tends to underemphasize responsibility, thereby generating a strange contradiction. On the one hand we have almost unlimited freedom to choose. On the other, when things go wrong, it is rarely *our fault*. Something or someone else is to blame: poverty, discrimination, a difficult childhood, the educational system, psychological abuse, the media, the government, junk food, or any other of the proliferating varieties of exculpation.[13] An employee, fired for consistently showing up late to work, sues his employers on the grounds that he is the victim of 'chronic lateness syndrome'. *The Economist* noted about the United States, 'If you lose your job you can sue for the mental distress of being fired . . . if you drive drunk and crash you can sue somebody for failing to warn you to stop drinking. There is always somebody else to blame.'[14]

There is much to be said for such a culture. It arises from the highest motives: sympathy, compassion, the desire to help, the urge to understand, the reluctance to be judgemental, a passion for justice; and these are all virtues. It is grounded in a range of scientific disciplines that has given us a deeper understanding of the causal processes behind human action. But taken to an extreme, it turns us into objects, not subjects. We become done-to, not doers; passive, not active. Locating the cause of our condition outside ourselves, we become chronically dependent on others, lacking the ability to break free from circumstance and become masters, not slaves, of our fate.

This is not, God forbid, to argue against compassion, which stands at the centre of the biblical vision of a good society. What it suggests, however, is that compassion itself must be guided by a duty to help the victim recover his or her capacity for independent action. I once spent a day at Sherborne House, a centre for young offenders in London.[15] The people I met – average age, 18 – had been committing crime for the previous eight or ten years. Yet by no stretch of the imagination could they be called evil. They had come from broken, often abusive, families. They had suffered violence, often from step-fathers. They were victims of circumstance. It would be easy to say that they should have exercised self-control, yet, knowing their family histories, it was hard to see how they could have learned it. They had a strong sense of morality: when I asked them what kind of father would they like to be when they had children, their answers were moving and passionate. They wanted to give their children everything their parents had not given them, especially time and care. When I asked the director of the centre what local communal networks of support they would have when they left, she looked blank. There were none. There is a famous African proverb: 'It takes a village to raise a child.' The young men of Sherborne House never had a village. They had not even had the consistent attention of their own parents.

What is striking about Judaism is not just its emphasis on responsibility but its insistence on elaborate support structures. Its welfare provisions sustained people going through hard times. The release of slaves after seven years, the remission of debts every seventh year, and the return of ancestral property in the Jubilee year, gave individuals the chance to begin again. The idea that the highest form of charity is to find someone a job speaks volumes about its understanding of human dignity – people do not *want* to be dependent. Jewish mysticism goes so far as to call the manna the Israelites ate in the wilderness 'the bread of shame', even though it came from God, because they did not have to work for it.

The ethic of responsibility structures Judaism's entire approach to the world. An obvious example is that biblical ethics is constructed in terms of responsibilities, not rights. Does this make a difference? Are rights not simply responsibilities seen from another point of view? 'Thou shalt not murder' creates a right to life. 'Thou shalt not steal' creates a right to property. The obligation to administer justice creates the right to a fair trial, and so on. That is true, but it omits one feature insufficiently alluded to in discussions of law.

Rights are passive, responsibilities active. Rights are demands we make on others, responsibilities are demands others make on us. A responsibility-based culture exists in the active mode. It emphasizes giving over receiving, doing not complaining. What is wrong with what Mary Ann Glendon calls 'rights-talk'[16] is that it draws on resources that only exist if we recognize responsibilities. It puts the cart before the horse. It neglects the moral commitments we need to create if rights are to be honoured at all. Rights are the *result* of responsibilities; they are secondary, not primary. A society that does not train its citizens to be responsible will be one in which, too often, rights-talk will be mere rhetoric, honoured in the breach not the observance.

One feature of the Jewish law of *tzedakah* has long fascinated me. Only one thing is as eloquent as the texts that speak of the duty to give – namely those that speak of the importance of *not receiving*. Here is Maimonides on the subject:

> A person should always exert himself and endure hardship rather than throw himself, as a dependant, on the community. The sages taught: 'Make your Sabbath a weekday, sooner than become dependent.' Even one who is learned and honoured should, if impoverished, work at various trades, yes, despicable trades, in order to avoid dependency. Better to strip the hides of beasts that

have sickened and died than to tell people, 'I am a great sage, my class is that of a priest, support me.' Thus spoke the sages.

Outstanding scholars worked as hewers of wood, carriers of beams, drawers of garden water, iron workers, blacksmiths, rather than ask anything of the community and rather than accept any proffered gratuity . . . One who is impoverished, but who endures privation and exerts himself, living a life of hardship rather than burden the community, will, before he dies of old age, possess the means out of which he will give help to others. Concerning such a person, it is written, 'Blessed is the man that trusts in the Lord.'[17]

In these lines, we hear the authentic voice of a religious tradition that has placed freedom of the will at the centre of its concerns. To give and not receive, to act rather than be acted on, to be free and not dependent on other human beings, to be dependent on God alone: these are what give Judaism its distinctive tone of voice. That is what makes *tzedakah* something other than charity. It is not merely helping those in need. It is enabling the afflicted, where possible, to recover their capacity for independent action. Responsibility lies at the heart of human dignity.

*　　　　　　*　　　　　　*

Two contemporary figures in psychiatry have done much to rehabilitate an ethic of responsibility. Aaron Beck is the founder of cognitive therapy, one of the most successful of therapeutic methods.[18] He came to the conclusion that dysfunctional behaviour is often accompanied by a series of barely conscious thoughts that determine people's emotional reaction. By changing our thoughts, 'reframing' our perceptions, we can transform our reactions. There is a strong connection between cognitive therapy and the Habad school of Jewish mysticism, which emphasizes the power of intellect (the letters H-B-D stand for the Hebrew words for wisdom, understanding and knowledge) over emotion. We can control what we feel by what we think. What makes Beck's approach refreshing is that it counters the Freudian insistence on the power of irrational feelings and subconscious drives. It restores the power of human agency by getting us to take responsibility for our cognitive processes.

Martin Seligman is one of the founders of positive psychology. When I met him he told me the story of how he came by the insight that changed his approach to the human mind – his equivalent of Newton's apple. He was clearing his garden one morning when his five-year-old daughter started throwing the weeds he had carefully piled up, into the air, dancing and singing at the same time. He told her to stop. She was ruining his work. She replied: 'Daddy, do you remember before my fifth birthday? I used to spend my time whining and complaining. On my fifth birthday, I decided I wasn't going to whine any more. And if I can stop whining, you can stop being such a grouch.'[19]

Seligman said that this was his epiphany. Until then he, like most psychiatrists, was involved in the treatment of negative syndromes: depression, anxiety, neurosis, psychosis. If I succeeded, he said, I had merely got the patient back to ground level. What if I looked at it the other way – not curing depression but creating positive states: happiness, fulfilment, exuberance, joy? He began studying people who had a positive approach to life. What they had in common, he found, was optimism, and this in turn had to do with their cognitive styles. They tended to see setbacks as temporary, not permanent; accidental, not essential; exceptional, not pervasive.[20]

Optimism worked. Pessimists turn out to have more depressive states, do less well at school and work, and suffer more from ill-health. Seligman even showed, through a close analysis of political speeches, that optimists won presidential elections. His crucial finding was that optimism and pessimism were not genetically determined. Like Beck, he looked closely at people's cognitive styles. Pessimism, he said, is *learned helplessness*, the view that what happens to you is inevitable and there is little you can do to change it. Pessimism and optimism are self-fulfilling prophecies. It is not that more bad things happen to pessimists than to optimists, but that optimists have a way of disregarding them, not letting them shape their view of reality. They have developed mental strategies for sustaining hope.

Seligman's conclusions are supported by findings from another field altogether: the relationship between culture and economic growth. In his majestic *The Wealth and Poverty of Nations*, Harvard economic historian David Landes poses the question: why is it that some countries have failed to grow economically while others have succeeded spectacularly? After more than 500 pages of close analysis, he reaches this conclusion:

> In this world, the optimists have it, not because they are always right, but because they are positive. Even when wrong, they are positive, and that is the way of achievement, correction, improvement, and success. Educated, eyes-open optimism pays; pessimism can only offer the empty consolation of being right.[21]

Landes ends by quoting the words of Moses cited above: 'I have set before you life and death, the blessing and the curse; therefore choose life'.

*　　　　　*　　　　　*

I sometimes wonder whether the Jewish sense of humour does not come from the same source, with the same motivation. The sociologist Peter

Berger calls humour a 'signal of transcendence'. He wrote a book about it called *Redeeming Laughter*, emphasizing its religious dimension.[22] A joke, he said, is 'a vignette of salvation'. [23] Humour is at its most intense among persecuted peoples. It is the weapon of the weak against the strong. What we can laugh at, momentarily, we do not fear. I once wrote that I could not go all the way with Roberto Benigni who made a comedy about the Holocaust and called it *Life Is Beautiful*. Its theme was that, in otherwise unbearable circumstances, humour keeps us sane. I argued that in Auschwitz, humour might have kept you sane but it would not have kept you alive. I was corrected by an Auschwitz survivor. He told me that in the camp, he and a fellow prisoner made a point of finding one thing each day about which they could laugh. That, he said, was what kept us alive. I was wrong, and acknowledge the fact.

Humour is the oldest form of cognitive therapy. Jewish humour in particular lives in its ability, at the last moment, to get us to see things differently, to reframe (it is no coincidence that Ludwig Wittgenstein, a philosopher of Jewish background, said that 'a philosophical work could be written entirely in the form of jokes'). Humour gives us a way out from what, until the last line, seemed an impossible situation. What we can laugh at, we can rise above. Humour is an assertion of humanity in the face of dehumanizing influences. It is a way of breaking the grip of fears that would otherwise hold us captive. It is, in its way, one of the supreme expressions of human freedom in the Beck, Seligman sense: freedom as the ability to redefine our situation. Those who can laugh at fate, redeem it from tragedy. One who rejects his enemy's interpretation of events cannot be made a victim. Psychologically, he or she remains free. Humour is first cousin to hope.

The Cambridge mathematician Alan Turing devised the famous 'Turing test' of artificial intelligence. If you can hold a conversation, by writing or speech, with a computer in another room and not know whether you are speaking to a person or a machine, the computer has passed the test: it is intelligent. I propose a more demanding test. Can a computer get the point of a joke? That is the real test of personhood. Humour is the ability to reconceptualize events and thus create the space to respond in freedom, not as the effect of a prior cause, but as a reflective, self-conscious agent. What Aaron Beck and Martin Seligman remind us of is the phenomenon of reflexivity: what governs human behaviour is not what happens to us but *how we perceive* what happens to us, and that is constrained only by the scope of our imagination. This entails that human behaviour can never be adequately explained by causal laws: neurophysiological, sociobiological, economic or sociological. A joke testifies to our ability to see things differently, and because we can do so, we are free. Humour is constitutive of humanity.

The philosopher Emmanuel Levinas was interned in a lumber camp for Jewish prisoners during the Second World War. His French uniform protected him from the worst Nazi violence, but he and his fellow prisoners were aware that, in the eyes of the Germans, 'We were subhuman, a gang of apes . . . A small inner murmur, the strength and wretchedness of persecuted people, reminded us of our essence as thinking creatures, but we were no longer part of the world.' Then something happened:

> For a few short weeks before the sentinels chased him away, a wandering dog entered our lives . . . He would appear at morning assembly and was waiting for us as we returned, jumping up and down and barking in delight. For him, there was no doubt that we were men.[24]

Levinas calls the dog 'the last Kantian in Nazi Germany' – a philosopher's joke, but enough to keep him sane.

This chapter has drawn together a number of themes – repentance and forgiveness, rights and responsibilities and the sense of humour, as well as touching on the psychological theories of Aaron Beck and Martin Seligman, and David Landes' account of economic history. What unites them is their opposition to learned helplessness. I have suggested that this is not unrelated to Jewish theology and to the monotheistic personality. By insisting that the various forces at work in the world are internal to the mind of God, biblical monotheism helped pave the way for a profound psychological transformation: the internalization of conflict. Once we locate the cause of our condition within ourselves, rather than 'out there' in external factors beyond our control, we enlarge the scope of human freedom. Responsibility is the negation of learned helplessness. It is a great weight to carry. But the alternative is heavier still.

NOTES

1. Viktor Frankl, *The Unheard Cry for Meaning: psychotherapy and humanism* (New York: Simon and Schuster, 1978), p. 61.
2. Jack Miles, *God: a biography* (London: Simon and Schuster, 1995), pp. 398–401.
3. Ibid., p. 401.
4. Ibid., pp. 397–8.
5. Maimonides, *The Guide for the Perplexed*, II:42; Rashbam, *Commentary* to Gen. 32:25, 29. Nahmanides, *Commentary* to Gen. 18:1 strongly dissents from Maimonides' reading of the passage, as does Hasdai Crescas. Gersonides, however, defends Maimonides' position.

6. Jean Anouilh, *Antigone*, quoted in J. A. Cuddon, *The Penguin Dictionary of Literary Terms and Literary Theory* (London: Penguin, 1992), p. 985.
7. Frank Kermode, *The Sense of an Ending* (Oxford: Oxford University Press, 2000).
8. Shakespeare, *Sonnets*, 129.
9. Rabbi Joseph B. Soloveitchik, 'Kol Dodi Dofek', in Bernard Rosenberg and Fred Heuman (eds.), *Theological and Halakhic Reflections on the Holocaust* (New York: Ktav, 1992), pp. 54–5.
10. Babylonian Talmud, *Berakhot* 5a.
11. Maimonides, *Mishneh Torah, De'ot* 7:8.
12. An English translation is available in: Abraham Rosenfeld, *The Authorised Kinot for the Ninth of Av* (London: I. Labworth, 1965).
13. On the 'junk food' defence, see James Q. Wilson, *Moral Judgment* (New York: Basic Books, 1997).
14. These examples are taken from Charles Sykes, *A Nation of Victims* (New York: St Martin's Press, 1993), pp. 3–24.
15. I was led to Sherborne House by Roger Graef's powerful book on the subject: *Living Dangerously: young offenders in their own words* (London: HarperCollins, 1993).
16. Mary Ann Glendon, *Rights Talk* (New York: Free Press, 1991).
17. Maimonides, *Mishneh Torah, Mattenot Ani'im* 10:17–18.
18. See Aaron Beck, *Cognitive Therapy and the Emotional Disorders* (London: Penguin, 1989); *Love Is Never Enough* (New York: Harper & Row, 1988); *Prisoners of Hate* (New York: HarperCollins 1999).
19. Martin Seligman tells this story in *Authentic Happiness* (New York: Free Press, 2002), p. 28.
20. Martin Seligman, *Learned Optimism* (New York: Pocket Books, 1998).
21. David Landes, *The Wealth and Poverty of Nations* (London: Little, Brown, 1998), p. 524.
22. Peter Berger, *Redeeming Laughter* (Berlin: Walter de Gruyter, 1997).
23. Peter Berger, *A Rumour of Angels* (New York: Anchor, 1969), p. 118.
24. Emmanuel Levinas, *Difficult Freedom* (Baltimore: Johns Hopkins University Press, 1997), pp. 152–3.

Chapter 14

The Faith of God

'A God of faith' (Deut. 32:4) – this means: God had faith in the universe and created it.
                                                                    (*Sifre*)

The book of Job is the strangest in the Bible, surely the most unusual book ever to be included in a canon of sacred texts. Tennyson called it 'the greatest poem of ancient and modern times'. Carlyle described it as 'one of the grandest things ever written'. Thomas Wolfe spoke of it as 'the most tragic, sublime and beautiful expression of loneliness which I have ever read'.[1] Yet these descriptions fail to capture the radical presence of the book in the context of the Bible as a whole. It is an expression, surely the most eloquent ever written, of doubt in the very axioms of which the Bible builds its faith: the meaningfulness of existence, and the justice of fate. William Safire, the American political commentator, wrote a book about it and called it *The First Dissident*. Job, he argues, is the first person in history to challenge the system, to speak truth to power, to bring charges against the establishment, the voice of authority, in the name of the individual. Its tone is 'a sustained note of defiance'.[2] Job is the role-model for those who have the courage to insist on justice against all those who defend the status quo and the powers-that-be. The book of Job is the space God makes for the human voice taken to its very limits and beyond – sacred scripture giving human protest its hour on the stage and conferring on it a lonely but unshakeable dignity. Job is a sustained cry of pain at the inequity of fortune: a cry that penetrates to the heart of heaven and threatens to shake the foundations of the world.[3]

Set in the land of Uz, the book opens with a serene picture of 'a man of blameless and upright life . . . who feared God and set his face against wrongdoing'. Job, when we first meet him, is a man with a large and loving family, considerable wealth in the form of flocks and herds, and a respected place in society. He was, we are told, 'the greatest man in all the East'. Quickly, however, the story moves to a conversation between God and Satan (not an independent force of evil in the Hebrew Bible, but 'the Accuser', counsel for the prosecution). God identifies Job as a model of piety. The Accuser, however, replies that he has every reason to be. Life has been good to him. God has given him reason to be thankful. 'But stretch out Your hand and touch all that he has, and then he will curse You to Your face' (1:11). Thus the trial begins.

In stroke after stroke, Job loses all he has: his herds, his flocks, then his children. Despite everything, Job keeps his faith. 'The Lord gives and the Lord takes away', he says; 'blessed be the name of the Lord' (1:21). Satan then tells God to afflict Job personally. He does. Job is smitten with 'running sores from head to foot'. His wife tells him to 'Curse God and die', but Job refuses. His friends come to comfort him. They sit with him for seven days until, tormented by their silence, Job finally breaks, and curses the day he was born (3:3).

Job's friends, Eliphaz, Bildad and Zophar, contend with him. God, they say, is just. There is no punishment without sin. Therefore Job must somehow be guilty. This, Job passionately denies. For more than 30 chapters the argument blazes in incandescent poetry. A new voice enters the conversation, that of Elihu, younger than the rest but no less opinionated. It may well be, he says, that there is suffering without sin but that does not mean it is unjust. It is God's tutorial in moral wisdom. Through it we may be saved from pride or checked from reckless conduct. 'Those who suffer He rescues through suffering, and teaches them by the discipline of affliction' (36:15). At this point God appears to Job 'out of the whirlwind' and for four chapters addresses him. Job eventually confesses, 'I have spoken of great things which I have not understood, things too wonderful for me to know . . . Therefore I melt away; I repent in dust and ashes' (42:3–6). The book ends with Job's fortunes restored. He has children again and lives to see four generations of descendants, eventually dying 'at a very great age'.

That, in brief, is the plot, but the problems in understanding it are legion. Job's fundamental challenge is never answered. Given the terms of the story, it could not be, because we know what Job's friends cannot: that he is innocent and his sufferings undeserved. Far from answering Job, God's speech, the longest in the Bible, is an unbroken series of questions, all rhetorical, none expecting or admitting a reply: 'Where were you when I laid the foundations of the earth?' 'In all your life have you ever called up the dawn or shown the morning its place?' 'Have you an arm like God's arm, can you thunder in a voice like His?'

God offers no explanation of Job's misfortunes, for there is none that would satisfy the demands of justice. Instead he shows Job the panoply of creation. Nor is this the creation of the first chapter of Genesis: a world of order at whose centre is humankind. The universe revealed in the closing chapters of Job is the most non-anthropocentric in the Bible. Job sees the planets and stars, the desert spaces, the wild animals – the mountain goat, the wild ass, the hawk, the vulture, leviathan and the crocodile – who live their lives untamed. This is a world not made for man nor there to be domesticated by him. 'Even the noticing beasts are aware', writes Rilke in the *Duino Elegies*, 'that we are not very securely at home in this interpreted world.'[4] What silences Job is not a vision of justice, an answer to his question or an explanation of his fate, but the sheer power of existence itself, the 'is'-ness of things. God, as Job meets him in the whirlwind, is the God of power, not the God of justice. What then becomes of the biblical project of an equitable order, a world where justice is to be found?

Then comes the denouement: a set of reversals no reader could possibly have anticipated. At the very moment Job admits he is wrong, God declares that he was right. His companions, who have consistently defended God, are told by God that they were wrong, 'because you have not spoken as you ought about Me'. The mind reels at the non-sequiturs and contradictions. What message is the book conveying? That fate is or is not just? That God does or does not answer those who call? That it is right or wrong to vindicate the ways of providence? That it is pious or impious to question? It is exceptionally hard to say.

*   *   *

Job is a difficult book because by its very terms it has presented Job, and us, with a question that is unanswerable. Job and his companions search for justice. However, we the readers know what Job and his friends cannot: there *is* no justice in Job's sufferings. That is made clear at the beginning. Job is not being punished for his sins. Indeed, it was his very righteousness that singled him out in the first place. That, incidentally, is why the sages were correct when they said that 'Job never existed; the story is merely an allegory.'[5] If the events of the book actually happened we would have to conclude, like Shakespeare's King Lear, that 'As flies to wanton boys, are we to the gods; They kill us for their sport.'[6] The book is the testing of a hypothesis: 'What would happen if . . . ?'

Job is rarely understood for a simple reason. We read it upside down. Yet the interpretive key has been there from the beginning:

> The day came when the members of the court of heaven took their places in the presence of the Lord, and the Accuser was there among them. The Lord asked him where he had been. 'Ranging over the earth', he said, 'from end to end.' Then the Lord asked the Accuser, 'Have you considered My servant Job? You will find no one

like him on earth, a man of blameless and upright life who fears God and sets his face against wrongdoing.' The Accuser answered the Lord, 'Has not Job good reason to be God-fearing? Have You not hedged him round on every side with Your protection, him and his family and all his possessions? Whatever he does You have blessed, and his herds have increased beyond measure. But stretch out Your hand and touch all he has, and then he will curse You to Your face.' Then the Lord said to the Accuser, 'So be it. All that he has is in your hands . . .' (Job 1:6–12)

On trial in the book of Job is not Job but God. The very idea sounds blasphemous. That is why the book has consistently been read against the grain, and why, read thus, it is unintelligible. Why do the righteous suffer? asked Moses, and Jeremiah, and Habakkuk. That is assumed to be the question at the heart of the book of Job, and to it, it offers no answer. How could it comfort the afflicted to be told that bad things happen for no good reason, because the Accuser is tormenting us, because we are innocent and because we have faith?

The question most often asked by theologians and philosophers is: how, given what we know of the world, can we be sure that God exists? The question asked in the book of Job (as in later rabbinic midrash) is the opposite: how, given what we know of God, can we explain that humankind exists? Why did a wise, good, all-knowing, all-powerful Creator, having constructed a universe of beauty and order, introduce into it one form of life, *Homo sapiens*, capable of destroying beauty and creating disorder? This is a surpassingly strange question, yet until we grasp its logic and force we will not understand the proposition at the heart of the book, and of the Jewish vision of humanity's role in the world.

Consider this: there are two creation narratives in the Pentateuch, the first, God's creation of the universe, the second, the Israelites' construction of the Tabernacle in the wilderness. The space allocated to these processes is utterly disproportionate. The Bible takes a mere 34 verses to describe the making of the universe. It takes between 500 and 600 verses to describe the building of the Tabernacle (Ex. 25–40), a small, portable, fragile building. In any other literature, the proportions would be reversed. What has fascinated humankind from the era of myth to the age of science is cosmology: How did the universe come to be? The Bible, having given the most influential account of all time – 'In the beginning, God created . . .' – reduces it to the barest outlines and rarely (except in Job itself and the 'creation' Psalms) returns to it again. There is a fundamental issue at stake. What kind of book is the Bible? What is its most fundamental theme? The question answers itself, and the answer is profoundly counterintuitive. *The Bible is not humankind's book of God; it is God's book of humankind*. It takes for granted that God can construct a home for humankind. The question that endlessly absorbs it is: can humankind construct a home for God?

Wittgenstein once rhetorically asked: What is your aim in philosophy? He replied: To show the fly the way out of the fly bottle. The fly is trapped in the bottle. It searches for a way out. Repeatedly it bangs its head against the glass until at last, exhausted, it dies. Had it been gifted with the power of reasoning it would have saved itself despair and death. If there is a way in there is a way out. The one thing the fly forgets to do is to look up. Insight is the capacity to see familiar things from an unfamiliar perspective. The way to understand Job is to *invert* the way it has often been understood. What if the truth at the heart of faith were the opposite of what we take it to be? What if, more significant than our faith in God, is God's faith in us?

*   *   *

When we use the word 'faith' in a religious context we naturally assume that it refers to our faith in God. Understandably so, for it is we who are finite in our understanding of the universe and the full perspective of history. It is we who must make the leap from the known to the unknowable, from the visible to the invisible, from what we see and infer to what lies beyond.

Using the philosophical categories we have inherited from ancient Greece, it makes no sense at all to speak of an act of faith on the part of God. God is omniscient and omnipotent, all-knowing and all-powerful. He is the unmoved mover, necessary being, the unchanging essence of reality. These propositions are surely true. Yet, as I have argued throughout, this is not God as we meet him in the pages of the Hebrew Bible. Instead it is God as a philosophical abstraction, detached from the human drama. But God is *not* detached from the human drama. He is intimately, even passionately, involved in it. That, as Judah Halevi put it,[7] is the essential difference between the God of the philosophers and the God of the prophets, though they are the same God whose parallel lines meet in infinity.

God as we encounter him in the Bible takes a risk monumental in its implications. He creates one being, humanity, capable itself of being creative. He creates, that is to say, a being in his own image. This act alters the whole nature of the universe. For there is now a life-form capable of language, thought, reflection, imagination and choice, able to conceive the idea of God, but also, given the nature of freedom and the human imagination, capable of rebelling against God. The implication is far-reaching in the most ultimate sense, for there is now one form of life that can choose between obedience and disobedience, good and evil, turning nature to good ends or destroying it altogether.

Human freedom and the self-consciousness that accompanies it are the great unknown and unknowable within the otherwise orderly processes of nature mapped by science. There can never be a science of freedom, for the concept is a contradiction in terms. Science is about causes, freedom about purposes. Science explains phenomena in terms of other phenomena that preceded them. Free action, by contrast, can only be understood in terms of the future we intend to bring about, not any past event, historical, biochemical or neurophysiological. To be sure, there are many influences on human behaviour: some genetic, others cultural and environmental. But they are *influences*, not *causes* in the sense in which the term is used in the natural sciences.

For almost every act we do, we could have chosen otherwise (the exception being those acts – from reflex movements to unwilling behaviour under threat of death – that are not free in such a way as to render their agent responsible for them. Jewish law calls such behaviour *ones*, 'action under coercion'). Often in the course of the history of ideas, human freedom has been called into question. Some believed in astrology. Philosophers like Spinoza and scientists like Comte thought that since we are physical beings in the material world, we are matter, and all matter is governed by laws of cause and effect. For neo-Darwinists, human action is genetically determined. As the most extreme proponent of this view puts it, human beings are a gene's way of producing another gene.[8] There were even figures within Judaism itself – the medieval philosopher Hasdai Crescas is the most famous example – who held that free will was an illusion and that the only operative principle in human affairs was divine providence. Maimonides, however, represented the mainstream when he emphatically rejected these views:

> Free will is bestowed on every human being. If one desires to turn toward the good way and be righteous, he has the power to do so. If one wishes to turn toward the evil way and be wicked, he is at liberty to do so . . . Every human being may become righteous like Moses our teacher, or wicked like Jeroboam; wise or foolish, merciful or cruel, niggardly or generous, and so with all other qualities . . . This doctrine is an important principle, the pillar of the Law and the commandments, as it is said, 'See I have set before you this day life and good, and death and evil', and again it is written, 'Behold, I set before you this day a blessing and a curse.' This means that the power is in your hands, and whatever a man desires to do among the things that human beings do, he can do, whether they are good or evil . . . If God had decreed that a person should be either righteous or wicked, or if there were some force inherent in his nature

194

which irresistibly drew him to a particular course . . . what place
would there be for the whole of the Torah? By what right or justice
could God punish the wicked or reward the righteous? 'Shall not
the Judge of all the earth act justly?'[9]

This means that we are responsible for what we do. It also means that we
are capable of recognizing and acknowledging our mistakes and choosing to act differently in the future. Hence the concept of repentance
(*teshuvah*). This entails that the future need not be like the past, and that
history is the arena of human development and growth. That much we
saw in an earlier chapter.

But there is another and more paradoxical consequence. *God, by entering the human situation, enters time, and thus uncertainty and risk.* The grant
of freedom to humanity was a fateful act of self-limitation on the part of
God – the Lurianic-mystical concept of divine self-effacement (*tzimtzum*).
The result is made clear almost at the beginning of biblical time:

> Then the Lord said to Cain, 'Why are you angry? Why is your face
> downcast? If you do what is right, will you not be accepted? But if
> you do not do what is right, sin is crouching at your door; it desires
> to have you, but you must master it.' Now Cain said to his brother –
> and while they were in the field, Cain attacked his brother Abel and
> killed him. (Gen. 4:6–8)

Here the entire paradox of the divine–human encounter is present in its
pristine form. God knew that Cain was jealous of Abel and planned to kill
him. That is why he spoke to him and warned him. Yet Cain did not listen.
The murder took place. How did God let it happen? To this the only
answer can be: a grant of freedom to X by a superior power, which is
suspended every time X acts in a way of which the superior power disap-
proves, is not a grant of freedom. This is a logical axiom true in all
possible worlds. God does not abandon the world. He speaks to humankind, he teaches us how to behave, he instructs us in the ways of justice
and equity, mercy and compassion. But if humankind closes its ears and
refuses to listen, there is nothing God can do, short of taking away
freedom, the very thing he made space for in creating humankind.

Creation inescapably involves risk. For us that is true of *all* acts of creation. Every technology can be misused, every form of art can become
idolatry. For God it is true of only *one* act of creation, namely the making
of humanity. That is why here alone in the biblical account of creation do
we find not a simple 'Let there be' but a deliberative prologue, 'Let us
make man in our image, in our own likeness . . .' as if to signal hesitation,
consultation, doubt. Several rabbinic texts develop this point. God consulted, they say, with the angels, who advised him not to make man.[10] The

sages understood what in philosophical discourse cannot be conceived: that – in some sense, however metaphorical – there can be a test of faith for God himself.

For philosophy the primary question relates to the existence of God. For Judaism the primary question relates to the existence of man. *Homo sapiens* is not simply an evolutionary variant of other forms of life. The use of language, the future tense, an ability to recall the remote past, self-consciousness, deliberative rationality – the powers that make *Homo sapiens* unique – are qualitative leaps, not quantitive developments. A lump of metal and a car may be composed of the same elements but they are not the same thing, or the same kind of thing. That we share many elements of our DNA with the primates does not mean that man is simply a naked ape or a gene-producing machine. This may be superficially plausible, but it is a fallacy none the less. Because we can conceive intentions and act on them, no purely causal explanation of human behaviour will ever be adequate. Creating humankind, God was taking a risk similar to that parents take when they give birth to a child, namely of bringing into existence something one cannot control. In making humankind God was taking the risk that one of his creations might turn against its Creator. Even for God, creation means the courage to take a risk.

There is a profound passage in the Babylonian Talmud that explains this precisely, and is the interpretive key that unlocks the mystery of Job:

> R. Judah said in the name of Rav: When the Holy One wished to create man, He first created a company of ministering angels and said to them, 'Is it your wish that we make man in our image?' They answered, 'Sovereign of the universe, what will be his deeds?' Such and such will be his deeds, He replied [God showed them in advance the course of human history]. They thereupon exclaimed, 'Sovereign of the universe, *what is man that You are mindful of him and the son of man that You think of him* (Ps. 8:5)?' At this, God stretched out His finger and consumed them with fire. The same thing happened with a second company of angels. The third company said to Him, 'Sovereign of the universe, what did it avail the former angels when they spoke to You? The whole world is yours; do whatever you wish.' God then created humankind. When it came to the era of the Flood and of the division [of tongues, i.e. the Tower of Babel] whose deeds were corrupt they said to Him, 'Sovereign of the universe, did not the first angels speak correctly?' God replied: '*Even to old age I am the same, and even to grey hairs I will forbear*' (Is. 46:4).[11]

The angels had reason on their side. Knowing in advance the course of human history, the prevalence of war over peace, corruption over justice, cruelty over compassion, what reason could there be for introducing into the universe a creature as wayward as man?

*   *   *

That essentially is what the Accuser says to God: 'This species you have created – humanity – has it repaid your trust? Has it reciprocated your generosity, honoured your name, heeded your word? Of course human beings worship you. Why should they not? They do so from selfish motives. They plant crops, therefore they pray for rain. They wage wars, therefore they pray for victory. They face a dangerous universe, therefore they pray for your protection. *But where is the pure disinterested love of man for God to vindicate God's self-negating, self-effacing love for man?*'

The author of Job sets out the problem with unparalleled boldness. He imagines the Accuser challenging God himself: 'Where is there even a single individual to justify the risk, the wager you took in creating humankind?' God's reply is Job. Here, he says, is a man without sin who loves God, keeps his commands, thanks him for the good and does no evil. The Accuser's reply is dismissive. 'How can Job be a vindication? You have blessed him, therefore he blesses you. But if you were to curse him, he would curse you. His is not disinterested love. It is egoism allied to good fortune. Remove his fortune and you will find that you will have erased his faith.'

Understood thus, the book of Job is not an anomaly in the Bible. It is neither out of place nor out of character. It focuses with laser-like intensity on the question God asks throughout the Bible, through the mouths of all his prophets. Given the love and blessings, rescues and redemptions he has bestowed on humanity, where is humanity's answering response? 'I reared children and brought them up, but they have rebelled against Me,' he says through Isaiah (1:2). 'The house of Israel and the house of Judah have been utterly unfaithful to Me, says the Lord' to Jeremiah (5:11). Multiplying proof-texts is unnecessary: this is *the* theme of the Bible. One of its most poignant expressions appears early in Genesis, when God seems to lose faith in the entire enterprise of humanity: 'When the Lord saw that man had done much evil on earth and that his thoughts and inclinations were always evil, He was sorry that He had made man on earth, and He was grieved to His very heart' (Gen. 6:5–6). What makes the book of Job unique is that it detaches this question from a historical context and turns it into a metahistorical dialogue. It invites us, the readers, to engage in a role-reversal. It asks us to imagine history and humanity from the vantage point of God. Is there even one person on earth who justifies God's hopes when he created man?

The question posed by the Accuser to God is: Is there a single individual capable of loving you unconditionally? Of trusting you even though you seem to have betrayed that trust? Of believing in justice despite the fact that he knows he has suffered injustice? To be sure, Abraham said, 'Shall not the Judge of all the earth do justice?' But he was speaking on behalf of others, not himself. And yes, he was willing to offer up his son, but he was spared that test: as he lifted his hand, you said Stop. Is there one human being able to look on the face of injustice and still believe in you – as you, looking on the face of man's injustice, still believe in humanity?

Job shows that faith. He does something astonishing, which ever since has been part of Jewish sensibility. *Though he defies God he does not lose faith in him.* Though he knows he has been unfairly treated he does not cease to talk to him:

> If He would slay me, I would not hesitate;
> I should still argue my cause to His face.
> This at least assures my success,
> That no godless man may appear before Him. (Job 13:15–16)

Job does not demand an answer. He seeks a hearing. He wants the chance to present his case before God in the tribunal of justice. His companions talk *about* God. Job talks *to* God. 'Show me that you exist, that you care about your creatures, that you are willing to reveal yourself to me. Show me that you are not a God who hides his face when people cry out in suffering and despair.' Job justifies God's faith in man. Despite the fact that he knows his suffering is unjust, he does not cease to talk to God, to argue, pray, challenge, debate, question and fight against wrong even to the very gates of heaven itself. He is capable of the sustained cognitive dissonance that lives at the very nerve centre of Jewish consciousness. God exists *and* evil exists (at least from the perspective of humankind). Job's comforters want him to deny evil. His wife wants him to deny God. He refuses both, because either would let him live at peace. But a world that contains evil is not one in which God wants us to live in peace.

Job's voice never left Judaism. It is present in the book of Lamentations, Psalm 44, the midrashic literature, the laments (*kinot*) of the Middle Ages, and post-Holocaust literature. One of its most reverberating echoes is the story told by the Jewish historian Solomon ibn Verga who lived through and chronicled the events of the Spanish expulsion:

> I heard from some of the elders who came out of Spain that one of the boats was infested with the plague, and the captain of the boat put the passengers ashore at some uninhabited place. And there most of them died of starvation, while some of them gathered up all their strength to set out on foot in search of some settlement.
> There was one Jew among them who struggled on afoot together with his wife and two children. The wife grew faint and died,

because she was not accustomed to so much difficult walking. The husband carried his children along until both he and they fainted from hunger. When he regained consciousness, he found that his two children had died.

In great grief he rose to his feet and said, 'O Lord of all the universe, you are doing a great deal that I might even desert my faith. But know you of a certainty that – even against the will of heaven – a Jew I am and a Jew I shall remain. And neither that which you have brought upon me nor that which you will yet bring upon me will be of any avail.'

Thereupon he gathered some earth and some grass, and covered the boys, and went forth in search of a settlement.[12]

Faith does not mean certainty. It means the courage to live with uncertainty. It does not mean having the answers, it means having the courage to ask the questions and not let go of God, as he does not let go of us. It means realizing that God creates divine justice but only we, acting in accord with his word, can create human justice – and our very existence means that this is what God wants us to do. For one who sets a hard challenge does not do so to punish, but because he believes in the one to whom he sets the challenge. At the heart of his call to responsibility – and *this* is the meaning of Job – is God's unshakeable faith in humankind.

*   *   *

One of the cruellest misrepresentations of Judaism is the claim that it is not a religion of love – despite the fact that the two great commands of love, 'You shall love the Lord your God with all your heart, all your soul and all your might' (Deut. 6:5) and 'You shall love your neighbour as yourself' (Lev. 19:18), both come from the Mosaic books. Judaism is a faith suffused with love, but infinitely transcending man's love of God is *God's love of humankind.* For this (in the necessarily anthropomorphic language which is the only one we know) he suffers every time human beings wrong one another, yet he is prepared to suffer rather than take back from humankind the gift of freedom he bestowed on us, which is necessarily freedom to do wrong as well as freedom to do right.

According to Judaism, the classic questions of theology have been framed upside down. *More than we search for God, God searches for us,* asking us, as he did to Adam and Eve, 'Where are you?' There is one rabbinic statement that sums up all this in three Hebrew words. It is based on the verse in Moses' final song, in which he speaks of the justice of God.

> The rock – His work is perfect
> For all His ways are just;

A God of faith without iniquity
Righteous and fair is He. (Deut. 32:4)

On the surface, this means that God is just. It is human beings who act
unjustly. To this day, the verse is part of the liturgy of the 'acceptance of
God's justice' (*tzidduk ha-din*) that we recite when someone dies.
However, one rabbinic interpretation of part of this verse sums up the
entire argument of this chapter. The halakhic midrash *Sifre* states: '"A
God of faith" – He who had *faith in the universe* and created it.'[13] Creation
was an act of faith on the part of God. This idea is the most profound theological insight I have ever encountered. Even God's creation, when it
involves endowing a creature with the capacity to act in freedom, involves
risk and therefore faith. More than we have faith in God, he has faith in
us. We are here because he wanted us to be, free because the Master-of-
all made space for our freedom. We are at home in the universe to the
extent that we make of our universe a home for God. To be sure, God's
faith in humanity is often betrayed, yet God responds: 'Even to grey hairs
I will forbear.' Though human beings inflict suffering on one another,
God does not give up on his creation. We are here because of an act of
supreme love on the part of the author of being. Despite the wrong we
do, he does not relinquish faith that we will change. However lost, he
does not cease to believe that one day we will find our way back to him.
For in his word he has given us the map, the guide, the way of return.
That is the theology of responsibility.

*   *   *

In 1942 a young Jewish woman from the Netherlands, Etty Hillesum, voluntarily went to the concentration camp at Westerbork to help the sick
and dying. She must have known that such courage would cost her life. It
did. A year later, in 1943, she was sent to the gas chambers of Auschwitz.
In the midst of that dark night, she wrote in her diary:

> I will go to any place on this earth where God sends me, and I am
> ready in every situation and until I die to bear witness . . . that it is
> not God's fault that everything has turned out this way, but our
> fault . . .
>
> Only this thing becomes more and more clear to me: that you
> cannot help us, but that we must help you, and in so doing we ulti-
> mately help ourselves. That is the only thing that matters: to save in
> us, O God, a piece of yourself . . .
>
> And with almost every heartbeat it becomes clearer to me that
> you cannot help us, but that we must help you and defend up to the
> last your dwelling within us.[14]

I do not know whether these were the only words that could be said at that time, but they speak to me with awesome power. It is we, only we, who can defeat the evil in the human heart. Like a parent to a grown-up child, God will not, may not, do it for us. But he made us, believed in us, and gave us his word to show the way. And there is no other way.

NOTES

1. Quoted in Nahum Glatzer (ed.), *The Dimensions of Job* (New York: Schocken, 1969), p. ix.
2. William Safire, *The First Dissident: the book of Job in today's politics* (New York: Random House, 1992), p. xiv.
3. There is, of course, a massive literature on Job. Moses Maimonides analyses it in *The Guide for the Perplexed*, III:21–2. Among recent commentaries, see Robert Gordis, *The Book of God and Man: a study of Job* (Chicago: University of Chicago Press, 1965); Edwin Good, *In Turns of Tempest: a reading of Job with translation* (Stanford, CA: Stanford University Press, 1990); Jack Miles, *God: a biography* (London: Simon and Schuster, 1995), pp. 308–28; Moshe Greenberg in Robert Alter and Frank Kermode (eds.), *The Literary Guide to the Bible* (London: Fontana, 1989), pp. 283–304.
4. Rainer Maria Rilke, *Duino Elegies*, trans. J. B. Leishman and Stephen Spender (London: Chatto & Windus, 1963), p. 25.
5. Babylonian Talmud, *Baba Batra* 15a; see Maimonides, *The Guide for the Perplexed*, III:22.
6. Shakespeare, *King Lear*, IV.i.36.
7. Judah Halevi, *Kuzari*, IV:3; trans. Hartwig Hirschfeld (New York: Schocken, 1964), pp. 199–200.
8. Richard Dawkins, *The Selfish Gene* (Oxford: Oxford University Press, 1989).
9. Maimonides, *Mishneh Torah, Teshuvah* 5:1–4.
10. See E. E. Urbach, *The Sages* (Jerusalem: Magnes Press, 1975), pp. 214–54.
11. Babylonian Talmud, *Sanhedrin* 38b.
12. Solomon ibn Verga, *Shevet Yehudah*, cited in Nahum Glatzer, *A Jewish Reader* (New York: Schocken, 1961), pp. 204–5.
13. *Sifre* to Deut. 32:4.
14. Etty Hillesum, *Etty: a diary 1941–43*, trans. Arnold J. Pomerans (London: Triad, 1985), p. 197.

Chapter 15

Redeeming Evil

The biggest miracle of all is the one that we, the survivors of the Holocaust, after all that we witnessed and lived through, still believe and have faith in the Almighty God, may His name be blessed. This, my friends, is the miracle of miracles, the greatest miracle ever to have taken place.

(Rabbi Yekutiel Yehuda Halberstam)[1]

Looking at his photograph I see a hassidic saint, one of those mystical leaders that Judaism has yielded in such abundance since the eighteenth century, a man with a long white beard, a frock coat and a gentle smile that seems both of this world and of the next. There is in that smile something profoundly affirming as if, were you to meet him, you would instinctively know that he would embrace you and assure you that all is well with the world and that you are part of that perfection. Yet this was no ordinary saint, no ordinary life, for I am looking at a picture of the late Rabbi Yekutiel Halberstam, the Klausenberger Rebbe who, during the Holocaust, lost his wife and eleven children.[2] I am looking at the face of Job.

I never met him. I would love to have been able to ask him where that smile and its warmth came from in one who saw what he saw and lost what he lost. What I have seen is what he built: the Laniado hospital in Netanya, Israel. Surviving the Holocaust, he vowed that he would dedicate himself to the saving of life. After many years of planning, he created the hospital, one of the finest in Israel. All that he cared for is embodied in the principles he insisted on in its running. It was to be a religious institution, run according to Jewish law and imbued with Jewish spirit. It was to treat all persons alike, Jew and Arab, Israeli and Palestinian. Staff were to be chosen not only for their medical excellence but also for their love of their fellow human beings. Every effort was to be made to relieve not just the physical suffering of patients but also their psychological and

202

spiritual distress. The hospital was to be animated by a spirit of compassion, kindness and sympathy. It was to be a place in which you should be able to feel the presence of the God of life.

Less than a mile away is the Park Hotel, Netanya, where in April 2002 guests were assembling in the dining room on the eve of Passover to begin the seder service, the oldest surviving ritual in the world, in which Jews remember the exodus from Egypt and thank God for their freedom. It was then that a suicide-bomber struck, killing 29 people and injuring hundreds of others. When I visited it months later, you could still see knives and forks embedded in the ceiling by the force of the blast. It was one of the worst terrorist catastrophes in the history of Israel, not only in terms of the numbers killed but in the cynicism of its assault on one of Judaism's most sacred times. Most of Laniado's doctors and nurses, specialists in the treatment of victims of terror, were at home getting ready to celebrate the festival. Within minutes they had assembled. The casualties were rushed to the operating rooms. Time was of the essence. Many lives were saved. I met some of them, still bearing the injuries they would carry with them for life, still mourning the members of their families they had lost. It was difficult not to feel, there and then, that you were witnessing a still-active struggle within the soul of humankind between the forces of life and death, order and chaos, love and hate. I thought of the phrase from the Song of Songs (8:6): 'Love is as strong as death.' Here, it was.

*　　　　　*　　　　　*

I never met the Klausenberger Rebbe, but I did meet the Rebbe of Lubavitch, Rabbi Menahem Mendel Schneersohn. When our first encounter took place, in 1968, I was still a university student. Profoundly affected by the anxious weeks leading up to the Six-Day War a year earlier, I had taken the decision to visit the United States where, I knew, there were many distinguished rabbis and Jewish thinkers. I wanted to ask them some of the questions I had about faith. Two years earlier, an American journal, *Commentary*, had invited 50 leading Jewish figures to reflect on the fundamentals of Judaism. Armed with a copy of the magazine and a bus ticket giving me unlimited travel for a month, I went in search of as many of the 50 I could find. In the end, I met most of them. One name kept coming up in our conversations: the Rebbe of Lubavitch. He, I was told, was one of the greats, and I should make every effort to meet him. Eventually I did. It was a meeting that changed my life.

The Rebbe, I learned, was the head of a relatively small Hassidic sect, known as Habad. The word itself was an acrostic formed of the initial letters of the Hebrew words for the three intellectual attributes, wisdom, understanding and knowledge. The Hassidim in general were known for their emphasis on emotion: serving God with joy. Habad had long been something of an exception. It was more reflective than the other sects, more committed to traditional Jewish study. It had its own complex and subtle theology, the work of its founder Rabbi Shneur Zalman of Ladi (1745–1813), one of the outstanding rabbinic figures of the second half of the eighteenth century, a master of law and mysticism alike.

The present Rebbe, who had led the movement since 1951, had done something unprecedented. Hassidic sects are usually closed groups, living in semi-detachment from society and other Jews, sustained by their own rich community life. Early into his leadership, Rabbi Schneersohn decided to send out emissaries – to university campuses and small communities throughout America. He began a series of campaigns. His followers would go out to business centres, hospitals and airports, seeking out Jews and getting them to perform a mitzvah, putting on tefillin, for example, or lighting candles in honour of the Sabbath. He extended his network beyond America, eventually sending his disciples to virtually every Jewish community on earth, including some that had never seen a rabbi before. By the time he died, in 1994, his impact on world Jewry was unequalled. Some of his followers thought he was the Messiah.

What moved him, I wondered, to do something no rabbi had done before – *evangelize?* The Christian term is inevitable: when the Rebbe began his work, there was no Hebrew equivalent. Jewish communities until then had relied on their own internal motivation. No one had conducted campaigns, sent out emissaries or communicated on a global scale as he had done. To be sure, there had been itinerant preachers, and in the thirteenth century Rabbi Moses of Coucy[3] had travelled throughout France encouraging Jews to greater observance, but nothing as far reaching and systematic as this. I sensed a profound instinct at work. This was a man who had lived through the almost total obliteration of the traditional heartlands of Jewish life during the Holocaust. From here on, Jewish life would survive in America and Israel if anywhere – and in neither of these places was it strong. In America, many Jews were deracinated. In Israel, most were secular. A momentous effort was needed to bring Jews back to Judaism and Judaism back to Jews. It occurred to me that there was something redemptive about the Rebbe's work. It came to me in the form of a sentence that seemed to sum up what he had set himself to do. *During the Holocaust Jews were hunted down in hate; the Rebbe had resolved to search them out in love.* Nothing could undo the evil of genocide, but something could help heal the wounds of those who survived. Hitler had tried to extinguish the Jewish flame. The Rebbe would try, with no less focused energy, to rekindle it.

Since then I have met many Holocaust survivors, ordinary men and women who had been plucked from ordinary life and brought to the gates of hell. I cannot begin to imagine what they suffered in those years, or the memories they carried with them since. Most of them, for several decades afterwards, simply refused to talk about their experiences, even to their own children. A university teacher with whom I had worked in the early 1970s committed suicide. I later discovered that he was a Holocaust survivor. There is a phenomenon known as *survivor guilt*. This is something more than the trauma of suppressed memory. It is the constant thought of the arbitrariness that led most to die and a few to live. Only late in their lives did the survivors begin talking about their experiences, anxious that the world should not forget the greatest crime of man against man. It was not only revisionist historians who sought to make people forget. There is something instinctive in us that makes us screen out the knowledge of evil, preferring to believe it never happened. Knowing that the day must come when no one with knowledge of those events would be alive, they became witnesses, writing their stories and telling them to the next generation.

What struck me most about the survivors was their absence of hate, their dedication to life, their desire not for revenge but for tolerance and understanding. There was something awe-inspiring about the way they had worked through their negative emotions, their trauma. Having lost most of their families, the survivors I knew had become an extended family among themselves, helping each other through the bad times when the unquiet ghosts of memory returned.

Gena Turgel is one of them. As a young woman she was sent, successively, to Plaszow, Auschwitz and Bergen-Belsen. She saw her sister and brother-in-law shot. In Plaszow she encountered Amon Goeth, the notorious character in *Schindler's List*, who shot people for fun. She lost many of her family. Only an iron determination to save her mother kept her alive. When Belsen was liberated by the British in 1945 one of the officers was a Jewish man, Maurice Turgel. They met, and within days he had proposed marriage. The Revd Leslie Hardman, the Jewish chaplain who was with the troops as they entered Belsen, officiated at their wedding. Gena came with her husband to London, where she has lived ever since.

In 1987 she wrote her biography, *I Light a Candle*,[4] and she has spent much of her time in recent years visiting universities and schools, recounting her experiences of the extermination camps. Most of the people to whom she speaks are not Jewish, and what she has to tell them often comes as a profound shock. Despite everything, most children do not know the details of those years. Yet what she conveys is not dark. Gena has no bitterness or hate or rage. There is something serene about her, a graciousness I find very moving. Though there are many questions of faith for which she has no answer, she profoundly believes that prayer helped her survive and that God was with her, giving her strength and hope. What she teaches, over and above the need for tolerance and the willingness to fight on behalf of those who are victims, is love of life itself. Every day is, for her, an unexpected gift. She knows that there were hundreds of moments at which she might have died. That too is something that, after Auschwitz, she feels a need to convey to her grandchildren's generation: a sense that time is precious and must be used to create good.

As part of a television documentary I was making, we filmed Gena with some of the children she had taught. I could see her effect on them. They were enthralled by her strength and will to live. During a break in the filming, she showed me a letter she had received that day from a Christian girl of 16 whose sister had heard Gena, and who – her interest whetted by what she heard – had read her autobiography. This is part of what she wrote:

> I have just finished reading your book . . . You gave a talk today . . . My younger sister, Polly, was there. When she brought the book home I began to read it and wasn't expecting the emotions I'm feeling now. Throughout the book I was in numb shock, I couldn't believe or possibly couldn't come to terms with what I was reading. As soon as I finished I cried. I'm still weeping now. I am in awe of you. Your courage and heightened spirits at the smallest glimmers of hope . . . Your mother sounded like an amazing woman too, no doubt she passed a lot of it on to you. I don't think anyone can ever comprehend the risks for your own life you took to save her. When you described her illness during the camp and how you looked after her I couldn't help but put myself and my mother in the situation . . .
>
> When you talked of your sister and her husband being in each other's arms as they were shot into their grave, I imagined me and my boyfriend in their position . . . They stood out as a symbol of love amongst the pain. The ending to your story shows there is hope for those that have suffered. The absolute strength you showed and the love and absolutely amazing story of your marriage and life after you were free is beyond words . . .
>
> Thank you for making me realise the trivial things I complain about are trivia. You have made me realise for the first time in my life the freedom I have, the luxuries I have. I never understood before that being able to open a window, eat hot food everyday, sleep in a comfortable bed at night and most of all, taking the people I love for granted, not realising how lucky I am to have them here, are very special things, things I will try to appreciate from now on . . .

To be able to emerge from the valley of the shadow of death and make a blessing over life is no small achievement. That is what I learned from the survivors.

In his essay 'Halakhic Man', Rabbi Joseph Soloveitchik speaks about the fluidity of time in Judaism. The past is not beyond reach, fixed, immutable. The halakhic personality inhabits 'a past still in existence, one that stretches into and interpenetrates with the present and the future'. By what we do now, we alter the character of what happened then. 'There can be a certain sequence of events that starts out with sin and iniquity, but ends up with *mitzvoth* and good deeds, and vice versa. The future transforms the thrust of the past.'[5] We cannot bring the dead back to life, but we can let their memory lead us into life. We can write a new chapter that connects their story to life.

I sense among some of the survivors an extraordinary gesture of *tikkun*, 'mending'. It is as if they had seen the tablets shattered, as Moses did, and had climbed back up the mountain to hew, with God, something new to replace what was lost. Lurianic kabbalah was a vision of cosmic catastrophe, but it was a healing vision. Somewhere among the debris, he taught, are fragments of divine light, and our task is to rescue them and restore them to their place in an ordered universe, a structure of fragile but recoverable harmony. The only way to fight evil the morning after the storm is to do good, countering hate with a no less determined love.

Instead of speaking about the Holocaust, the great leaders of religious Jewry after the Destruction – the 'brand plucked from the burning' – gathered their disciples and told them to marry and have children. They built schools and academies and communities. Painfully, slowly, but with iron will, they reconstructed the lost centres of Eastern European Jewish life on Israeli and American soil. They did not build museums and memorials. They built living memorials. Every Jewish child was a life redeemed from the grave, a ghost brought back to the land of the living. One day this story will be told in awe, and that is what I feel today, seeing the grandchildren of those who survived. The Talmud says of Rabbi Hanina ben Teradyon, burned alive with his Torah scroll during the Hadrianic persecutions of the early second century, that he told his followers who watched him die: 'I see the parchment burning, but the letters are flying back to heaven.'[6] The body can be destroyed, but the spirit remains. The lost letters of the Holocaust have been rewritten in the Torah scroll made up of Jewish lives, and they tell a story of indomitable faith. They have rewritten the book of Job in our time.

Yaffa Eliach was 4 years old when, on two days in September 1941, the entire Jewish population of her town, Eishyshok in Lithuania, was taken out and shot. Of almost 5,000, only 29 survived. Of the Jewish community that had been there for 900 years, all was destroyed. She became a historian and, in time, one of the members of the President Carter's Holocaust Commission. One day she was flying over Lithuania looking down at the town, when she took a decision that was to occupy her for the next seventeen years. She would gather every fragment that remained of the community – photographs, diaries, memories. She wanted to create a memorial to those who died, made up of images of life, not death; not emaciated survivors and piles of corpses but vivid recollections of the people who had once worked and prayed, studied and argued, dreamed and hoped in its houses and streets.

It was a search that took her across the world. Eventually she created the gallery of photographs that today forms the Tower of the Life in the Holocaust Museum in Washington. She wrote the story of the town in a book, *There Once was a World.* It was an extraordinary labour of love.[7] An elderly rabbi I knew, who had grown up in Radun, four miles away from Eishyshok, read a review I had written of the book in the national press and asked if he could borrow it. I saw him sit there, looking at the photographs, his eyes filled with tears. Yaffa ended the book with the hope of her late father that 'at least the people, and perhaps even God, will remember that there once was a world filled with faith, Judaism, and humanity.'

The survivors were part of a tradition that did not dwell on the past. By and large, Jews did not allow themselves to be weighed down by the burden of resentment or desire for revenge. What they carried was grief and a deep perplexity about the justice of the world and the logic of those who claimed to worship the God of love but who, for centuries, accused Jews of crimes they had not committed, kept them locked in ghettos, expelled them, burned them at the stake or massacred them in pogroms. Jews confined their tears to a handful of days in the year, when they remembered those who had died, so that they should not have died unrecalled, unheard. The Judaism I know always was a faith suffused with love and celebration, and a hope so resilient that it could survive any catastrophe. We do not redeem evil by hate. We redeem it by a faith in life so strong that it has the courage to bring children into a world that has known overwhelming suffering and yet is prepared to take the risk to begin again.

*   *   *

I met Yoni Jesner in Jerusalem in January 2002. He was 19 years old, just beginning his second year in a rabbinical academy. We had brought together a group of 300 British students, but he stood out among them as a leader, a young man with quiet inner strength and a sense of humour that drew people to him and brought out the best in them. I knew of his reputation from the community in Glasgow where he had grown up. Already he was something of a legend. He worked with the young and the old, he took children's services in the synagogue, taught in its classes, ran the local youth group and was a volunteer in the burial society, helping prepare the dead for burial (he left behind him a touching notebook of principles by which he led his life. It contained such thoughts as 'Never say "Obviously" or "Of course" . . . Don't bore people by complaining . . . Always buy presents at least a week in advance'). A brilliant student, he had decided to become a doctor and already had a place at medical school. Despite his love of Jewish learning, his first priority was to dedicate his life to saving life. Like many others in Jewish history, he saw medicine as a religious vocation.

Yoni was travelling on the no. 4 bus in Tel Aviv on 19 September 2002 when the suicide-bomber detonated his belt: fifteen pounds of explosive, made more devastating by the addition of bolts and nails. Six were killed, dozens of others maimed. Yoni was rushed to hospital and placed on a life-support machine, but he had been brain-dead since the moment of impact. I clearly remember the shock that went round our community when we heard the news. Yoni had been a role-model to his contemporaries. They had followed the news from Israel, the suicide bombings that were happening on an almost daily basis at that time, but never had it come so close, striking someone they knew. We quickly arranged a service of prayers and Psalms that afternoon. The room was packed, the atmosphere intense. He was still in intensive care, but we knew there was no hope.

Ari, his brother in London, caught the next flight to Israel. Quickly, after consulting Yoni's rabbi, the family came to a decision. Yoni had wanted to save life. They would donate his kidneys, liver and spleen for transplantation. Among those whose life was transformed was Yasmin Abu Ramila, a 7-year-old Palestinian girl from east Jerusalem who had been on dialysis for two years awaiting a compatible transplant. That was an extraordinary deed – to save the life of someone on the other side, one of whose people had just murdered a member of your family. It takes exceptional courage to come to such a decision in the midst of grief; but acts like these are fragments of redemption.[8]

Daniel Pearl was a journalist working for the *Wall Street Journal*. Since 1996 he had been a foreign correspondent, serving first in London, then Paris, then Bombay. Born in Princeton, New Jersey, where his father was a distinguished computer scientist, he had led a charmed life, excelling at literature, sport and music – he was a gifted violinist. He was also, I later discovered, someone with an immense trust in people. Incapable of malice himself, he never suspected it in others. It was to prove his fatal weakness. On 23 January 2002 he was kidnapped in Karachi, Pakistan, while covering a story. On 21 February he was murdered in the most gruesome manner, his captors videoing the entire scene while his throat was cut and his head severed. Before they killed him they made him say to the camera, 'My father is Jewish, my mother is Jewish, I am Jewish.'

I came to know his father Judea through a book he published in Daniel's memory. Though neither father nor son was religious, Judea wanted those last words to serve as an inspiration to young Jews, to be proud of what they were and not to be intimidated. He wrote to many people throughout the Jewish world, asking them simply to say what their Jewish identity meant to them. The book *I am Jewish* is a moving testimony, a series of simple declarations of faith.[9] The Daniel Pearl Foundation that Judea created is dedicated to reconciliation. Among its projects are bursaries for young Pakistani journalists to come to America to study and learn something of its culture and lessen their sense of alienation. It organizes concerts throughout the world, using music, as Daniel did, to bring people together. But Judea wanted to go further: to engage directly with the world of Islam that had harboured Daniel's killers.

I met Judea in London together with the Islamic scholar Professor Akbar Ahmed. I had earlier been in e-mail contact with Professor Ahmed after I had written to express my admiration for his *Islam Under Siege*, a work of great sensitivity and moderation.[10] I did not know the two men knew one another, but I subsequently discovered that they had sought each other out because of their shared commitment to reconciliation, and also because Ahmed was from Karachi, the scene of Daniel's abduction and death. Together we visited, first a Muslim, then a Jewish school in London, and I was deeply impressed by their determination to chart a new path of Jewish–Islamic understanding. I asked Judea what motivated him. He was blunt and direct. 'If I were to fight hate with hate, I would only create more hate. Therefore I fight it with love. That is my tribute to Daniel's memory.'

The late Dr David Applebaum was a man of unusual piety. My brother knew him, admired him and told me about him. A distinguished Talmudic scholar and a deeply devout Jew, he was a favourite disciple of Rabbi Aaron Soloveitchik, who urged him to spend his life in the academy, studying religious texts and teaching others. As Yoni Jesner was later to do, he refused on the grounds that saving life takes precedence over all other commands. He became a doctor. He specialized in emergency medical treatment for victims of terror attacks. He treated every victim equally, Israeli or Palestinian, Christian, Muslim or Jew. He was head of Jerusalem's emergency medical service and won an award from Israel's president for bravery in saving lives. There were times when, after a suicide bombing, he operated on casualties in the street because he knew they would not survive the ambulance drive to the hospital.

He had just returned to Jerusalem from a visit to New York, where he had been lecturing to doctors on caring for the victims of terrorist attacks. He was, like most Jews, deeply devoted to his family. Despite the pressures on him, he would spend time each week studying Talmud with his children. Wednesday 10 September 2003 was to have been one of the happiest of his life. He was scheduled to stand under the bridal canopy at the wedding of his daughter Nava. The night before, a bomb exploded at the Café Hillel in Emek Refaim, Jerusalem. Arriving at the scene, rescue workers were puzzled not to see Dr Applebaum there. He was usually one of the first to arrive. Eventually they discovered why. He and his daughter were among the dead. He had taken her out for a coffee the night before the wedding. The next day, instead of standing under the bridal canopy together, they were buried together. A few months later, I went to Israel to the hospital where he had worked, to deliver a speech in his memory. His work continues: the patient task of saving life, because life is holy. He worked to save what others sought to destroy, and his memory – as the traditional Jewish saying puts it – will be a blessing.

I have told these stories, because in the end, stories are where theology comes off the page and begins to transform the landscape of human possibility. The faith that counts is the faith made real in lives, in deeds and words that heal some of the wounds of a fractured world. Evil can never be justified as the will of God, but it can be redeemed, even if never ultimately undone. These were some of the people – Job's successors in a post-Holocaust world – who justify God's faith in humankind.

NOTES

1. Quoted in Yaffa Eliach, *Hasidic Tales of the Holocaust* (New York: Avon, 1982), p. 228.
2. The story is told in Judah Lifschitz, *The Klausenberger Rebbe: the war years* (Southfield, MI: Targum Press, 2003).
3. Rabbi Moses of Coucy, *Sefer Mitzvot Hagadol*, positive command 5.
4. Gena Turgel, *I Light a Candle* (London: Grafton, 1987).
5. Rabbi Joseph B. Soloveitchik, *Halakhic Man*, trans. Lawrence Kaplan (Philadelphia: Jewish Publication Society of America, 1983), pp. 114–15.
6. Babylonian Talmud, *Avodah Zarah* 18a.
7. Yaffa Eliach, *There Once Was a World* (Boston: Little, Brown, 1998). The story of the massacre is also told in Avraham Aviel, *A Village Named Dogali-shok* (London: Valentine Mitchell, 2004).
8. Yoni's story is told in David Horovitz, *Still Life with Bombers: Israel in the age of terrorism* (New York: Knopf, 2004).
9. Judea and Ruth Pearl (eds.), *I Am Jewish: personal reflections inspired by the last words of Daniel Pearl* (Woodstock, VT: Jewish Lights, 2004).
10. Akbar S. Ahmed, *Islam Under Siege: living dangerously in a post-honor world* (Cambridge, UK: Polity, 2003).

Part 3

The Responsible Life

Chapter 16

Transforming Suffering

Ultimately, man should not ask what the meaning of his life is, but rather must recognize that it is *he* who is asked. In a word, each man is questioned by life; and he can only answer to life by *answering for* his own life; to life he can only respond by being responsible.

(Viktor Frankl)[1]

Three ways are open to a man who is in sorrow. He who stands on a normal rung weeps, he who stands higher is silent, but he who stands on the topmost rung converts his sorrow into song.

(Rabbi Menahem Mendel of Kotzk)[2]

The late Sue Burns suffered from a rare condition called osteosclerosis, progressive deterioration of the spine. Its effect was devastating. She was completely unable to stand or sit, even in a wheelchair. As her condition worsened, she was condemned to spend her life horizontally, permanently confined to bed and in almost constant pain. More than most she had reason to believe that life had dealt her the unkindest of blows.

I met her on one of my visits to care homes, in this case a centre for those who suffered from the most severe forms of debilitation. From the first moment I saw her, I realized that Sue was extraordinary. She greeted me with a radiant smile, like sunshine on a grey day. It seemed to come from deep within, as if she were celebrating being alive. At first I could not understand it. The contradiction between her fate and her mood was total. How, given her condition, was she so obviously at peace with the world and herself?

After we parted, the director of the home told me her story. Early on in the course of her illness, she had decided to dedicate her life to helping others as incapacitated as herself. There were only two problems: unable to move, she could not visit them and they could not visit her. So she set about bringing the world to her bedside. She had two phone lines installed. She taught herself how to use a computer and databases (this was in the late 1980s and early 1990s, before e-mails and the Internet were easily available or widely used, but she had enough with which to begin). From her bed she began building a network of relationships that became the *Tikvah* ('Hope') Help Line.

She contacted people who, like her, suffered serious illness or handicap. She became their adviser, mentor and friend. She spoke to them regularly, helping them through crises, advising them on available resources, lifting them when they felt low. She devoted time to working for Jewish Care, the superb welfare agency of British Jewry which ran the home where she lived. Towards the end of her all-too-short life, she was awarded an MBE by the Queen for her outstanding work. She became the first person to be taken into Buckingham Palace on a hospital bed and receive her honour lying down. Characteristically, she said to those who congratulated her that the award was not for her; she had merely been delegated to receive it on behalf of her fellow sufferers. She had no time for self-regard at all.

In the years I knew her I never saw her without that radiant smile, not even at our last meeting. She had asked to see me, and when I arrived she told me, with total calm, that she was about to die. Her body was exhausted and could no longer continue the struggle. She did not complain. Gently, knowing that the moment was hard for me as well as for her, she said goodbye, her graciousness, dignity and defiant humour intact to the end. Quietly, undemonstratively, Sue was a heroine of the spirit. She taught me, as she taught others, what it is to defeat tragedy. The sages once said that the ark in the wilderness 'lifted those who lifted it'.[3] They thought they were carrying the ark. In fact it was carrying them. Sue Burns lifted herself by lifting others.

I never asked her what gave her the strength to live as she had done. I think she knew the truth stated by Kierkegaard when he said: 'The door to happiness opens outwards.'[4] She never gave her illness the chance to turn her in on herself or feel sorry for her condition. She turned outward, caring for other people's suffering, and in so doing was able to forget her own, or at least, prevent it from demoralizing her. But I suspect she knew more – that at some time she had said to herself: There must be a reason why this has happened to me. It is God's way of enabling me to do something I could not have done otherwise. She found purpose in her suffering. Those who have a *why* for life, said Nietzsche, can put up with any *how*. That was Sue Burns, who took affliction and turned it into a blessing.

*   *   *

The person who did most to turn this insight into a systematic psychology was the late Viktor Frankl. Born in Vienna in 1905, he was deported with the rest of his family to the concentration camp at Theresienstadt in 1942, and spent the next three years in extermination camps, among them Auschwitz and Dachau. He and one sister were the only members of the family to survive. It was during this time he made the discovery that later became his life work.

Already a distinguished neurologist, he preserved his sanity by observing his fellow prisoners, as if he and they were taking part in an experiment. He noticed the various phases they went through. The first was shock and complete disillusionment. The Nazis with demonic detail began by dehumanizing the prisoners in every conceivable way. They took from them everything that gives people a vestige of humanity: their clothes, shoes, hair, even their names. They seized Frankl's most precious possession, a scientific manuscript containing his life's work. Frankl says that at this point, 'I struck out my whole former life.'[5]

The second stage was apathy, a complete dulling of the emotions, without which it would have been impossible to survive at all. People became automata, hardly living, merely existing from day to day. It was then that Frankl asked the fateful question. Was there any freedom left to a person who has been robbed of everything: dignity, possessions, even the power of decision itself? The Jewish victims of earlier persecutions had been given a choice: convert or die. During the Holocaust there was no choice. *What remained once you had lost everything there was to lose?* Frankl realized that there was one freedom that can never be taken away:

> We who lived in concentration camps can remember the men who walked through the huts comforting others, giving away their last piece of bread. They may have been few in number, but they offer sufficient proof that everything can be taken from a man but one thing: the last of the human freedoms – to choose one's attitude in any given set of circumstances, to choose one's own way.[6]

The freedom that remained was *the decision how to respond.* Frankl survived by constantly analysing what was happening to himself and others and helping them find a reason to continue to live. One of the most deadening conditions in the camps was what he called 'futurelessness', the total absence of hope. Frankl recalls that 'A prisoner marching in a long column to a new camp remarked that he felt as if he were walking in a funeral procession behind his own dead body.'[7]

Two of his fellow inmates were contemplating suicide. By conversing with them he was able to get each to see that they had something still to do. One had published a series of books on geography, but the series was not yet complete. A task awaited him. The other had a daughter abroad who loved him devotedly and longed to see him. A person awaited him. In both cases, what was essential was the realization that there was something to be done that could be done by no one else.[8] This knowledge gave meaning, not to life in general, but to *this* life, mine, unique and irreplaceable. This became the core of an insight Frankl was to turn, after the war, into a new school of psychotherapy. He called it *logotherapy*, from the Greek *logos*, meaning 'word' in the broadest sense – the spiritual dimension of human life, that which endows life with a sense of purpose. He summarized his teaching in the title of his most famous book: *Man's Search for Meaning*.

If a life could be meaningful even in Auschwitz, it could be meaningful anywhere under any circumstances.

> We must never forget that we may also find meaning in life even when confronted with a hopeless situation, when facing a fate that cannot be changed. For what then matters is to bear witness to the uniquely human potential at its best, which is to transform a personal tragedy into a triumph, to turn one's predicament into a human achievement.[9]

That, for Frankl, meant restoring to psychoanalysis a spiritual dimension (he was at pains to point out that he did not mean 'religious'; he himself was a religious man, but he regarded the spirit as an essential dimension of human life as such, religious or otherwise).

Whatever our fate, we always have a choice between seeing it as a tragedy devoid of meaning, or as a possibility to achieve something positive. This we can do in three ways: by creating a work or doing a deed; by experiencing something or encountering someone; or by the attitude we take toward unavoidable suffering. He gives one example of a man he treated for depression. He had had a long and happy marriage, and two years after his wife's death was still unable to come to terms with the loss:

> I asked him quite simply: 'Tell me what would have happened if you had died first and your wife had survived you?' 'That would have been terrible', he said. 'How my wife would have suffered!' 'Well, you see,' I answered, 'your wife has been spared that, and it was you who spared her, though of course you must now pay by surviving and mourning her.' In that very moment his mourning had been given a meaning – the meaning of a sacrifice.[10]

Homo sapiens is the meaning-seeking animal, Frankl argued. But to preserve meaning in desperate circumstances we must be able, or be helped, to do a number of things. First is the refusal to believe that we are victims of fate. Frankl rejected determinism in all its forms. 'Of a pair of identical twins, one became a cunning criminal, while his brother became an equally cunning criminologist. Both were born with cunning, but this trait in itself implies no values, neither vice nor virtue'[11] (Frank Abagnale Jr, whose story is told in the book *Catch Me If You Can*, was a cunning criminal who *became* a cunning criminologist).[12]

Second is the knowledge that there is more than one way of interpreting what happens to us – more than one way (though Frankl does not use this phrase) of *telling the story* of our life. The depressed widower saw his fate as bereavement, which it was. Frankl helped him to see it as a way of sparing his wife's suffering, which it also was. He turned the grief outward. Events never carry with them their own interpretation. Frankl survived the concentration camps by refusing to let his captors define his situation. You can regard me as worthless, he seems to say to the Nazis, but you cannot force me to share your opinion. Eleanor Roosevelt once said, 'No one can make me feel inferior without my permission', and it is a permission we can refuse to grant.

Third, despite the fact that Frankl focuses on the freedom that is within us, he insists that *meaning lies outside us*. It is a call from somewhere else:

> In the last resort, man should not ask, 'What is the meaning of my life?' but should realise that he himself is being questioned. Life is putting its problems to him, and it is up to him to respond to these questions by being responsible; he can only answer to life by answering *for* his life. Life is a task. The religious man differs from the apparently irreligious man only by experiencing his existence not simply as a task, but as a mission. This means that he is also aware of the taskmaster, the source of his mission. For thousands of years that source has been called God.[13]

Whether we are religious or irreligious, there is something we are *called on to do*, something no one else can do – not here, not now, not in these circumstances, for this person. Discovering that task is not easy. There are depressive states in which we simply cannot do it on our own ('A prisoner cannot release himself from prison', says the Talmud[14] about depression). But once we have found it, our life takes on meaning and we recover the will to live. That is what I and others saw in Sue Burns. She suffered a terrible fate, but she had turned it into a task. She had found what she was called on to do.

*   *   *

In Frankl's psychotherapy, we find one of the deepest dimensions of the ethics of responsibility. The word 'responsible' is related to *response*. It is an answer to a question posed by another. The Hebrew word for responsibility, *achrayut*, comes from the word *acher*, which means an 'other'. Responsibility is not something that comes from within but is always a response to something or someone outside us. In his *The Responsible Self*, Richard Niebuhr writes: 'Responsibility affirms: God is acting in all actions upon you. So respond to all actions as to his action.'[15] He adds, 'We are most aware of our existence in the moment, in the now, when we are radically acted upon by something from without, when we are under the necessity of meeting a challenge with an action of our own, as is the case in every important decision.'[16] The responsible life is one that responds. In the theological sense it means that *God is a question to which our lives are an answer.*

God's first question to humankind was, 'Where are you?' (Gen. 3:9). That is the question heard by those who have internalized the ethic of responsibility. Faith is *a form of listening*, and what we hear in the still silence of the soul is God's question: 'What have you done with the gift I gave you, of life? How have you used your time? Have you lived for yourself alone or have you lived also for others? Is your primary question, What can the world give me? or is it, What can I give to the world? Have you sought blessing, or have you *been* a blessing?'

Frankl was not a kabbalist, but his work exemplifies a deep sense of *tikkun*. There are some sufferings that can be ended, but there are others that can only be fought with the power of the imagination. The search for meaning represents one of the deepest truths of the human condition, namely that what affects us is not what happens to us but how we *perceive* what happens to us, and that is not independent of our will. We are not billiard balls or atoms or genes, responses to stimuli, mere effects of a prior cause. We are free because our response depends on our perception, and that can always be revised. You can imprison the body but not the mind.

What *tikkun* represents is the faith that in every evil there is a fragment of good that can be rescued and redeemed. Every profound experience of suffering is a form of *dis*integration. The world we had taken for granted is no longer there. Something is missing, lost. A bond connecting us to reality has broken, and the result is cognitive crisis. What is happening to us contradicts what we had previously assumed about the basic goodness and givenness of the world. *Tikkun* is *re*-integration. That is where mysticism meets psychotherapy and transforms it.

It was Philip Rieff, in his book *The Triumph of the Therapeutic*, who noted that classic psychotherapy, Freudian and Jungian, is the opposite of traditional methods of healing. In the past people were healed by becoming reintegrated in the community. The therapeutic stance distances the individual from the community in order to perform the work of integration within the self.[17] A key figure in this transformation was Rousseau. For Plato and Aristotle, as for the great religious faiths, happiness and well-being are achieved within community. 'It is not good for man to be alone.' For Rousseau the reverse was the case. Community is a burden from which the individual has to liberate himself. We are born free; society places us in chains. Logotherapy, by contrast, is a reversion to an older faith. 'The true meaning of life', wrote Frankl, 'is to be found in the world rather than within man or his own *psyche* . . . Human existence is essentially self-transcendence rather than self-actualization.'[18] Meaning takes place when something within us responds to something outside us: *not when we choose but when we are chosen.*

One example of countertherapeutic healing is the Jewish law of mourning. Bereavement forces us in on ourselves. The week of *shiva*, during which we are visited by neighbours and friends and rarely left alone, forces us out of ourselves and back into the land of the living. It helps mend the broken bonds of relationship. *Shiva* is a form of reintegration, a radical insistence that it is not in and by ourselves that we are able to restore the meaningfulness of a life, but in the company of others. ('Hell', said Sartre, 'is other people.' For Judaism hell is the *absence* of other people, solitary confinement in the prison of the self.) Mourning in Judaism is a process of *tikkun*, healing the fractures caused by suffering and loss, evil and injustice.

At the end of the book that bears his name, Job admits that he was wrong: God was right. 'Surely I spoke of things I did not understand, things too wonderful for me to know.' Then, in what looks like a complete reversal of the plot, God declares that Job was right and his comforters, who defended God, were wrong. He tells them to apologize to Job and ask him to pray for them, which they do. God then gives back to Job all that he has lost, and more. He has another seven sons and three daughters, as if to compensate for those he lost during his trial. He dies comforted and honoured, 'old and full of years'.

Commentators have been puzzled by this apparently false happy ending. It looks, they say, absurdly contrived. It was tacked on because the book as it stood was unbearably painful and bleak. (Beethoven suffered a similar fate with his B Flat minor quartet, opus 130. The ending, a vast movement known as the *Grosse Fugue*, was too austere. His audience wanted something light and cheerful. The alternative final movement, graceful but undemanding, was the last thing he wrote.) The conclusion of the book of Job, they argue, was a later addition.

I disagree. Job never finds an answer to his question because, as I argued in an earlier chapter, the book is not about Job's faith in God but about God's faith in man. God is not Job's answer; Job is God's answer. The meaning of the final chapter is that Job, having lived through a world-without-sense, a world seemingly without God, finds reintegration by experiencing God. *He finds, not an answer, but a presence*, and in re-establishing his relationship with God he is not convinced, but healed.

Job, after meeting God in the whirlwind, is not one who now knows why evil happens. He has become a person able to reaffirm life despite the existence of evil. He now has the greatness of soul to pray for those who afflicted him. He has the courage to have children – and in Judaism this is the ultimate courage, *God's* courage – despite the fact that the world is full of suffering and doubt. The most fundamental answer to the apparent meaninglessness of life is not found but lived. Doing good, we discover good. Only in action do we find the truth beyond action; only in caring for others (in Job's case, praying for others) do we heal the jagged edges in our soul. In the classic rabbinic interpretation of the words said by the Israelites when they accepted the covenant with God, 'We will do; *then* will we understand.' Judaism is not about the truths we know, but about the truths we live.

*   *   *

The Israeli violinist Yitzhak Perlman contracted polio at the age of 4. Ever since, he has had to wear metal braces on his legs and walk with crutches, yet he became one of the great virtuosi of our time. On one occasion, the story is told, he came out onto the stage at a concert to play a violin concerto. Laying down his crutches, he placed the violin under his chin and began tuning the instrument when, with an audible crack, one of the strings broke. The audience were expecting him to send for another string, but instead he signalled the conductor to begin, and he proceeded to play the concerto entirely on three strings. At the end of the performance the audience gave him a standing ovation and called on him to speak. What he said, so the story goes, was this: '*Our task is to make music with what remains.*' That was a comment on more than a broken violin string. It was a comment on his paralysis and on all that is broken in life.

The history of music has many such stories. I think of Beethoven who, profoundly deaf in his later years, wrote some of the most sublime music ever written and whose late quartets, for me, are little less than the sound of heaven itself. I think of Smetana (whose *Ma Vlast* inspired the music of Naftali Herz Imber's 'Hatikvah', national anthem of the State of Israel), who suffered from tinnitus so severely that it tipped him over the edge into insanity; of Chopin, so ill from tuberculosis that he constantly coughed blood; of the Spanish composer Joaquín Rodrigo, blind from the age of 3, who wrote masterpieces for the guitar; and of Paul Wittgenstein, brother of the philosopher Ludwig Wittgenstein, a concert pianist who lost his right arm during the First World War but who continued to play, and for whom Ravel, Prokofiev, Richard Strauss and Benjamin Britten wrote works for the left hand.

Happiness, these lives seem to say, is not the absence of suffering but the ability to take its fractured discords and turn them into music that rescues from the darkest regions of the soul a haunting yet humanizing beauty – surely the supreme achievement down here on earth. Some of the greatest Psalms come from this realm of pain, as do the finest works of art. As Frankl wrote: 'If there is meaning in life at all, then there must be a meaning in suffering. Suffering is an ineradicable part of life, even as fate and death. Without suffering and death, human life cannot be complete.'[19]

He also wrote, 'It is not from the length of its span that we can ever draw conclusions as to a life's meaningfulness. We cannot, after all, judge a biography by its length, by the number of pages in it . . . Sometimes the "unfinisheds" are among the most beautiful symphonies.'[20] I learned that from Adele (not her real name). She was my age. I first met her in the 1970s when she came to some lectures I was giving. You couldn't miss her. She was tall, with the most striking appearance. There was a sense of drama about everything she did. She dressed with theatrical flourish. Her voice was resonant, musical. In her company the atmosphere became more vivid and colourful, charged with energy. Everyone sensed it.

In those days she and her husband James seemed to lead a charmed life. They were successful, intelligent and charming. They had a lovely home and whatever they did, they endowed with panache. Nor did they keep their happiness to themselves. They had a gift for friendship. In the synagogue, Adele sought out the lonely, invited them to a meal, and drew them into her circle. Their Sabbath table was always full of guests. Their home was open and you never knew who you would find there.

Then things started to go wrong. They suffered a series of personal setbacks. One by one the bricks out of which they had built their life began to crumble. Their business failed. She discovered that she was unable to have a child. Then came the final blow. Adele discovered she had cancer. Many treatments were tried; none worked. She knew she was going to die, and die young.

It was then that she became something extraordinary. She refused to be afraid. Not once in those last years and months did she let her sufferings affect her public face or private faith. She became yet more sensitive to others. Her hospitality grew. Racked with pain, she commanded her face to smile. Despite losing her hair because of chemotherapy, she continued to walk tall. It was an act of pure will, day by day, hour after hour.

She had come to a conclusion. If God had decided that her chapter on earth was to be a short one, she would make every paragraph and sentence count. Immortality, she had once heard a rabbi say, lies not in how long you live but in *how* you live. That became her guiding principle.

223

However few days were left, each was a gift of God and she would use it to the full – to celebrate life and be a blessing to others. It is easy to say these things, but to see someone live them was awe-inspiring.

As the months passed, she grew weaker and more emaciated. One Friday afternoon I rang to see how she was. James answered the phone. She was, he said, not well enough to speak.

'Tell her', I said, 'that I pray for her every day.'

'I know', he said, 'but I don't think she's going to survive the weekend.' I hoped he was wrong, but from the tone of his voice I knew he was not.

What happened next, I heard later. She had decided that since this was going to be her last Sabbath on earth, she would celebrate it to the full. She invited all her closest friends. Too frail to sit at the table, she sat in her wheelchair and smiled as they sang the blessings and her favourite Sabbath songs. That night, having thanked God for life, she died.

She had seen the angel of death face to face and said: 'You may take me, but you will not defeat me, nor will you intimidate me.' There are people who teach us how to live. Adele taught us how to die: undefeated, undiminished, thanking God for everything, for existence, for love, to the very end.

To be a Jew is to carry the name Israel, meaning one who 'struggles with God and with men and prevails'. That name was born in one of the most haunting episodes in the Bible. Left alone at night, fearing the meeting he was about to have the next day with his brother Esau, Jacob wrestled until dawn with an unnamed adversary. As night faded and the first glimmerings appeared on the horizon, the stranger asked Jacob to release him. 'I will not let you go until you bless me' (Gen. 32:26), Jacob said.

That is the wrestling match each of us has to undergo when evil threatens or tragedy strikes. Faith is *the refusal to let go* until you have turned suffering into a blessing. At that moment Jacob became a different person with a new name. Sue Burns, Viktor Frankl, Yitzhak Perlman, Adele, heroes of the spirit, refused to let go. R. Nahman of Bratslav taught a parable:

> Sometimes when people are joyous and dancing, they grab a man from outside the dancing circle, one who is sad and melancholy, and force him to join them in their dance. Thus it is with joy: when a person is happy, his own sadness and suffering stand off on the side. But it is a higher achievement to struggle and pursue that sadness, bringing it too into the joy, until it is transformed . . . you grab hold of this suffering, and force it to join with you in the rejoicing, just as in the parable.[21]

That is what they did, transforming suffering, making even the angel of death join, for a moment, the dance of life.

Notes

1. Viktor Frankl, *Man's Search for Meaning* (New York: Washington Square Press, 1985), p. 131.
2. A. J. Heschel, *A Passion for Truth: reflections on the founder of Hasidism, the Kotzker and Kierkegaard* (London: Secker and Warburg, 1974), p. 283.
3. *Tosefta, Sotah* 8:6.
4. Viktor Frankl (see this chapter) frequently quotes this dictum in the name of Kierkegaard. This is evidently his own free translation of Kierkegaard's statement: 'Alas, fortune's door does not open inward so that one can push it open by rushing at it, but it opens outward, and therefore one can do nothing about it.' Søren Kierkegaard, *Either/Or*, trans. Howard Hong and Edna Hong (Princeton, NJ: Princeton University Press, 1987), p. 23.
5. Frankl, *Man's Search for Meaning*, p. 33.
6. Ibid., p. 86.
7. Frankl, *The Doctor and the Soul: from psychotherapy to logotherapy* (London: Souvenir Press, 2004), p. 104.
8. Ibid., p. 107.
9. Frankl, *Man's Search for Meaning*, p. 135.
10. Frankl, *The Doctor and the Soul*, p. 13.
11. Ibid., p. 17.
12. Stan Redding and Frank W. Abagnale, *Catch Me If You Can* (New York: Grosset & Dunlap, 1980).
13. Frankl, *The Doctor and the Soul*, p. 13.
14. Babylonian Talmud, *Berakhot* 5b; *Nedarim* 7b; *Sanhedrin* 95a.
15. H. Richard Niebuhr, *The Responsible Self* (Louisville, KY: Westminster John Knox Press, 1999), p. 126.
16. Ibid., p. 94.
17. Philip Rieff, *The Triumph of the Therapeutic* (London: Chatto & Windus, 1966), pp. 48–65.
18. Quoted in Reuben Bulka, *Work, Love, Suffering, Death* (Northvale, NJ: Jason Aronson, 1998), p. 10.
19. Frankl, *Man's Search for Meaning*, p. 88.
20. Frankl, *The Doctor and the Soul*, p. 53.
21. *Likkutim* II: 23. Quoted in Arthur Green, *Tormented Master: a life of Rabbi Nahman of Bratslav* (New York: Schocken Press, 1981), p. 142.

Chapter 17

The Chaos Theory of Virtue

One can acquire a share in eternity in a single hour.

(Babylonian Talmud)[1]

A single moment can retroactively flood an entire life with meaning.

(Viktor Frankl)[2]

In their screenplay for the film *About Schmidt,* Louis Begley and Alexander Payne weave a beautifully subtle tale of contemporary self-discovery. Warren Schmidt (played in the film by Jack Nicholson) is a 66-year-old assistant vice-president of an insurance company in Omaha, Nebraska, who, following retirement and his wife's death, is forced to confront the meaninglessness of his life, its petty deceptions and betrayals and the failure of his relationships with his wife and daughter.[3] It is a film of closely observed humour, which makes bearable the intense sadness of its portrait of a mean-spirited man who has done nothing to earn a place in other people's affections.

Its master-stroke involves the use of a minor incident which, until the film's closing scene, seems no more than a narrative device. The one positive thing Schmidt has done in retirement is to answer a television appeal to adopt a 6-year-old child in Tanzania by sending a monthly cheque to pay for his treatment and schooling. Along with the cheque, he sends a letter telling the boy, Ngudu, about himself. This provides the film with its narrative voice, allowing its central character to reflect aloud on what is happening to and within him. In the final minutes, Schmidt is driving home after his daughter's wedding, a match he tried but failed to prevent. Overwhelmed by a sense of failure, he writes Ngudu another letter, his requiem for an inconsequential life:

> I know we're all pretty small in the big scheme of things . . . What in the world is better because of me? . . . I am weak and I am a failure . . .

226

there's just no getting around it . . . Soon I will die . . . maybe in
twenty years, maybe tomorrow, it doesn't matter . . . When everyone
who knew me dies too, it will be as though I never even existed . . .
What difference has my life made to anyone? None that I can think
of . . . none at all.

Just then he receives a note from Tanzania, from the nun who has been
looking after Ngudu. Thanking Schmidt for his cheques and letters, she
tells him about the boy. He cannot write, she says, but he has sent
Schmidt a drawing instead. It shows two stick characters, obviously the
boy and Schmidt. They are holding hands, and the sun is shining.
Schmidt slowly realizes he has done one good deed in his life, after all.
He really did help a child far away whom he has never met. He begins to
weep – overwhelmed by the good he might have done but did not, and by
the single act of charity he might not have done but did – and with that
scene the film ends.

By contemporary standards it is a daring statement. One reviewer
called it a 'trumpet-blast of defiant non-irony'.[4] But it is a moment of
great cinematic and moral power. The sages had a saying for this idea:
There are some who acquire their share of eternity in a lifetime, others
who win it in a single hour. One generous act can redeem a life.

*   *   *

There is a corollary moment in the Bible. It freeze-frames, as it were, a
critical moment in one person's life, showing what is at stake in a single
moment of moral choice. The person concerned is one of the great
might-have-beens of the Bible: Jacob's eldest son Reuben.

The background is the childhood of Joseph, Jacob's child by his second
wife, Rachel. Jacob had loved Rachel at first sight. He agreed with her
father Laban to work seven years for her. The Torah uses a lovely phrase at
this point: the seven years 'seemed to him like a few days because of the
love he had for her' (Gen. 29:20). Then comes the great betrayal. The
night after the wedding, Jacob wakes up to discover that he has married
Leah, Rachel's elder sister, not Rachel herself. He protests to Laban, 'Why
have you deceived me?' Laban replies insouciantly: 'It is not done *in our
place* to give the younger before the elder' (Gen. 29:25–6). The implication is clear: the deceiver has been deceived. Jacob had disguised himself
to take the blessing of his elder brother Esau from their blind father Isaac.
What he did has now been done to him. Jacob eventually marries Rachel
as well, but the ripples of the deception extend across the years. Leah,
unloved, is blessed with children. Rachel remains infertile. There is
tension between the sisters. Eventually Rachel has a child, Joseph, and the
rivalry between the sisters is transferred to the next generation.

Jacob loves Joseph, and cannot help showing his favouritism, to the hurt and slight of his other sons. The vignettes of Joseph as an adolescent are less than endearing. He tells tales to his father about his brothers. He has dreams in which his family bow down to him, and worse – he reports them. His father tolerates his behaviour and even gives him a token of his love, a richly embroidered cloak, the famous 'coat of many colours', the sight of which acts as a constant provocation to the other sons.

One day, as his brothers are tending the flocks far from home, Jacob sends Joseph to see how they are doing. It will be, we sense, a fateful encounter. The brothers see Joseph from afar, and the sight of the cloak enrages them. They realize that, alone with no one to see them, they can kill Joseph and construct a tale that will be impossible to disprove. Only one brother, Reuben, protests. At this juncture the narrative slows down to ensure that we notice every detail of the scene that follows. It then does something that has no parallel anywhere else in the Torah. It makes a statement that *cannot* be read literally. What it says is this: 'Reuben heard *and saved him* from their hands' (Gen. 37:21). Almost immediately, we discover that he did not. He tried, but failed. The text states the might-have-been. Reuben *intended* to save Joseph. He made an effort, but it was not good enough. In a subtle but unmistakable way the text is telling us about something larger than Reuben and Joseph. It is making a statement about the moral life itself: we never know the consequences of our actions. Reuben came close to heroism at that moment – but not close enough. On that one failure the whole future history of Israel turned.

Reuben's plan was simple. He told the brothers not to kill Joseph but to let him die: '"Let's not take his life", he said. "Don't shed any blood. Throw him into this cistern here in the desert, but don't lay a hand on him"' (Gen. 37:21–2). The text then – again unusually, for it is rare for the Torah to describe a person's intentions – explains what he had in mind: 'Reuben said this *to rescue him from them* and take him back to his father.' His plan was to come back to the pit while the brothers' attention was elsewhere, lift him out and take him home.

What happens next is obscure, though the outcome is clear. Joseph is taken from the pit and sold to a passing caravan of merchants who carry him to Egypt to be sold as a slave – though whether the deed is done by the brothers at the suggestion of Judah, or by passing Midianites, is impossible to determine. Reuben, who has been elsewhere during the episode, returns to the pit to rescue Joseph but finds him gone. He is bereft. 'When Reuben returned to the cistern and saw that Joseph was not there, he tore his clothes. He went back to his brothers and said, "The boy is not there! Where can I turn now?"' (Gen. 37:30). Commenting on the episode, an enigmatic midrash states the following: 'If Reuben had only known that the Holy One, blessed be He, would write of him, "And Reuben heard and saved him from their hands", he would have picked him up on his shoulders and carried him back to his father.'[5] What this means is far from obvious. But the comment is profound. It contains the key to the story of Reuben's life and much else besides.

Who and what is Reuben, Jacob's eldest son? A careful examination of the various scenes in which Reuben appears allows us to build up a picture of his character. He is the man of good intentions that fail to achieve their aim. In the first scene we see him as a child in the fields during the wheat harvest. He finds some mandrakes – an aphrodisiac – and brings them back to give to his mother Leah. He knows Jacob loves her less than Rachel, and feels it with all the preternatural sensitivity of an eldest son. He hopes that, by means of the mandrakes, Leah will be able to win Jacob's attention, perhaps even his love. The gesture backfires. Rachel sees the mandrakes and wants them for herself, precipitating a bitter exchange in which Leah says to her, 'Wasn't it enough that you took away my husband? Will you take away my son's mandrakes too?' (Gen. 30:15). Intending only good, Reuben provokes an argument between the sisters, the only one recorded in the Bible.

In the next scene, Rachel has died, prematurely and young. A strange incident then takes place. The text is cryptic: 'When Israel [i.e. Jacob] was living in that region, Reuben went in and lay with his father's concubine Bilhah, and Israel heard of it . . .' (Gen. 35:22). Read literally, it suggests that Reuben took his father's place in Bilhah's tent – an act of displacement, as we discover later in the Bible when Absalom does the same with his father David's concubine (2 Sam. 16:21). Rashi, the medieval commentator, prefers a gentler explanation. When Rachel died, Jacob, who had slept in her tent, moved his bed to the tent of Bilhah, her handmaid. This, for Reuben, was the final insult to his mother Leah. It was bad enough that Jacob preferred her sister Rachel, but intolerable that he should prefer her handmaid to his mother. He therefore *moved the beds*.[6] Even according to this interpretation, however, it is clear that Jacob misunderstood the act and believed that Reuben had in fact usurped his place. He never forgot or forgave the incident, recalling it on his death-bed:

> Reuben, you are my firstborn,
> My might, the first sign of my strength,
> Excelling in honour, excelling in power.
> Unstable as water, you will not excel,
> For you went up onto your father's bed,
> Onto my couch and defiled it. (Gen. 49:3–4)

Earlier, at the time of the event itself, the text uses an unusual stylistic device. After the words, 'And Israel heard of it', the Masoretic text indicates a paragraph break in the middle of a sentence. The effect is to signal a silence, a total breakdown in communication. Reuben must surely have known how badly his father thought of him, for this explains the depth of his despair when his attempted rescue of Joseph failed. As the eldest of the sons he bore primary responsibility for Joseph's safety when he was with them away from home. Not only had he not rescued Joseph, but he now knew that nothing would restore him to Jacob's esteem.

The key to Reuben's character lies in his earliest childhood. Jacob resented the fact that he had been tricked into marrying Leah. When he finally marries Rachel, the Torah says in a passage of great pathos:

> When the Lord saw that Leah was not loved, He opened her womb, but Rachel was barren. Leah became pregnant and gave birth to a son. She named him Reuben ['see, a son'], for she said, 'It is because the Lord has seen my misery. Surely my husband will love me now.' She conceived again, and when she gave birth to a son she said, 'Because the Lord heard that I am not loved, He gave me this one too.' So she named him Shimon. (Gen. 29:31–3)

Leah hoped that the birth of a son would make Jacob love her. She is still voicing the same wish when her second son is born. Reuben has to carry with him through life the awareness of his mother's slight. This results in the lack of confidence that causes his several efforts to mend relationships within the family to fail.

Hence the fateful significance of the meeting between Joseph and the brothers – not only for Joseph and Jacob, but for Reuben and the future fate of the family. At the critical moment, his conscience does not fail him but his resolution does. Instead of saving Joseph boldly and immediately, he defers the moment and devises a stratagem that will buy him time. In that hesitation, more was lost than Joseph. So too was Reuben's chance to become the hero he might and should have been. Everything turned on that moment. Had Reuben acted decisively, Joseph would have returned home safely. He would not have been sold into Egypt, and the *entire sequence of events that led to the exile and enslavement of the Israelites* would not have taken place. History would have been different. We never know the counterfactual conditionals, the might-have-beens, that would have set the sequence of events on a different course. But here, with great emphasis, the Bible draws our attention to the moment of choice. Reuben knew what ought to be done – the text makes this clear – but he delayed, and in that moment the chance of changing history was lost.

Hence the midrash. Had Reuben known that the Torah would write of him, 'And Reuben heard and saved him from their hands' – had he been aware that his intention was known and valued by God – he would have carried it through into action. *If only we knew the good that lies within our reach*, the effect a single action may have on the lives of others . . . but we do not, and the result is that much we could have done remains undone. In a single moment of arrested intention, Reuben lost his chance of greatness. One act can change the world. More often than we know, what we do or fail to do has far-reaching consequences.

*   *   *

In the midst of his presentation of the laws of *teshuvah* (repentance) Maimonides makes a remarkable statement. He has been speaking about the balance of a life. Each of us, he says, has merits and demerits, good deeds and bad, and our lives are judged as a whole – at the end of life, and also every year on Rosh Hashanah, the New Year. He continues:

> Even though the blowing of the shofar on the New Year is a biblical decree, it none the less contains a deep meaning, as if to say: Awake, sleepers, from your sleep; rouse yourselves, slumberers, from your slumber. Examine your deeds, return in repentance and remember your creator. Those who forget the truth in the vanities of time and spend their years on meaningless pursuits that neither profit nor save, look to your souls and improve your ways and works. Let each leave his ways that are bad and thoughts that are not good. *Therefore throughout the year everyone should regard himself and the world as if evenly poised between innocence and guilt.* If he commits a sin he tilts the balance of his fate and that of the world to guilt, causing destruction. If he performs a good deed he shifts the balance of his fate and that of the world to innocence, bringing salvation and deliverance to others. That is the meaning of [the biblical phrase] 'the righteous person is the foundation of the world' (Prov. 10:25), namely that by an act of righteousness we influence the fate of, and save, the world.[7]

This is a fascinating passage. Without an alarm-call from heaven, Maimonides says, we can sleepwalk through our days, and adds that one act can change a life, transform a world. How so? Our acts and interventions have ripples of consequence – spiritual, psychological – that are vast but of which, for the most part, we are unaware. Could Sara Kestenbaum, when she made the simple gesture of bringing out drinks and food to welcome a family of black children to her neighbourhood, have known that this would change the life of one of them, and that he, by his teaching and writing, would influence many others? Obviously not. She could not have known it because the human future is inherently unknowable. Nor could she have intended it, because if she had, her act would have been calculating instead of simply being kind. There are some effects we can only achieve if we do not intend to achieve them.

So there is a truth we can neither be aware of, nor act on, all the time even though it is true all or most of the time. What we do affects others, and cannot but affect others. We give them comfort or leave them feeling inadequate and alone. We embarrass them or make them feel they belong. A smile can lift a person for a day. A cutting comment can leave a scar that lasts a lifetime. A word of encouragement can open up for someone a possibility, a source of energy, they did not have before. Of such passing moments are our images of the world made. By such micro-interactions we have an effect on other lives.

Maimonides' account, Talmudic in origin, of human behaviour is an early anticipation of chaos- or complexity-theory, best known through meteorologist Edward Lorenz's 1963 description of the 'butterfly effect' – the idea that the beating of a butterfly's wing in Australia can cause a tornado in Kansas or a monsoon in Indonesia.[8] So interwoven are the chains of cause and effect in complex systems that there is no natural equilibrium, no way of foretelling what the result of an event will be. Small acts can have large outcomes. Maimonides' assertion is chaos theory applied to human behaviour.

But of course we rarely think in such terms. We act, most of the time, without regard for these chains of consequences. We live in the moment, for the moment, within the parameters of the moment. This means that much of the significance of our acts and their effects on others is hidden from view. That is what Maimonides means when he says that we spend much of the year sleepwalking. A dream is a set of thoughts taking place in the mind without connection to reality outside. In that sense, says Maimonides, a great deal of our waking life is like a dream. We find it difficult to stand outside the moment and view the scene from the vantage point of someone else, let alone to see it *sub specie aeternitatis* ('from the perspective of eternity'). That is why we have a special time of the year when we undergo this focused act of attention. It is called Rosh Hashanah, the New Year.

On the New Year we engage in a specific meditation. We think of God as a judge in a courtroom passing a verdict on our life. Will we, or will we not, merit a stay of sentence from mortality and be granted another year? That depends on how we have used the greatest gift of God, time itself. Rosh Hashanah and Yom Kippur are festivals of time – *individual* time as opposed to the collective Jewish experience of time (history) that is the subject of the three pilgrimage festivals, Pesach, Shavuot and Sukkot. The questions we ask ourselves on Rosh Hashanah are about the use of time. Did we use it to a purpose, or did we merely exist? Did we use it for ourselves or for higher ends? Did we bring blessing into a life other than our own?

Here Jewish thought rises to the summit of faith in the significance of the individual. *One act can change a world. A moment can vindicate a life.* There is a view, implicit in many philosophies and mysticisms, that nothing we can do as individuals can affect history, change the course of the world, make a difference in the scheme of things. Measured against the universe and eternity, our lives are dust on the surface of infinity and to believe otherwise is infantile illusion. The only person we can affect is ourselves, and the only way to live with our insignificance is to accept it and gather what pleasures we may in the all too brief span of years we call a life.

But there is another and deeper truth, that even if our life is only the beating of a butterfly's wing, we can set something consequential in motion. We cannot change the world altogether in one go, but we can have an effect, one act at a time, one day at a time, one person at a time. That is what it is, intimates Maimonides, to be awake: to know that our acts make a difference, sometimes all the difference in the world.

*   *   *

It was the worst crisis in Moses' life. Incited by the 'mixed multitude', the Israelites complain about the food: 'If only we had meat to eat. We remember the fish we ate in Egypt at no cost – also the cucumbers, melons, leeks, onions and garlic. But now we have lost our appetite; we never see anything but this manna' (Num. 11:5).

It was an appalling show of ingratitude, but not the first time the Israelites had behaved this way. Moses' reaction takes us by surprise. For once, the hero of the Exodus experiences something recognizably like despair:

> Why have You brought this trouble on Your servant? What have I done to displease You, that You put the burden of all these people on me? Did I conceive all these people? Did I give them birth? Why do You tell me to carry them in my arms, as a nurse carries an infant, to the land You promised on oath to their forefathers? Where can I get meat for all these people? They keep wailing to me, 'Give us meat to eat'. I cannot carry all these people by myself; the burden is too heavy for me. If this is how You are going to treat me, put me to death right now – if I have found favour in Your eyes – and do not let me face my own ruin. (Num. 11:11–15)

It is an extraordinary outburst, and a puzzling one. Moses had faced and overcome such difficulties before. Each time, God had answered the people's requests. He had sent water from the rock, manna from heaven, and quails driven by the wind. Moses knew this. Why did this outburst of the people induce in him a complete breakdown? Equally strange is God's reaction:

> Bring me seventy elders who are known to you as leaders and officials among the people. Make them come to the Tent of Meeting that they may stand there with you. I will come down and speak with you there, and I will take of the spirit that is on you and put the spirit on them. They will help you carry the burden of the people so that you will not have to carry it alone. (Num. 11:16–17)

To be sure, this is a response to Moses' complaint, 'I cannot carry all these people by myself'. Yet both complaint and response are puzzling. How would the appointment of elders address the crisis Moses was undergoing? He did not need deputies to help him find meat. Either it would appear by a miracle, or it would not appear at all. Nor did he need help in sharing the burdens of leadership. Already, on the advice of his father-in-law Jethro, he had created a leadership infrastructure: heads of thousands, hundreds, fifties and tens. How would a new appointment of 70 elders make a difference?

And why the emphasis in God's reply on *spirit*: 'I will take of the spirit that is on you and put the spirit on them'? The elders did not need to become prophets to help Moses in carrying out the burdens of leadership. Prophets help only in knowing what guidance to give the people – and for this one prophet, Moses, is sufficient. To put it bluntly: either the 70 elders would deliver the same message as Moses or they would not. If they did, they would be superfluous. If they did not, they would undermine his authority, precisely what, in the event, Joshua feared.

Yet it worked. Reading the text closely, we see that from this moment onward, Moses' despair disappeared. He was transformed. Immediately afterward, it is as if a new Moses stands before us, untroubled by even the most serious challenges to his leadership. When two of the elders, Eldad and Medad, prophesy not in the Tent of Meeting but in the camp, Joshua senses a threat to Moses' authority and says, 'Moses, my lord, stop them!' Moses replies, with surpassing generosity of spirit, 'Are you jealous for my sake? Would that all the Lord's people were prophets and that the Lord would put His spirit on them' (Num. 11:29).

In the next chapter, when *his own brother and sister*, Aaron and Miriam, start complaining about him, he does nothing – 'Now Moses was a very humble man, more humble than anyone else on the face of the earth' (Num. 12:3). Indeed, when God became angry at Miriam, he prayed on her behalf. The despair has gone. The crisis has passed. These two subsequent challenges were far more serious than the request of the people for meat, yet Moses meets them with confidence and equanimity. Something has taken place between him and God and he has been transformed.

The reason for Moses' despair is this: the people had complained before. But that was before the momentous events that firmly established the fact of God's presence in their midst: the crossing of the Red Sea, the revelation at Mount Sinai and the construction of the Tabernacle. They were no longer a group of runaway slaves. They had become 'a kingdom of priests and a holy nation'. They had come through some of the most transformative experiences in the history of the people Israel. Hence Moses' exasperation. To be sure, they had complained about the food before, but they were a different people before. What caused Moses' spirit to break was the fact that, as soon as they had left the Sinai desert to begin the journey again, they reverted to their old habits of complaint *as if nothing had changed.* If the revelation at Sinai, the experience of divine anger at the Golden Calf and the long labour of building the Tabernacle had not changed them, what would? Moses' anguish is all too intelligible. For the first time since his mission began, he could see defeat staring him in the face. Nothing – so it seemed – not miracles or deliverances, revelations or creative labour, would change this people from complaints about food into recognition of the unique ethical–spiritual destiny to which they had been called. Perhaps God, from the perspective of eternity, could see a sign of hope in the future. Moses, the human being, could not. 'I would rather die', he says, 'than spend the rest of my life labouring in vain.'

There are moments in the life of any transformative leader when hope is eclipsed by clouds of doubt – not about God, but about the people and above all about oneself. Am I deceiving myself when I think I can change the world? I have tried, I have given the best of my energies, yet nothing seems to alter the depressing reality of human frailty and lack of vision. I have given the people the word of God himself, yet they still complain, thinking only about the discomforts of today, not the possibilities of tomorrow. Such despair (Winston Churchill, who suffered from it, called it 'the black dog')[9] can affect the greatest (not only Moses prayed to die; so did Elijah, Jeremiah and Jonah). Moses *was* the greatest. Therefore God gave him a unique gift.

He let Moses see the influence he had on others. For a moment God took 'the spirit that is on you and put it on them' so that Moses could see the difference he made to one group, the 70 elders. Once he had seen that, he needed nothing more: not their help, nor their prophecy. All he needed was a transparent insight into how his spirit had communicated itself to them. He saw a fragment of the difference he had made. Little could Moses have known that he, who encountered nothing in his lifetime but complaints, challenges and rebellions, would have so decisive an influence that more than 3,000 years later, the descendants of those he led would still be studying and living by the words he transmitted, that he had helped forge an identity more tenacious than any other in history, that in the full perspective of hindsight he would prove to have been one of the greatest leaders who ever lived. He did not know these things; he did not *need* to know these things. All he needed was to see, if only for a moment, that 70 elders had internalized his spirit and made his message their own. That was enough to know that his life was not in vain. He had disciples. His vision was not confined to him. He had planted it in others. They would continue his work after his lifetime. That was sufficient for him, as it must be for us. Once Moses knew this, he could face any challenge with equanimity.

That is what I discovered when my late father died and we – my mother and brothers – were sitting *shiva*. Repeatedly, people would tell us of kindnesses he had done for them, in some cases more than 50 years before. I have since discovered that many people who have sat *shiva*, have had similar experiences. How moving, I thought, and how sad, that my father was not there to hear their words. What strength it would have given him to know that despite the hardships he faced, the good he did was not forgotten. How tragic it is that we so often keep our gratitude to ourselves, speaking it aloud only when the person to whom we feel indebted is no longer here, and we are comforting his or her mourners.

That is the human condition. We never really know how much we have given others – how much the kind word, the thoughtful deed, the comforting gesture, change lives and are never forgotten. In this respect, if no other, we are like Moses. He too was human. He had no privileged access into other people's minds. Without a miracle, he would not have known the influence he had on those closest to him. All the evidence seemed to suggest otherwise. The people, even after all God had done for them, were still ungrateful, querulous, quick to criticize and complain. But that was on the surface. For a moment he was granted a glimpse of what was beneath the surface. Moses saw how his spirit had entered others and lifted them, however briefly, to share his vision.

If that was enough for Moses, it is enough for us. Dylan Thomas wrote:

> Though lovers be lost, love shall not;
> And death shall have no dominion.[10]

We never know the good we do, still less the chain of consequences to which it gives rise. But this is the only legacy worth leaving: the trace we leave on other lives, and they on others in turn. Sometimes a single act, like the beating of a butterfly's wing, can reverberate in incalculable ways. That is what Maimonides taught and what might, had Reuben known it, have changed his life and history.

NOTES

1. Babylonian Talmud, *Avodah Zarah* 18a.
2. Viktor Frankl, *The Doctor and the Soul: from psychotherapy to logotherapy* (London: Souvenir Press, 2004), p. 58.
3. Louis Begley, *About Schmidt* (New York: Alfred A. Knopf, 1996); *About Schmidt*, directed by Alexander Payne (New Line Cinema, 2002).
4. Peter Bradshaw, 'Review of About Schmidt', *The Guardian* (London), 24 January 2003.
5. *Leviticus Rabbah* 34; *Ruth Rabbah* 5; *Tanhuma (Buber), Vayeshev* 13; *Yalkut Shimoni, Ruth* 604.
6. Rashi, *Commentary* to Gen. 35:22.
7. *Mishneh Torah, Teshuvah* 3:4.
8. See Edward N. Lorenz, *The Nature and Theory of the General Circulation of the Atmosphere* (Geneva: World Meteorological Organization, 1967); *The Essence of Chaos* (Seattle: University of Washington Press, 1993). See also J. Gleick, *Chaos: Making a New Science* (New York: Penguin Books, 1987).
9. Anthony Storr, *Churchill's Black Dog and Other Phenomena of the Human Mind* (London: HarperCollins, 1997).
10. Dylan Thomas, 'And Death Shall Have No Dominion', in *Collected Poems 1934–1952* (London: J. M. Dent, 1952), p. 68.

Chapter 18

The Kind of Person
We Are

> When I was young, I wanted to change the world. I tried, but the
> world did not change. Then I tried to change my town, but the town
> did not change. Then I tried to change my family, but my family did
> not change. Then I knew: first, I must change myself.
>
> (R. Israel Salanter)[1]

I met David and Rachel when I was appointed to my first congregation. I
did not notice them immediately. They sat at the back of the synagogue.
They were inconspicuous, but gradually I began to realize that they were
the most important people there. Quietly they helped transform it from
a congregation into a community.

What used to happen was this: whenever a stranger appeared in the
synagogue, they would go up to them and greet them, give them a prayer
book and invite them to sit next to them. At the end of the service they
would invite them back for lunch. Their home, I discovered, was an open
house. Every Shabbat their table would be full of strangers. More arrived
during the course of the afternoon. Other members of the synagogue
would drop in. Newcomers would find themselves, in the course of a
single day, integrated into the community. They turned strangers into
friends.

They were the congregation's Abraham and Sarah, watching out for
passers-by, as did their biblical precursors, so that they could invite them
to eat and rest awhile. They were redeemers of loneliness. Eventually they
left the community and moved to Jerusalem, where they continued to do
the same for people there. Like the best of the good, they saw nothing
unusual in what they did, and were embarrassed when anyone thanked
them. They reminded me of the Jewish tradition of the *lamed-vovniks*, the
'thirty-six' righteous people on whose merits the world depends. The
one thing they have in common is that they have no idea that they are

exceptional. They are the kind of people in whom God takes special delight.

There is a danger in a religion like Judaism, with so many clear-cut rules for highly specific situations, that we may forget that there are areas of life which have no rules, only role-models, but which are no less religiously significant for that. One of the great Jewish mystics, Rabbi Leib Saras, used to say that he travelled to Rabbi Dov Baer of Mezeritch, not to learn biblical interpretations but to see how the Rabbi tied his shoelaces. The Talmud speaks of the 'foolish' Jews of Babylon who 'stand in the presence of a Torah scroll but not in the presence of a great human being'.[2] A great sage *is* a living Torah scroll. There are text-books and there are text-people. We learn virtue less by formal instruction than by finding virtuous people and observing how they live. Sometimes we make a difference less by what we do than by what we are.

*　　　　　　*　　　　　　*

We can identify the moment at which this idea became self-conscious in Judaism. In his law-code, the *Mishneh Torah*, Moses Maimonides was highly innovative in his presentation of Jewish law. What he taught had always been there, but some of it had not been formulated in a systematic way before. One of the most striking examples is the book he entitled *Hilkhot Deot*, 'the laws of ethical character'. This is how he begins:

> Every human being has many character traits, and they differ greatly from one another, being exceedingly divergent. One person is irascible, perpetually angry, while another may have a tranquil disposition and does not become angry at all – if he does get angry, he is only mildly so and only rarely during a period of several years. One may be exceedingly haughty, while another is humble in the extreme . . . In the same way they differ in other traits. There are, for example, the cheerful and the melancholy, the miserly and the generous, the cruel and the merciful, the soft-hearted and hard-hearted, and so on.[3]

Maimonides recognizes that character is not like behaviour. We choose what to do, but we do not choose the kind of person we are. Many aspects of our personality are not the results of conscious decision:

> Some character traits a person has from birth, in virtue of his physical nature. Others are such that he is disposed to acquire them more easily than their alternatives. Some traits are not innate, but

have been learned from other people, or are self-originated as the result of an idea that has entered the person's mind, or because he has heard that a certain character trait is good for him and that it is proper to acquire it, and he trains himself in it until it is firmly established within him.[4]

None the less, Maimonides distinguishes between genetic *determinism* and *influence*. Our character is not immutable. We can change. This is Maimonides' programme of character formation:

> A person should habituate himself in these character traits until they are firmly established in him. Time after time, he shall perform actions in accordance with the traits that are the mean between extremes. He shall repeat them continually until performing them is easy for him and they are no longer burdensome, and these character dispositions are firmly established in his soul.[5]

We become what we do. One who is irascible must accustom himself to stay calm. A coward must risk danger. A miser must repeatedly give. My late father was intensely shy. To defeat what he saw as a failing in himself, he used to force himself to go up to strangers and engage them in conversation. As a child, I used to find this embarrassing, but he was showing me what it is to become what you strive to be. *We are responsible for our character.* That is Maimonides' point. Moral education is the acquisition of good habits, not just the learning of rules. Just as no book will teach you how to play the piano, so no formal instruction will make you ethical. As we learn a language by speaking, or a game by playing, so we learn virtue by doing virtuous deeds.

The idea is profound. One of the key texts of the Renaissance was Pico della Mirandola's *Oration on the Dignity of Man*, usually taken as the first expression of humanism in European culture. Pico's argument is that *Homo sapiens* has a unique place in the universe. Alone among life-forms, we are free to become what we choose. Pico's starting-point is Genesis. He imagines God addressing Adam in the following words:

> Adam, we give you no fixed place to live, no form that is peculiar to you, nor any function that is yours alone. According to your desires and judgments, you will have and possess whatever place to live, whatever form, and whatever functions you yourself choose. All other things have a limited and fixed nature prescribed and bounded by our laws. You, with no limit or no bound, may choose for yourself the limits and bounds of your nature ... We have made you neither of heavenly nor of earthly stuff, neither mortal nor

immortal, so that with free choice and dignity, you may fashion yourself into whatever form you choose.[6]

This was a turning-point in the history of the West, a decisive break with the Platonic idea of fixed forms and essences, and a return to a more Judaic conception of human freedom. Mirandola's words chime perfectly with those of the great twentieth-century Jewish thinker, Rabbi Joseph Soloveitchik: 'The most fundamental principle of all is that man must create himself.'[7]

Maimonides goes further. For him, this is the way we fulfil the command of *imitatio Dei*, emulating God, 'walking in his ways' (Deut. 28:9). Indeed, he argues that it is for this reason alone that the Bible attributes character traits to God, speaking of him as merciful, gracious and so on. Maimonides the philosopher held as a matter of principle that God lies beyond the reach of language. The infinite cannot be described in the language of finitude. Why then does the Torah run the constant risk of anthropomorphism, by speaking of God in human terms? To tell us, says Maimonides, not something about God but about *us* – how we should behave, what kind of relationships we should have with people.[8] That is why the sages said, 'Just as God is gracious, so shall you be gracious; just as God is merciful, so shall you be merciful.'[9] The Bible tells us that God is gracious *in order that* we should aspire to grace. God-talk for Maimonides is not ontological but ethical. It is not about *what God is* but about *what we should aim to be*.

No one had set out a Jewish virtue-ethic in quite these terms before, and shortly after Maimonides' death, his son Abraham, Chief Rabbi of Egyptian Jewry, was sent a question. His correspondent challenged Maimonides' approach to ethics. One of his questions was this: surely 'walking in God's ways' is not a specific imperative. It is a general statement meaning, 'obey his word, keep his commands'. Maimonides himself had laid down as one of the rules for enumerating the commands that purely general statements were not to be counted, only specific laws with precise parameters. His decision to count 'walking in his ways' as a command in its own right seemed to go against his own principles of jurisprudence.

After dealing with technical issues of biblical interpretation, Rabbi Abraham makes a subtle and far-reaching point:

> After the verse has already stated, 'If you keep God's commands', it adds 'and you shall walk in his ways' because in respect of this requirement it is possible to think that it is not obligatory in the way that the other commands are obligatory, for they are about action whereas 'you shall walk in his ways' concerns character traits

(*middot*). This has been explained by the tradition: 'Just as he is gracious, so you be gracious'. [Thus character traits are one thing, acts another] despite the fact that the point of these character traits is the actions to which they give rise. This is something which is hard to understand at first.[10]

Rabbi Abraham understood the originality of his father's ethics. Maimonides saw that Judaism contains an ethic of virtue,[11] not just a set of rules of behaviour. It is *not just about what we do but also about the kind of person we are called on to become.* The Torah is more than law. It is narrative as well. Law divides reality into simple categories: right and wrong, innocent or guilty, permitted or forbidden, liable or exempt. We need narrative to instruct us in the many situations in which there are no simple answers – conflicts, for example, between right and right, or choosing the lesser of two evils, or deciding which loyalty should take priority. Through narrative we see how people respond to crisis and challenge: one with courage, another with vacillation, one with authority, another with gentleness, one with defiant resignation, another prepared to accept a setback for the sake of long-term victory. Law yields rules, narrative produces role-models. Within Judaism there are both: laws and narratives, codes and stories. Judaism is full of stories because it recognizes the limits of law in teaching us how to live.

Yet on the face of it, Rabbi Abraham's questioner was right. What is a hero if not one who performs courageous acts? What is generosity if not sharing one's wealth with others? Once you have specified the actions, what is the significance of the remainder: character, disposition, temperament, personality? Surely Maimonides is guilty of the error known as a category-mistake. The late Gilbert Ryle, who coined the phrase, used as his example a foreign tourist who has been taken by a guide through Oxford. He sees the colleges, their cloisters and quadrangles, and at the end of the tour, he says to the guide, 'I've seen the colleges. Now show me the university'. What he has not understood is that the university *just is* the colleges.[12] So too Maimonides seems not to understand that character *just is* our actions. There is nothing over and above what we do that is worthy of a separate command.

Maimonides is right, however, and importantly so. When we interact with people, much of what matters has less to do with *what* we do than *how*. When we turn to a counsellor, we want not only technical proficiency (a matter of rules) but also sensitivity, sympathy, an ability to listen and enter into our distress (traits of character). When we vote for a politician we know that he or she will face problems that cannot be foreseen. We look therefore to qualities of character. Does she have basic integrity, seeking to serve, not just to exercise power? Does he have the strength to stand firm under pressure, not wavering at times of crisis?

So important is character to human relationships that we are genetically disposed to be sensitive to its cues.[13] We notice gestures, postures,
body language, tone of voice, mood, attitude. We instinctively know
whether the person facing us is listening to us, respects us, is trying to
understand who we are and how we see our situation. Character is not
marginal to the ethical life but of its essence – for the very reason that
rules alone are insufficient. There are rules of sonata form, but they do
not yield a Beethoven. There are formulas for writing sonnets, but not
everyone is a Shakespeare. There are rules of the moral life, but they are
not sufficient to produce a hero or a saint. Thus, Maimonides' son was
correct when he said that acts are one thing, character traits another
'despite the fact that the point of these character traits is the actions to
which they give rise'. There are two distinct challenges in the ethical life.
We are called on to *obey* God in what we do. We are asked to *imitate* God
in what we are.

The difference was brought out strikingly by one of the great figures of
East European piety, Rabbi Naftali Zvi Yehudah Berlin (1817–93). In the
preface to his commentary to the Pentateuch, he raised a series of questions: What is the place of Genesis in Jewish life? Why is it known to
tradition as 'the Book of the Upright'? Why was the Second Temple
destroyed, despite the piety of the Jews of that time? His comments are
fundamental:

> [The people of Second Temple times] were righteous and pious
> and laboured in the Torah. But they were not upright in their deal-
> ings with the world. Thus, as a result of the baseless hatred in their
> hearts, they suspected anyone who did not act in accordance with
> their opinions of being a Sadducee and a heretic. The result was
> murder and other evils, until eventually the Temple was destroyed.
> It is about this that Moses vindicates divine justice, for the Holy
> One, blessed be He, is upright and does not tolerate righteous
> people such as these unless they act uprightly in their dealings
> with the world rather than perversely, even though their intention
> is for the sake of heaven, for this causes the ruination of the world
> and the destruction of society.
>
> This was the merit of the patriarchs, that besides the fact that
> they were righteous and pious and loved God to the utmost extent,
> they were also *upright*. In their relations with Gentiles – even the
> worst idolaters – they acted out of love, and sought their good, for
> this enables the world to endure. Thus we find that Abraham,
> though he hated their wickedness, prostrated himself in prayer for
> the people of Sodom, for he wanted them to survive . . . Similarly
> we see how readily Isaac let himself be placated by his enemies,
> and on the basis of a few apologetic words from Avimelech and his

companions, he made his peace with them. So too we find with Jacob who, though he knew that Laban sought to destroy him, spoke to him gently, on which the Midrash says, 'Better the anger of the patriarchs than the humility of their descendants.' Thus we learn much from the way the patriarchs conducted themselves with civility.[14]

The Jews of the late Second Temple period kept the laws but failed to educate their characters. The result was that their very piety, when it became heresy-hunting, became divisive and destructive. Faith must instruct not just what we do, but what we are.

*   *   *

No less fascinating is what Maimonides goes on to say next. He lists the various character traits we should strive to have, and how we can fail to acquire them. Following Aristotle, he points out that there are two ways, not one, in which we can fail: by having *too little* of the trait in question, or by having *too much*. So, for example, courage is opposed not only to cowardice (fearing too much) but also foolhardiness (fearing too little). One who takes unnecessary risks, endangering himself and others, is not courageous but irresponsible. Virtue is a matter of judgement and balance, weighing considerations and deciding between them. Aristotle called this 'the golden mean'. Maimonides, in the same spirit, called it 'the middle way'.

Maimonides then asserts that there are two types of ideal, two models of the religious personality. He calls them respectively the *hakham* and the *hassid*, respectively the 'sage' and the 'saint':

> Every person whose character traits all lie in the mean is called a sage [*hakham*]. Whoever is exceedingly scrupulous with himself, inclining a little toward one extreme or the other, away from the character trait of the mean, is called a saint [*hassid*].
>
> How so? Whoever moves away from a haughty heart to the opposite extreme so that he is extremely lowly in spirit is called a saint; this is the measure of saintliness. If he moves only to the mean and is humble, he is called a sage. The same applies to all other character traits. The saints of old used to direct their character traits away from the middle way toward [one of] the two extremes . . . This is the meaning of 'within the line of the law'.[15]

There is law, and there is 'within the line of the law' – action beyond the call of duty. The sage does what he is commanded, the saint goes further. Maimonides then says something unexpected:

244

We are commanded to walk in these middle ways which are the good and right ways. As it is said, 'You shall walk in His ways.' Thus they taught us in explaining this command: Just as He is called gracious, so you be gracious. Just as He is called merciful, so you shall be merciful. Just as He is called holy, so you be holy . . . Since these terms applied to the Creator refer to the middle way that we are obliged to follow, this way is called 'the way of the Lord'. That is what Abraham taught his sons, as it is said, 'For I have known him so that he will instruct his children and his household after him to keep the way of the Lord by doing justice and righteousness.'[16]

The inference is inescapable: *The sage is greater than the saint.* This is the opposite of what we would have expected. If courage, loyalty or generosity are virtues, then one who manifests them to an extreme is surely greater than one who displays them in moderation. Is not one who acts beyond the call of duty more virtuous than one who merely does his duty? Were the prophets advocates of 'the middle way'? Aristotle was – but he belonged to a Hellenistic culture of reason, balance and harmony, while Maimonides represents a tradition of revelation, devotion and piety.[17] His ethical system is predicated on God himself. Religious ethics is surely more inclined to value extremes of piety over moderation. To understand Maimonides on this point – and it is an important one – we must follow him through three steps of an argument.

The first is that, according to him, the task of the religious life is dual: perfection of the body and perfection of the soul. The second is higher, but it cannot be achieved without the first. It is impossible to reach spiritual heights if you are suffering from lack of food or shelter, if you are in poverty or pain. Because our physical needs cannot be met without collaborative activity on the part of many people, we need *society*. The first task of faith is therefore to create social order by 'removing all violence from our midst' and by 'teaching every one of us such good morals as must produce a good social state'. We are social animals; hence our first task is to create a good and gracious society. A Jewish ethic is first and foremost a social ethic, an ethic of the group, not just the individual.[18]

It follows, secondly, that part of what religion teaches us is *how to be part of a society*. When the Torah describes God as being 'compassionate and gracious, slow to anger, abounding in love and faithfulness', it mentions these attributes because 'they are required for the good government of a country'.[19] God, who cares for humanity as a whole, acts for the benefit of humanity as a whole. That involves striking a balance between justice and mercy, law and compassion, retribution and forgiveness.

'Walking in God's ways' therefore means involvement in society, which is why Maimonides favoured the sage over the saint. *The sage is concerned with the perfection of society. The saint is concerned with the perfection of self.* The sage knows that in any human group there are conflicts – of temperament and conviction, interest and ambition – and they can only be resolved by balance, compromise and mediation. That is the gift of the sage. His wisdom is to give each person and situation its due: to reward the good, discourage the bad and ensure that decisions are taken that enhance the group rather than taking the side of one individual against another.

The sage has the *social* virtues: justice, fairness, integrity, patience, a love of peace, an ability to hear both sides of an argument and weigh conflicting situations. He or she does not act out of emotion but on the basis of careful deliberation of what is best for all concerned. A zealot, said the Rebbe of Kotzk, cannot be a leader. To be a leader one has to cultivate those traits the Torah ascribes to God: compassion and grace, patience and forgiveness, and the other 'attributes of mercy'.

The saint is engaged in an altogether different enterprise. He or she is less concerned with the group than with his or her personal relationship with God. If the focus of the sage is social, that of the saint is psychological and spiritual. As Maimonides explains, the saint knows how unruly the emotional life can be, and therefore takes extra precautions to avoid temptation or risk. It is easy to fall prey to pride, therefore the saint errs on the side of self-abasement. It is easy to be selfish, therefore the saint inclines to over-generosity. The body has strong passions and desires, so the saint goes further than others in denying himself pleasures of the body.

The sage is the personality-type associated with the Torah's first aim, perfection of society. The saint is part of its second, perfection of the soul. In a famous essay on Tolstoy, Isaiah Berlin wrote about the difference between the hedgehog and the fox. 'The fox knows many things. The hedgehog knows one big thing.'[20] In Maimonidean ethics, the sage is a fox, the saint a hedgehog. The sage knows many things: the competing pressures and conflicting interests of life within the group. He or she builds a family, creates a home, has a career and takes part in the affairs of the community. The saint knows one big thing: the longing to be close to God. While the sage is interested in the world outside, the saint is preoccupied by the world within, the 'strife of the spirit', the yearning for inner perfection. One can imagine a society of sages. It is impossible, until the Messianic Age, to imagine a society of saints.

A saint, knowing that 'the more possessions, the more anxiety',[21] may be tempted to give all he has away and live in poverty. That is a noble act – but what about his wife and children? A saint may forgive all, but what if she is a judge? Shimon bar Yohai, the second-century saint, regarded it as a neglect of Torah to engage in a worldly occupation. But what if everyone acted in accordance with his teaching? The result would be destitution. Saints are noble individuals, but saintliness cannot be the ethic of a society – and Judaism *is* the ethic of a society.

The greatness of Maimonides is that he understood that there is more than one way of serving God. The sage embodies wisdom, the saint piety. The saint may be closer to God, while the sage is closer to doing what God wants us to do, namely bring his presence into the shared spaces of our collective life. Maimonides valued the life of the saint, the semi-recluse who abandons the world in order to live in close and uninterrupted contact with God. He wrote critically about social life and its trivial pursuits. He went so far as to say that only the patriarchs and Moses were able to unite their thoughts with God in the midst of their daily concerns. Life in society *is* a distraction from the single-minded pursuit of spiritual depth.

Yet for all this, Maimonides elevates the sage over the saint because of his engagement with the world. That was the life Maimonides himself chose. His horizons were vast. He wrote not only some of the masterpieces of rabbinic literature, but also texts on logic, astronomy and medicine. He became one of the great physicians of his day. He answered questions from Jewish communities around the world. He was *de facto* leader of Egyptian Jewry and was consulted also by many non-Jews. Though he hated controversy he was unafraid to take challenging stances, intellectual or communal. Critical of worldly pursuits, he none the less believed that we were placed in society to make a difference to society. To do so is 'to walk in God's ways'.

In his poem 'The Choice', W. B. Yeats wrote:

> The intellect of man is forced to choose
> Perfection of the life, or of the work . . .[22]

Maimonides acknowledged this dilemma and wrestled with it. The saint chooses perfection of the *life*; the sage is summoned to the *work* – and it was to the latter that Maimonides ascribed the greater religious dignity. For he believed in the God who intervened to save a people from slavery, set them on the path to freedom, and taught them how to honour the freedom and dignity of others. Those who 'walk in God's ways' are socially involved. They fight battles, seek peace, work for the underprivileged and excluded and do not merely contemplate justice but struggle to achieve it. More than any other rabbinic figure in the Middle Ages, Maimonides gave religious depth to the complex, conflict-ridden world of work, leadership, community-building and the public square. Without devaluing the saint, Maimonides showed us another way.

He also showed how this choice, of segregation from or integration with society, plays out in terms of character. It needs a special set of virtues to live in the world – the virtues of the sage, not the saint. Closed communities can exercise control over their members by social sanction. Open communities demand a different approach: persuasion, not compulsion; argument, not anathemas; moderation and balance rather than extremism and zealotry. They need people who, as the rabbis ruled, sometimes place peace above truth, who draw others close – as did David and Rachel, the couple with whom this chapter began – by kindness, hospitality and generosity of spirit.

*　　　*　　　*

It is all too easy to compartmentalize the religious life. There are sacred times and places: Sabbath, the festivals, the synagogue, the home. And there are contexts – work, colleagues, the wider society – when we play our allotted roles and live by other rules. The result is a divided personality and a sense of disconnection between inner and outer worlds. It does not have to be like this.

Rabbi Isaac Hutner (1907–80) was one of the great rabbinic personalities of the twentieth century. In 1954 he received a letter from a young man who was leaving a religious seminary to begin a secular career. The prospect was causing him distress. In the seminary he had found a sheltered environment within which he felt the intensity of a life devoted uninterruptedly to study. Pursuing a career seemed like a compromise that could only lead to a loss of single-mindedness. He was, he said, fearful of leading 'a double life'. Rabbi Hutner wrote him a powerful, dissenting reply:

> I want to tell you that in my opinion the internal struggles about which you write have their source in a mistaken understanding of the matter. The general impression one receives from your words is that you are working on the assumption that pursuing a 'secular career' means leading 'a double life'. It is unnecessary to tell you that I would never agree to your leading a double life. One who rents a room in a house in which to live, and [at the same time] pays for a room in a hotel in which to be a guest is certainly leading a double life. But one who rents an apartment with two rooms is not leading a double life but a broad life.
>
> I remember once visiting the hospital in Jerusalem where [a certain Orthodox doctor worked] and I saw him approach a patient who was just about to undergo an operation. He asked him for the name of his mother so that he could say a prayer on his behalf for the success of the operation. When I mentioned this to one of the outstanding Torah sages in Jerusalem, he exclaimed, 'How enviable to be such a Jew with so great an opportunity to serve as a vehicle for the glory of heaven!' Tell me, beloved friend, is a doctor, about to perform an operation on a patient, who says a chapter of Psalms for the safe recovery of his patient, leading a double life?

Beloved friend, God forbid that you should see yourself as leading a double life. [The sages say that] 'Whoever prolongs the word "One" [in the first verse of the *Shema*, Deut. 6:4], prolongs his days and years.' Therefore throughout your life you should be one of those who 'prolongs the "One"' – [focusing on] unity, not duality. It would grieve me very much if this point were not apparent to you. Many dots scattered here and there certainly constitute a multiplicity, but the same number of dots ordered around a single point at the centre form one circle. This is your duty in life, to place at the centre of your life the 'One', and then you need have no worry about dualities. Every new dot you acquire will then merely expand the circle, but its unity will remain.[23]

It is a beautiful response and goes to the heart of the subject of this chapter. What we take with us wherever we go is our character, and it makes all the difference if it has been educated and sensitized. There is a tendency in contemporary culture, fed by many influences, to see character as given, an immutable fact. Self-esteem becomes self-acceptance. We are what we are. The Judaic ethic speaks in a different accent. We become what we strive to be. Character is like the block of marble out of which Michelangelo carved his Moses. It may take many years, a lifetime, but as we chip away the abrasive edges, the dysfunctional reactions, the faults and weaknesses, what emerges is *life as a work of art*.

To be gracious, thoughtful, sensitive, attentive; to have integrity, courage and psychological strength; to be able to respond to different people in different ways, knowing what each needs to fulfil his or her part in the scheme of things – is to come as close as we can to living in the world as God lives in the world. We imitate God not just by what we do but also by the kind of person we become. We carry our faith with us wherever we go, and our character affects every interaction we have. Our lives are changed by people. There are those who heal by their simple ability to listen, others to whom we turn for wise advice. Some have the gift of cheering us when we feel low, others of inspiring us by their enthusiasm and passion. Each of us has unique gifts of character, but they need to be honed and refined. A great golfer used to say, when asked how he won a tournament, 'I was lucky', and would then add, 'But it's a funny thing: the harder I practise, the luckier I get.' Character is a matter of fortune, but we can make a fortune as well as inherit one. The kind of person we are is testimony to the ideals in which we believe. If I were to sum up what faith asks us to be, I would say: a *healing presence*. That is the common factor among the many different lives that have inspired me.

NOTES

1. I have not been able to track the source of this quotation: I have heard it attributed to several teachers, most often to Rabbi Israel Salanter. It is a widely shared idea. Tolstoy said, 'Everyone thinks of changing the world, but no one thinks of changing himself', and Gandhi: 'You must be the change you wish to see in the world.' To Confucius is attributed the saying: 'To put the world in order, we must first put the nation in order; to put the nation in order, we must put the family in order; to put the family in order, we must first cultivate our personal life; we must first set our hearts right.' Arnold Glasow said it most pithily: 'Improvement begins with I.'
2. Babylonian Talmud, *Makkot* 22b.
3. Maimonides, *Mishneh Torah, Laws of Ethical Character*, 1:1.
4. Ibid., 1:2.
5. Ibid., 1:7.
6. Pico della Mirandola, 'On the Dignity of Man', in E. Cassirer, P. O. Kristeller and J. H. Randall (eds.), *The Renaissance Philosophy of Man* (Chicago: University of Chicago Press, 1948), pp. 224–5. See also Charles Taylor, *Sources of the Self* (Cambridge: Cambridge University Press, 1989), pp. 199–200.
7. Rabbi Joseph B. Soloveitchik, *Halakhic Man*, trans. Lawrence Kaplan (Philadelphia: Jewish Publication Society of America, 1983), p. 109.
8. Maimonides, *Laws of Ethical Character*, 1:6. See also *The Guide for the Perplexed*, I:54.
9. *Sifre, Ekev* 49 to Deut. 10:12.
10. *Responsa Rabbi Abraham ben HaRambam*, ed. A. H. Freimann (Jerusalem: Mekize Nirdamim, 1937), no. 63, pp. 65–8.
11. The classic text on virtue ethics is Aristotle, *The Nicomachean Ethics*, trans. J. A. K. Thomson (London: Penguin Classics, 2004). The revival of the virtue tradition in modern philosophy is due to the impact of Alasdair McIntyre, *After Virtue* (London: Duckworth, 1981). See also Roger Crisp (ed.), *How Should One Live? Essays on the Virtues* (Oxford: Clarendon Press, 1996); Roger Crisp and Michael Slote (eds.), *Virtue Ethics* (Oxford: Oxford University Press, 1997).
12. Gilbert Ryle, *The Concept of Mind* (Harmondsworth: Penguin, 1963), pp. 13–25.
13. See Matt Ridley, *The Origins of Virtue* (London: Viking, 1996).
14. Rabbi Naftali Zvi Yehudah Berlin, *Ha'amek Davar*, Introduction to Gen. (Jerusalem: El Hamekorot, 1975), p. 1.
15. *Laws of Ethical Character*, 1:4–5.
16. Ibid., 1:5–7.
17. This was the critique of Samuel David Luzzatto (1800–65), who was critical of what he saw as Maimonides' over-indebtedness to the Greek tradition in his account of ethical character. See Noah H. Rosenbloom, *Luzzatto's Ethico-psychological Interpretation of Judaism* (New York: Yeshiva University, 1965).

18. Maimonides, *The Guide for the Perplexed*, III: 27.

19. Ibid., I: 54.

20. Isaiah Berlin, *The Hedgehog and the Fox* (London: Phoenix, 1992).

21. *Mishnah, Avot* 2:7.

22. W. B. Yeats, 'The Choice', in Norman Jeffares (ed.), *W. B. Yeats: selected poetry* (London: Macmillan, 1984).

23. R. Yitzhak Hutner, *Pahad Yitzhak, Iggerot u-Mikhtavim* (New York: Gur Aryeh, 1998), no. 94, pp. 184–5.

Chapter 19

Who Am I?

When I die and go to the world to come, they will not ask me, Zusya, why were you not Moses? They will ask me: Zusya, why were you not Zuysa?

(Rabbi Zusya of Hanipol)[1]

Moses' *second* question to God at the burning bush was, 'Who are You?' His first was 'Who am I?' – 'Who am I that I should go to Pharaoh and bring the Israelites out of Egypt?' (Ex. 3:11). He did not stop there. He said, 'Lord, I am not a man of words, neither in the past nor now that You have spoken to Your servant. I am slow of speech and tongue.' I find it extraordinary that the greatest Jewish leader of all time thought he was inadequate, not up to the task: 'Please', he said, 'send someone else' (Ex. 4:1–13).

Nor was this true of Moses alone. Isaiah, when charged with his mission, said, 'I am a man of unclean lips' (Is. 6:5). Jeremiah said, 'I cannot speak, for I am a child' (Jer. 1:6). Jonah tried to run away. According to one commentator, that is what Jacob was doing when he found his way blocked by the man/angel with whom he wrestled at night.[2] Twice David, Israel's greatest king, echoed Moses' words, 'Who am I?'[3] These were not figures possessed of a sense of destiny, determined from an early age to achieve fame. They doubted their own abilities. There were times when they felt like giving up. Moses, Jeremiah and Jonah reached points of such despair that they prayed to die. They became heroes of the moral life against their will. There was work to be done – God told them so – and they did it. It is almost as if a sense of smallness is a sign of greatness.

The first question asked in lectures and books on ethics is usually: 'Why be moral?' – as if the greatest roadblock on the way were selfishness, egocentricity, indifference. I suspect, however, that the real question is 'Why me?' Who am I to do the noble deed, the courageous act? I am just an ordinary person, not the kind you read about in books. But the great people, the *lamed-vovniks*, those who change lives and mend the fractures of the world, just *are* ordinary persons who think there is nothing special about them and what they do.

Lionel Trilling made an interesting observation in his *Sincerity and Authenticity*:

> I once had occasion to observe in connection with Wordsworth that in the Rabbinical literature there is no touch of the heroic idea. The Rabbis, in speaking of virtue, never mention the virtue of courage, which Aristotle regarded as basic to the heroic character. The indifference of the Rabbis to the idea of courage is the more remarkable in that they knew that many of their number would die for their faith.[4]

A similar story could be told about the majority of the heroes of the Holocaust, the people who saved lives. According to researchers, they were 'neither saints nor ideologues but ordinary people with an extraordinary willingness to alleviate suffering when they encountered it'.[5]

There is a famous phenomenon known as the Genovese effect. It owes its name to the incident in 1964 when Kitty Genovese was stabbed to death in a New York suburb. Dozens of her neighbours heard her cries for help but none came to her rescue. At the time, appalled commentators interpreted their failure as apathy, callousness or the effect of urban anonymity in which we do not 'love our neighbours as ourselves' because we simply do not know who our neighbours are. However, two social scientists, Bibb Latané and J. M. Darley, staged a series of 'emergencies' (physical collapse, fire alarms, thefts) in stores and offices and came to a remarkable discovery. In every case, a lone bystander was more willing to intervene and help than was a group of bystanders.[6] Often, we fail to act because we think someone else will, or should, or is better qualified than I am. More than evil or indifference, the fundamental moral problem is, 'Why me?' What connects me to this person in need? What gives me the right or duty to intervene?

The hassidic master Rabbi Solomon of Karlin (1738–92) said something beautiful and unexpected: 'The greatest *yetser hara* [inhibition against doing good] is that *we forget that we are children of the King.*'[7] We are not no one. We are here because God brought us into being in love and gave us work to do, saying in his still, small voice: 'Bring a fragment of my presence into other lives.' What made Moses and Jeremiah and David special was not that they had a high opinion of themselves – the opposite was the case – but that they heard and heeded the cry of human suffering. For them, injustice was not a fact but a call. They believed, not in themselves, but in the cause. They knew that when someone is drowning, you don't stop to ask who is the best swimmer. You jump in. Leadership is response-ability, the ability to respond.

In 1968 a young man met the then Rebbe of Lubavitch, Rabbi Menahem Mendel Schneersohn, at his centre in New York. The visitor was a British university student, halfway through an undergraduate course in philosophy. His studies had raised a number of intellectual questions about religion, and he wanted to find thoughtful people with whom to discuss them. During his summer vacation he made a trip to America, searching out rabbis whose writings he had read. Throughout his travels, a name kept coming up in conversation. You must meet – he was told – the Rebbe of Lubavitch, one of the great leaders of the Jewish world. He went to the Rebbe's centre in Eastern Parkway, Brooklyn, and told one of his followers that he wanted to meet the great man. The hassid laughed. There are thousands of people who want to see the Rebbe, he said. Every moment of his day is full. The student persisted. He gave the hassid the phone number of his aunt in Los Angeles. 'I will be there in three weeks' time', he said. 'If you can arrange a meeting, please let me know.'

Three weeks later a call came through: the Rebbe can see you, the man said, this Thursday evening. The student boarded a Greyhound bus, travelled for three days, and arrived in New York. Finally admitted to the Rebbe's presence, he was surprised. He had assumed that he was about to meet a charismatic leader. Instead, he spoke quietly, unassumingly, as if the most important person in the room were the student. The young man asked his questions; the Rebbe gave replies. Then he did something unexpected. He turned the conversation round. He began asking the student questions: what was he doing to strengthen Jewish life in the university where he was studying? Was he befriending other students and drawing them close?

The young man was taken by surprise. He was not a leader. He had never seen himself as one, or wanted to be one. He had come to the Rebbe to ask philosophical questions, not to be recruited to a religious task. Yet the Rebbe was insistent. He was inviting the British student to get involved, take the initiative, accept responsibility. As he himself put it later: 'I had been told that the Rebbe was a man with thousands of followers. After I met him I understood that the opposite was the case: *A good leader creates followers. A great leader creates leaders.* More than the Rebbe was a leader, he created leadership in others.'

The impact of the meeting was not immediate. The student returned home and continued his studies. But the Rebbe's questions continued to echo in his mind. At the time, his intention was to become an economist, or a lawyer, or an academic. Yet he could not rid himself of the feeling that the Rebbe had said something important, *personal.* Jews were disaffiliating. Fewer and fewer were finding in Judaism intellectual stimulus or ethical inspiration. The Rebbe translated that fact into a challenge, a situation into a call: 'Things are going wrong. Are you willing to be one of those who helps to put them right?' Years later, still troubled by the question, the young man began studying at a religious seminary. Eventually he became a rabbi, then a teacher of rabbis, then a chief rabbi, then the writer of the words you are reading now. This book is part-payment of a debt I incurred to a great Jewish leader many years ago.

You don't have to be special to heed the call. All you need is the ability to listen – to the poor, the ill, the lonely, the homeless, the neglected, the excluded, the people whose voices go unheard; or to the challenge unmet, the problem unsolved, the things that need doing but remain undone. That is what religious listening is. It is what, in the Bible, God does. He hears the silent sadness of Leah, unloved by Jacob, and gives her a child. He hears the cry of the Israelites in Egypt, broken by slavery, and brings them out to freedom. It is no accident that the greatest Jewish command is *Shema Yisrael*, 'Hear, O Israel.' The moral life, the life that transforms lives, begins in the ear, in the act of listening.

The first Rebbe of Lubavitch, Rabbi Schneur Zalman, was once imprisoned by the Russian government. In those days, the late eighteenth century, there was intense opposition within East European Jewry to the Hassidic movement. Its opponents, the *mitnagdim*, were not above resorting to slander in their attempts to suppress the new populist pietism. The Rebbe was accused of treason and thrown in jail awaiting trial. The prison warden, struck by the saintliness of his prisoner, decided to ask him a question that had long troubled him in his reading of the Bible. 'It says in Genesis that when Adam and Eve sinned, God asked them, "Where are you?" God knows all, sees all, so why did he need to ask, "Where are you?"'

'Do you believe', asked the Rebbe, 'that the words of the Bible apply not only to that time but to all time?'

'Of course', the warden replied.

'Then God's question', continued the Rebbe, 'was not meant for Adam and Eve alone, but for all of us, including you and me. Of you, who work here, now, in this prison, God is asking "Where are you?"'

The warden smiled and said, 'Well answered.' But inwardly he trembled. Life is God's question: Where are you?

*   *   *

Shortly after 9/11, I received a letter from a woman in London whose name I did not immediately recognize. The morning of the attack on the World Trade Center, I had been giving a lecture on ways of raising the status of the teaching profession, and she had seen a report about it in the press. This had prompted her to write and remind me of a meeting we had had eight years earlier.

She was then headteacher of a school that was floundering. She had heard some of my broadcasts, felt a kinship with what I had to say, and thought that I might have the answer to her problem. I invited her, together with two of her deputies, to our house. The story she told me was this: morale within the school, among teachers, pupils and parents alike, was at an all-time low. Parents had been withdrawing their children. The student roll had fallen from 1,000 children to 500. Examination results were bad: only 8 per cent of students achieved high grades. It was clear that unless something changed dramatically, the school would have to close.

We talked for an hour or so on general themes: the school as community, how to create an ethos and so on. Suddenly, I realized that we were thinking along entirely the wrong lines. The problem she faced was practical, not philosophical. I said: 'I want you to live one word – *celebrate*.'

She turned to me with a sigh: 'You don't understand – we have *nothing* to celebrate. Everything in the school is going wrong.'

'In that case', I replied, '*find* something to celebrate. If a single student has done better this week than last week, celebrate. If someone has a birthday, celebrate. If it's Tuesday, celebrate.' She seemed unconvinced, but promised to give the idea a try.

Now, eight years later, she was writing to tell me what had happened since then. Examination results at high grades had risen from 8 to 65 per cent. The roll of pupils had risen from 500 to 1,000. Saving the best news to last, she added that she had just been made a Dame of the British Empire – one of the highest honours the Queen can bestow – for her contribution to education. She ended by saying that she just wanted me to know how one word had changed the school and her life.

She was a wonderful teacher, and certainly did not need my advice. She would have discovered the answer on her own anyway. But I was never in any doubt that the strategy would succeed. We grow to fill other people's expectations of us. If they are low, we remain small. If they are high, we walk tall. The idea that each of us has a fixed quantum of intelligence, virtue, academic ability, motivation and drive is absurd. Not all of us can paint like Monet or compose like Ravel. But we each have gifts, capacities, that can lie dormant throughout life, until someone awakens them. We can all achieve heights of which we never thought ourselves capable. All it takes is for us *to meet someone who believes in us more than we believe in ourselves.* Such people change lives. That is what the Lubavitcher Rebbe did for me.

I came to understand this through a remarkable individual: Lena Rustin, who died in December 2004. Lena was a speech therapist specializing in the treatment of stammering. Most people who work in this field concentrate on teaching stammerers various techniques: how to deal with hard consonants, run words into one another, and so on. Lena Rustin, however, came to the conclusion that to cure speech dysfunction she had to address the person, not just the symptom. The people she treated were young children, but she involved the entire family – especially the parents – in the programme. Early on, she taught the parents to recognize the single most counterintuitive fact about dysfunctional behaviour.

She put them through a mental exercise. She told them to visualize the single most precious object they possessed. She then told them to imagine that they came home one day to discover that it had been stolen. She asked them to tell her what they felt. They would describe their reactions – shock, grief, distress, something close to bereavement. 'Now you understand', she said, 'what your child will feel like on losing its stammer.' Without fail, the parents were bewildered. They had assumed, rightly, that their child *wanted* not to stammer. It caused them problems, embarrassed them, interfered with their relationships. All that was true, Lena would say, but by now your children's stammer has become part of their identity, and when they lose it, it will feel like losing a limb. Change, even for the better, is painful. That is why I need your help, she told the parents. You have to create an environment in which your child will have the courage to change.

The word she taught them was *praise*. She told them that every day, they must catch each member of the family doing something right, and say so, specifically, positively and thankfully. She did not go into deep explanations, but it was clear what she was doing. She was creating, within each home, an atmosphere of mutual regard and continuous positive reinforcement. She wanted the parents to shape an environment of self-respect and self-confidence, not just for the stammering child but for every member of the family, so that the whole atmosphere of the home was one in which people felt safe to change and help others to do so.

Listening to her, and watching her in action, I realized that she had discovered a solution not just for stammering but for life itself. My intuition was confirmed in an immediate and surprising way. I had been filming her at work for a television documentary. There had been tensions among the camera crew. Things had gone wrong at various stages during the production, and people were blaming one another. After we left Lena, the crew – whether consciously or unintentionally, I never discovered which – started praising one another. Immediately, the atmosphere was transformed. Those days were among the most enjoyable I have ever spent.

The Mishnah tractate *Avot*, known as 'The Ethics of the Fathers', contains a passage that long puzzled me:

Rabbi Johanan ben Zakkai had five pre-eminent disciples: Rabbi Eliezer ben Hyrcanus, Rabbi Joshua ben Chananya, Rabbi Jose the priest, Rabbi Shimon ben Netanel, and Rabbi Elazar ben Arakh. He used to recount their praise: Eliezer ben Hyrcanus – a cemented cistern which loses not a drop. Joshua ben Chananya – happy is she who bore him. Jose the priest – a most pious man. Shimon ben Netanel – a man who fears sin. Elazar ben Arakh – a spring flowing with ever-increasing vigour.[8]

What is odd about the passage is that it occurs in a text about ethics. Why do we need to know who Rabbi Johanan ben Zakkai's students were? That belongs to history, not ethics. Understanding Lena Rustin's methods, however, I had the answer. Johanan ben Zakkai knew how to praise. That is how he was able to raise such extraordinary disciples. His tributes were not generic. In each case, he identified the student's specific gifts. Rabbi Eliezer ben Hyrcanus was a man of memory, Rabbi Elazar ben Arakh was creative, and so on. By identifying what each could become, he helped them achieve it. The ethical message was clear. Praise is an essential part of moral education. The best teachers are not necessarily those with a gift for instruction. They are people who value their students, identify their potential, and get them to believe in themselves.

Sometimes this has extraordinary results. Ruth Lehman is the creator of a school for children with mental handicap called *Kisharon*. The word is Hebrew and means ability, capacity, skill. She deliberately chose the name to create a paradigm-shift in our understanding of children with special needs. Most people see what they lack. She wanted everyone associated with the school to see what they have and what, with the right training and love, they are capable of giving. Her educational philosophy flows directly from her religious faith: she believes that all of us are created for a purpose, and if we lack some abilities, we still have others. The children blossom under her care.

Andrew Mawson is a Christian minister who has transformed an old and declining church in the East End of London into one of the most active community complexes in Britain: the Bromley-by-Bow Centre. It now runs 125 activities each week on a three-acre site in the middle of one of the poorest housing estates in London. It includes a nursery and family projects, a health centre, a range of arts and educational projects, seven social businesses and a restaurant. Its facilities are used by people of many different faiths and it has revitalized the entire neighbourhood. People are drawn to Andrew for the same reason as children are attracted to Ruth Lehman. He told me that wherever social workers see a problem, he sees an opportunity.

He met Sheila (not her real name) in the course of his work ('What's your method of reaching people?' I asked him. 'Gossip', he replied). He was working on one of his first projects, building a nursery. It lacked a kitchen. 'Does anyone have any ideas?' he asked. Sheila said, 'I always dreamed of running my own café.' She was at that time an unemployed single mother. Andrew said, 'Invite my wife and me over for a meal and let's taste your cooking.' She did. The meal was good. He said, 'I will give you a room in the church, facing the street. We'll get some of the locals to do the carpentry. I'll raise the money for a cooker, and let's take it from there.' He did. It went well. They expanded it, and then made it larger still until it became the focal point of the community, the place where people met. The new and magnificent restaurant was opened by Prince Charles. While this was happening, Sheila was developing new interests. One day she said, 'I've always wanted to get a university degree.' She had left school without qualifications. Andrew persuaded a university to admit her. She went on to achieve first-class honours in social psychology. She had grown in a way she could have had no hope of doing until Andrew came along.

Meanwhile, Andrew recognized what was happening to Sheila. The practical experience of creating the restaurant had transformed her. He began to think that if it worked for her, it could work for other people in similar situations. That is how he came to establish what he calls a *communiversity* – a community-based university where people who left school early learn by doing. It is linked to several London colleges and now has 400 students. Peter (not his real name) is a young man who joined the programme. He too had no qualifications, but when Andrew asked him what he dreamed of doing, he said, 'I've always wanted to run a radio station.' Andrew persuaded Coca-Cola to back the project, which is how 3BC (Bromley-by-Bow Centre) came into being. It was a great success, and out of it came a wide range of new relationships with young people in the area. Andrew's method is simple: he discovers people's passions, and backs them by finding them resources, creating teams and most of all by getting them to believe that they can do what they dream of doing. He has changed hundreds of lives. I no longer find it difficult to believe in the existence of angels. Ruth Lehman and Andrew Mawson are two.

*　　　　　*　　　　　*

What applies to people is true of situations. We never know in advance when the opportunity will arise to do the transformative deed, and what it might involve. Amos Oz is one of Israel's greatest novelists, and the most articulate person I have ever met. He is a secular Jew, profoundly so, yet had he lived in an earlier age, I can imagine him as one of Israel's prophets. I came to know him because of my long-standing concern about the secular–religious divide in Israeli society. We became friends and have conducted a public dialogue, as well as several private ones, to show that mutual respect is possible across that particular border.

In his autobiography, *A Tale of Love and Darkness*, he tells the story of his father, a man who could read sixteen languages and speak eleven, a brilliant scholar who, because there was only one university in Israel at the time, never rose above the job of assistant librarian. A disappointed man, he dedicated his spare time to writing a book, *The Novella in Hebrew Literature*, into which he poured all his frustrated energies. Eventually it was complete, and he would rush every day to the local post office, anxious to receive the first copies. They came. He invited his closest friends – including the novelist Israel Zarchi who lived in the same apartment block – to celebrate. Oz continues:

> Father's happiness lasted for three or four days, and then his face fell. Just as he had rushed to the post office every day before the package arrived, so he now rushed every day to Achiasaf's bookshop in King George V Avenue, where three copies of *The Novella* were displayed for sale. The next day the same three copies were there, not one of them had been purchased. And the same next day, and the day after that.
>
> 'You', Father said with a sad smile to his friend Israel Zarchi, 'write a new novel every six months, and instantly all the pretty girls snatch you off the shelves and take you straight to bed with them, while we scholars, we wear ourselves out for years on end checking every detail, verifying every quotation, spending a week on a single footnote, and who bothers to read us? If we're lucky two or three fellow-prisoners in our own discipline read our books before they tear us to shreds. Sometimes not even that. We are simply ignored.'

The days passed. No copies were sold. Oz's father no longer spoke about his disappointment, but it was there 'like a smell':

> And then suddenly, a couple of days later, on Friday evening, he came home beaming happily . . . 'They're sold! They've all been sold! All in one day! Not one copy sold! Not two copies sold! All three sold! The whole lot! My book is sold out – Shakhna Achiasaf is going to order some more copies from Chachik in Tel Aviv! He's ordered them already! This morning! By telephone! Not three copies, another five! And he thinks that is not going to be the end of the story!'

His father and mother went out to celebrate, leaving young Amos in the care of Zarchi, the novelist downstairs:

> Mr Zarchi sat me down on the sofa and talked to me for a bit, I don't remember what about, but I shall never forget how I suddenly noticed on the little coffee table by the sofa no fewer than four identical copies of *The Novella in Hebrew Literature*, one on top of the other, like in a shop, one copy that I knew Father had given to Mr

Zarchi with an inscription, and three more that I just couldn't understand, and it was on the tip of my tongue to ask Mr Zarchi, but at the last moment I remembered the three copies that had just been bought today, at long last, in Achiasaf's bookshop, and I felt a rush of gratitude inside me that almost brought tears to my eyes. Mr Zarchi saw that I had noticed them and he did not smile, but shot me a side-long glance through half-closed eyes, as though he were silently accepting me into his band of conspirators, and without saying a word he leant over, picked up three of the four copies on the coffee table, and secreted them in a drawer of his desk. I too held my peace, and said nothing either to him or to my parents. I did not tell a soul until after Zarchi died in his prime and after my father's death . . .

Oz adds:

I count two or three writers among my best friends, friends who have been close to me and dear to me for decades, yet I am not certain that I could do for one of them what Israel Zarchi did for my father. Who can say if such a generous ruse would have even occurred to me. After all, he, like everyone else in those days, lived a hand-to-mouth existence, and the three copies of *The Novella in Hebrew Literature* must have cost him at least the price of some much-needed clothes.[9]

I am grateful to Amos for permission to quote the story at length because it so beautifully illustrates a concept that ought to exist in ethics but doesn't: *original virtue.* Sin is rarely original, but a good deed sometimes is. The episode needs no further comment, but I add one. I have never done an act as thoughtful as Mr Zarchi, but I have found one idea deeply helpful: divine providence. Just as every life has a task, so every day brings an opportunity. If we are where we are because God wanted us to be, then there must be, in every situation, something he wants us to do, some act of redemption he wants us to perform. I found the best way of knowing what it is, is to turn the situation upside down. I used to hope that people would praise my work; then I realized that what I was here to do was to praise the work of others. There were times when, in crisis, I would await the reassuring word from a friend, until I suddenly saw that I should be the one giving reassurance. The discovery changed my life. That was when I knew that we experience pain to sensitize us to the pain of others. Turning our emotions outward, we can use them as the key to free someone else from the locked room of suffering or disappointment or grief.

*　　　　　　*　　　　　　*

Immanuel Kant famously defined morality as the universal imperative: 'Act only on a maxim through which you can at the same time will that it should become a universal law.'[10] Perhaps that is what morality is to the mindset of reason. There surely are universal imperatives. We all know them. Don't murder. Don't injure the innocent. Don't rob or steal. Don't lie. Those are the rules we learned as children, and if we failed to learn them, others quickly taught us. The interesting part of the moral life, the grown-up part, comes not in universals but particulars.[11] It speaks to me, here, now: this person, in this situation, at this time. It knows my name. It calls to me, not to the person next to me. It says: there is an act only you can do, a situation only you can address, a moment that, if not seized, may never come again. God commands in generalities but calls in particulars. He knows our gifts and he knows the needs of the world. That is why we are here. There is an act only we can do, and only at this time, and that is our task. The sum of these tasks is the meaning of our life, the purpose of our existence, the story we are called upon to write. God's call is almost inaudible. I translate the biblical phrase, 'a still, small voice' (1 Kings 19:12) as 'the voice we can only hear if we are listening'. But it is there, and if, from time to time throughout our lives, we create a silence in the soul, we will hear it.

There is no life without a task; no person without a talent; no place without a fragment of God's light waiting to be discovered and redeemed; no situation without its possibility of sanctification; no moment without its call. It may take a lifetime to learn how to find these things, but once we learn, we realize in retrospect that all it ever took was the ability to listen. When God calls, he does not do so by way of universal imperatives. Instead, he whispers our name – and the greatest reply, the reply of Abraham, is simply *hineni*: 'Here I am', ready to heed your call, to mend a fragment of your all-too-broken world.

NOTES

1. Martin Buber, *Tales of the Hasidim: early masters* (New York: Schocken, 1947), p. 251.
2. Rashbam, *Commentary* to Gen. 32:23.
3. 1 Sam. 18:18; 2 Sam. 7:18.
4. Lionel Trilling, *Sincerity and Authenticity* (Cambridge, MA: Harvard University Press, 1972), p. 85.
5. James Q. Wilson, *The Moral Sense* (New York: Free Press, 1993), p. 38.
6. Bibb Latané and John M. Darley, 'Group inhibition of bystander intervention', *Journal of Personality and Social Psychology* (1968) 10:215–21; *The Unresponsive Bystander: why doesn't he help?* (New York: Appleton-Century-Crofts, 1970).

7. See Judah Goldin, 'Introduction', to S. Y. Agnon, *Days of Awe* (New York: Schocken, 1965), p. xxvii.
8. Mishnah, *Avot* 2:8.
9. Amos Oz, *A Tale of Love and Darkness* (London: Chatto & Windus, 2004), pp. 129–31.
10. H. J. Paton, *The Moral Law: Kant's Groundwork of the Metaphysic of Morals* (London: Hutchinson, 1948), p. 84.
11. Compare Michael Walzer's sharp observation: 'Philosophical discovery is likely to fall short of the radical newness and sharp specificity of divine revelation. Accounts of natural law or natural rights rarely ring true as descriptions of a new moral world. Consider Nagel's discovery of an objective moral principle: that we should not be indifferent to the suffering of other people. I acknowledge the principle but miss the excitement of revelation. I knew that already.' Michael Walzer, *Interpretation and Social Criticism* (Cambridge, MA: Harvard University Press, 1987), p. 6.

Chapter 20

On Dreams and Responsibilities

Each time a man stands up for an ideal, or acts to improve the lot of others, or strikes out against injustice, he sends forth a tiny ripple of hope, and crossing each other from a million different centres of energy and daring, those ripples build a current that can sweep down the mightiest walls of oppression and resistance.

(Robert Kennedy)[1]

The twenty-first century confronts humanity with challenges of a scale and scope that seem to defy solution. There are the environmental problems: global warming, the erosion of the biosphere, the destruction of rain forests and the greatest extinction of species since civilization began. There is the growing inequality between rich and poor: in some parts of the world, affluence beyond the dreams of previous generations; in others, nations and entire regions wracked by poverty, illness, drought, homelessness, illiteracy and despair. Each day, 30,000 children die of preventable diseases. One hundred and five million of the world's children do not go to school. Forty million suffer from HIV/AIDS. Three hundred million farmers are unable to trade fairly because of trade barriers. Half the world lives in poverty. Americans spend more on cosmetics, and Europeans on ice-cream, than it would cost to provide schooling and sanitation for the two billion people who currently go without both.[2]

Then come the political problems: ethnic conflict, civil wars, successive waves of asylum-seekers, the proliferation of violence and international disorder. There is the danger posed by failed, failing and rogue states, and the sheer difficulty – after wars such as those in Afghanistan and Iraq – of building stable regimes, with the rule of law and respect for human rights, to take the place of failed dictatorships or tyrannies. Meanwhile terror, inspired by groups such as Al Qaeda, has become a global threat, undermining the security of every life in one country after another, encouraging the spread of religious extremism and barbaric acts of violence against the innocent. Worst of all is the fear that these factors may come together in the form of weapons of mass destruction – chemical, biological or nuclear – reaching the hands of groups who have no compunction against mass murder in the name of God and the apocalypse. The Chinese curse – 'May you live in interesting times' – seems likely to ring true for the foreseeable future.

These problems are so vast, so interconnected and global, that they lie beyond the reach of nation states, even superpowers like the United States and the European Union. How then can you and I make a difference? Taken individually, we are no more than a grain of sand on the sea shore, a wave in the ocean, dust on the surface of infinity. Because we are confronted with these problems daily on our television screens, we are faced with constant cognitive dissonance. We want to help, but there is all too little any of us can do. Under such pressures, the mind turns inward, seeking satisfaction within the self, or fulfilment within the narrow circle of family or friends, or salvation within the closed community.

That inward turn is evident in almost all Western societies today. It takes radically different forms – from consumerism, to 'spirituality' and the exploration of the self, to aggressively anti-modern forms of religious practice and belief. These phenomena could not be less alike yet they have one thing in common: they are an attempt to create safe space, a shelter from the world outside, a haven in a heartless world. In Christopher Lasch's poignant phrase, we seek 'psychic survival in troubled times'.[3]

I have argued in this book for the opposite response. Now, of all times, we should be holding out the hand of friendship to strangers, help to those in need. Power entails responsibility, and the immense power generated by modern technology, medicine, instantaneous worldwide communication and the global economy will call for responsibility on the same scale. We can make a difference, and *only* we can make a difference. Without the unforced contributions of people of good will, politicians are powerless and international resolutions so many well-meaning words spent upon the air.

At the heart of this book has been a metaphor, coined in a hilltop village in north Israel in the sixteenth century by a Jewish mystic, in the aftermath of one of the great human tragedies of the Middle Ages, the Spanish Expulsion. Rabbi Isaac Luria framed a vision of hope in the midst of catastrophe. The divine light which initially flooded creation proved too strong. There was a 'breaking of the vessels', as a result of which fragments of God's light lay hidden under the rubble and wreckage of disaster. It is our task, he said, to 'heal' or 'mend' the world by searching for those fragments and rescuing them, one by one. It was a lovely image, because it refused to accept the fractures of the world as incurable, but neither did it suppose that repair would be instantaneous, easy or dramatic.

Like the people I have written about, and like Loren Eiseley's story of the starfish, Lurianic kabbalah proposed a redemption of small steps. God does not ask us to save the world, entire and alone. On the contrary: the attempt to 'force the end' usually results in violence and disaster. Instead, God asks us to do what we can, when we can. We mend the world one life at a time, one act at a time, one day at a time. A single life, said the rabbis, is like a universe.[4] Change a life, and you begin to change the world. Every generous deed, each healing word, every embracing gesture brings redemption nearer. Each is a letter we write in the book of life.

We can make a difference. It must have seemed absurd at the time to think that the leader of a group of slaves, escaping to freedom across a barren wilderness more than 3,000 years ago, could deliver a message that would eventually transform the moral landscape of the West. In a later age, a handful of prophets kept the Jewish spirit alive at times of catastrophe and near-despair. An even smaller handful of survivors rebuilt Jewish life after the Holocaust, having come eyeball to eyeball with the angel of death. There is not one movement, not one shift in the world's conscience, that did not begin with a few individuals daring to think the not-yet-thought, speak the courageous word, do the different deed. The word 'impossible' did not exist in their vocabulary. It should not exist in ours.

Long ago, in the desert, Moses assembled the people and told them they were about to construct a sanctuary that would become the visible home of the divine presence in their midst. Then he made a strange remark:

> When you take a census of the Israelites to determine their numbers, each one shall be counted by giving an atonement offering for his life. In this manner, they will not be stricken when they are counted. Everyone included in the census must give a half shekel . . . (Ex. 30:12–13)

Evidently, it was dangerous to count the Israelites. Why? Normally, when nations take a census, they do so because they believe that there is strength in numbers. The Jewish people have never found strength in numbers. Moses told them that they were 'among the smallest of all the nations' (Deut. 7:7). They still are. The American writer Milton Himmelfarb once remarked that the entire population of world Jewry is smaller than the statistical error in the Chinese census. How then was their strength to be measured? The biblical answer is surpassingly beautiful: ask people to give, then count their contributions. A people can be numerically small, yet its contributions may be vast.

Moses added one small detail: each, he said, should give *half* a shekel. By this, he was saying: never think that you need to do it all. Each of us must be conscious that we can't complete the task: we need someone else to make the shekel whole. But neither is our contribution insignificant. We contribute our half, confident that others will join us, perhaps inspired by what we do. We can change the world, but we need partners, and the best way of finding them is to lead by personal example. Virtue is contagious. One good deed begets another. What is important is that we begin. I remember how, as a new student, I paid my first visit to the university library. Two dons had arrived at the entrance at the same time. One said to the other, 'After you.' The other replied, 'No, please, after you.' It was wonderfully polite, and could have gone on for ever. When it comes to suffering and injustice, however, we need not the 'After you' school of leadership, but 'After me'.

*　　　　*　　　　*

All too often in recent years, the face religion has presented to the world has been unlovely: either strident and aggressive, or weak and vague. Yeats' lines come to mind:

> The best lack all conviction, while the worst
> Are full of passionate intensity.[5]

There is no need for this. Neither strategy offers a road map to redemption. Neither is adequate to heaven's call in our day. Against the fundamentalisms of hate, we must create a counter-fundamentalism of love – knowing, without hesitation or equivocation, that this is what God wants us to do: to heal his fractured world.

This has been a religious book, a Jewish book, and I make no apologies for either fact; but the truth is that each of us has a contribution to make, whether we are religious or secular, Jewish, Christian or Muslim, whether we represent the great non-Western traditions or more modern forms of spirituality. All I have aspired to do in this book is to articulate one voice in the conversation, knowing that no human voice can express the totality of wisdom, and there is none from which we cannot learn.

If the religious voice has one thing to say above all others it is that each of us counts. I am notoriously bad at names. I see familiar people and forget what they are called. So one line in the book of Psalms always inspires in me a certain awe. It says of God that 'he counts the number of the stars and calls them each by name' (Ps. 147:4). To call someone or something by a name is to endow it with significance for what it uniquely is. God *knows who we are*. The god of the Greek philosophers knew things in general, but not in particular: classes but not individuals, types but not persons. The dazzling assertion at the heart of the Hebrew Bible is that God 'turns his face toward us' (Num. 6:26), knowing, loving and

267

challenging each of us in our singularity. None of us is replaceable, sub-stitutable, dispensable. There are deeds we can do that can be done by no one else. That vision is not unique to Judaism – and even if it were, I hope it can be shared by everyone, for no more powerful assertion has ever been made of the dignity of the individual and the potential majesty of a human life. There are some six billion people alive on earth as I write, but no power on earth can rob each one of us of our categorical value in the eyes of God.

In the Bible, when God revealed himself to Abraham, Jacob and Moses, he began simply by calling them by name. Their response – at once the most primal and profound – was simply to say *hineni*, 'Here I am.' Life is God's question. We are his answer. It may be a good answer or a bad one, but it is the only answer there is. God does not need to know, or be assured by us, that he is God. He needs to know that we hear his call, that we are ready to rise to his challenge and that we are willing to take into our own hands the responsibility with which he has entrusted us, empowered and given strength by that very trust itself.

This is a religious vision but you do not have to be religious to share it. There is a hassidic story about a disciple who once asked his teacher: 'Rabbi, do you believe that God created everything for a purpose?' 'I do', the rabbi replied. 'In that case, rabbi, why did God create atheists?' The rabbi paused and smiled. 'God created atheists to remind us never to accept the existence of evil. Sometimes we who have faith have too much faith. We accept the evils of this world as the will of God. They are not the will of God, which is why God created atheists to cure us of this illusion.'

The religion in which I believe is a counterintuitive, morally revolu-tionary force. In the last chapter of his eloquent book, *The Rebel*, Albert Camus wrote:

Rebellion indefatigably confronts evil, from which it can only derive a new impetus. Man can master, in himself, everything that should be mastered. He should rectify in creation everything that can be rectified. And after he has done so, children will still die unjustly even in a perfect society. Even by his greatest effort, man can only propose to diminish, arithmetically, the sufferings of the world. But the injustice and the suffering of the world will remain and, no matter how limited they are, they will not cease to be an outrage . . . Confronted with this evil, confronted with death, man from the very depths of his soul cries out for justice.[6]

Those words might almost be a summary of this book, with one differ-ence. What Camus saw as a revolt *against* God in the name of humanity, Judaism sees as a rebellion against the worst instincts of humanity in the name of God himself. His is the voice that never ceases to ask why the world-that-is is not yet the world-that-ought-to-be. *Faith is the question.* Our deeds are the only adequate answer.

And what of those who are not religious, who question whether there is justice and a Judge? Blaise Pascal (1623–62), one of the most brilliant minds of the seventeenth century, had already invented probability theory before turning, at the age of 30, to religious pursuits. He is best known for the so-called 'Pascal's Wager' in which he brought together his two loves, the mathematical calculation of risk and the life of faith.[7] Either God exists, he argued, or he does not. If we live irreligiously and then discover, when we die, that we were wrong, we face endless torment in hell. If we live religiously, then if God exists we will face an eternity of bliss when we die, and if he does not, we will merely cease to be. The low-risk strategy is to live religiously, for at least this spares us from the worst possible outcome.

I admire Pascal. His *Pensées* are one of the classics of religious litera-ture, and of course his Wager is more positive and subtle than I have made it seem. But if I were to attempt my own wager, I would make it far more modest. I would say to the unbeliever: either God exists or he does not. If he does, we will be rewarded for the good we do. If he does not, we will still be rewarded, for there is no greater reward than the knowledge that you have healed some of the pain of this deeply fissured world, miti-gated some of its injustice, cured even a fraction of its ills.

And that is the point. Happiness can never be obtained by being pursued. Like the coming of the Messiah in Jewish tradition, it is one of those things that only comes when you are not thinking about it. It comes from a life well lived, in pursuit of the good for its own sake. There is something deep within us that leads us to feel implicated in the fate of others. Is this sympathy, empathy, benevolence, compassion, conscience, duty, enlightened self-interest, the impartial spectator, what sociobiologists call reciprocal altruism or what I call the covenant of human solidarity? I don't know, but it is close to the heart of what we are, of what it is to be human. Neither pleasure nor desire, success nor fame, wealth nor power, can remotely rival it as a source of satisfaction or self-respect.

Many people have said it. 'Everyone can be great', said Martin Luther King, 'because everyone can serve.' 'Only a life lived for others is a life worthwhile', said Albert Einstein. 'He who wishes to secure the good of others has already secured his own', said Confucius. And Edmund Burke: 'Nobody made a greater mistake than he who did nothing because he could do only a little.' And perhaps most beautifully, Isaiah, in words that Jews have read for almost 2,000 years on the 'Sabbath of Consolation' after the day we mourn the destruction of the Temple in Jerusalem:

Even youths grow tired and weary,
and young men stumble and fall;
but those who hope in the Lord
will renew their strength.
They will soar on wings like eagles;
they will run and not grow weary,
they will walk and not be faint. (Is. 40:30–1)

The paradox of altruism is that the hope we give others returns to us undiminished and enlarged. Perhaps faith is only created in the doing, happiness in the giving and meaning in the courage to take risks for the sake of an ideal. All I know is that the greatest achievement in life is to have been, for one other person, even for one moment, an agent of hope.

*   *   *

The greatest danger facing Western societies today is the sense of powerlessness, of a world running out of control, of problems too great to solve and hatreds too deep to cure. This is what Robert Kennedy alluded to just before he uttered the words that stand at the head of this chapter. He spoke about 'the danger of futility; the belief there is nothing one man or one woman can do against the enormous array of the world's ills'.[8] The politics of despair is the worst kind there is. The sense of powerlessness is all too easily manipulated by those hungry for power. Fear can be quickly turned into anger, rage, violence, terror, xenophobia and paranoia in one direction, or capitulation and cowardice, defeatism and appeasement in the other. When Franklin D. Roosevelt said, 'The only thing we have to fear is fear itself', he was uttering a truth that has not yet lost its salience in the twenty-first century.

The only antidote to fear is responsibility: the refusal to believe that there is nothing we can do, the decision never to take refuge in blaming others, making them the scapegoats for our frustrations and fears. It is easy to complain: to say it is someone else's fault. Courage is born the moment we decide not to complain but instead to make a personal protest against the evils of the world by doing good, however slight. An ethic of responsibility yields individuals of astonishing resilience – people able to survive any setback and face any future without fear. For the last fourteen years I have carried with me, in my diary, the words of an earlier Roosevelt (Theodore), which have given me strength in dark days:

It is not the critic who counts,
Not the man who points out how the strong man stumbles,
Or where the doer of deeds could actually have done them better.
The credit belongs to the man who is actually in the arena,

Whose face is marred by dust and sweat and blood,
Who strives valiantly,
Who errs and comes short again and again –
Because there is no effort without error and shortcomings –
But who does actually strive to do the deed,
Who knows great enthusiasm, great devotion,
Who spends himself in a worthy cause,
Who at the best knows in the end the triumph of high achievement
And who, at the worst, if he fails, at least fails while daring greatly –
So that his place shall never be with those cold and timid souls
Who know neither victory nor defeat.[9]

To know that God empowers us to take risks, forgives our failings, lifts us when we fall and believes in us more than we believe in ourselves – that is one way, the best I know, to write, in the record of our days, a story worth leaving as our legacy to those who come after us, of whose future we are the guardians.

Every good act, every healing gesture, lights a candle of hope in a dark world. What would humanity be after the Holocaust were it not for the memory of those courageous few who saved lives, hid children, rescued those they could? There were times when the gift of a crust of bread – even a smile – gave a prisoner the will to live. A single message of support can tell threatened populations that they are not alone. One act of hospitality can redeem a lonely life on the brink of despair. A word of praise can give strength to someone losing the will to carry on. We never know, at the time, the ripple of consequences set in motion by the slightest act of kindness.

'A little light', said the Jewish mystics, 'drives away much darkness.' And when light is joined to light, mine to yours and yours to others, the dance of flames, each so small, yet together so intricately beautiful, begins to show that hope is not an illusion. Evil, injustice, oppression, cruelty do not have the final word. Perhaps it is true that 'from the crooked timber of humanity no straight thing was ever made'. But do we need to be straight to point upward? Do we need to be perfect to be good? All I can say is what I feel: that the people I have met who have lit candles in other people's lives have given me the strength to carry on. I confess: I have never had a crisis of faith in God, but there were times when I came close to losing faith in humanity. It was the sheer decency – what Yiddish calls *menschlichkeit* – of ordinary people who restored it. Every generous or gentle or courageous deed begets others, inspires others, initiates a transformation. A single act, performed for its own sake out of love, gives us – wrote Maimonides – a share in the world to come.[10]

*　　　　　*　　　　　*

I have spent much of my life thinking about life, observing people, reading books, searching for teachers and exemplars, trying to distinguish between what ultimately matters and what merely seems to matter at the time. I make no claims to wisdom, but this I have learned:

- that each of us is here for a purpose;
- that discerning that purpose takes time and honesty, knowledge of ourselves and knowledge of the world, but it is there to be discovered. Each of us has a unique constellation of gifts, an unreplicated radius of influence, and within that radius, be it as small as a family or as large as a state, we can be a transformative presence;
- that where *what we want to do* meets *what needs to be done*, that is where God wants us to be;
- that even the smallest good deed can change someone's life;
- that it is not the honours we receive that matter, but the honour we give;
- that what counts is not how much wealth we make but how much of what we have, we share;
- that those who spend at least part of their lives in service of others are the most fulfilled and happiest people I know;
- that there is no greater gift we can give our children than to let them see us sacrifice something for the sake of an ideal;
- that religions reach their highest levels when they stop worrying about other people's souls and care, instead, for the needs of their bodies;
- that no religion that persecutes others is worthy of respect, nor one that condemns others, entitled to admiration;
- that we honour the world God created and called good by searching for and praising the good in others and the world;
- that nothing is gained by less-than-ethical conduct. We may gain in the short term but we will lose in the long, and it is the long term that counts;
- that moral health is no less important to the quality of a life than physical health;
- that a word of praise can give meaning to someone's life;
- that, putting others down, we diminish ourselves; lifting others, we lift ourselves;
- that the world is a book in which our life is a chapter, and the question is whether others, reading it, will be inspired;
- that each day is a question asked by God to us;
- that each situation in which we find ourselves did not happen by accident: we are here, now, in this place, among these people, in these circumstances, so that we can do the act or say the word that will heal one of the fractures of the world;

- that few are the days when we cannot make some difference to the lives of others;
- that virtue does not have to be conspicuous to win respect;
- that the best do good without thought of reward, understanding that to help others is a privilege even more than it is an opportunity;
- that cynicism diminishes those who practise it;
- that self-interest is simply uninteresting;
- that it is not the most wealthy or powerful or successful or self-important who make the greatest difference or engender the greatest love;
- that pain and loneliness are forms of energy that can be transformed if we turn them outward, using them to recognize and redeem someone else's pain or loneliness;
- that the people who are most missed are those who brought hope into our lives;
- that the ability to give to others is itself a gift;
- that we can make a difference, and it is *only* by making a difference that we redeem a life, lifting it from mere existence and endowing it with glory;
- that those who give to others are the closest we come to meeting the divine presence in this short life on earth;
- that the best way of *receiving* a blessing is to *be* a blessing;
- and that if we listen carefully enough – and listening is an art that requires long training and much humility – we will hear the voice of God in the human heart telling us that there is work to do and that he needs us.

'Good represents the reality of which God is the dream', wrote Iris Murdoch.[11] 'In dreams begin responsibilities', wrote W. B. Yeats.[12] Judaism is the guardian of an ancient but still compelling dream. To heal where others harm, mend where others destroy, to redeem evil by turning its negative energies to good: these are the mark of the ethics of responsibility, born in the radical faith that God calls on us to exercise our freedom by becoming his partners in the work of creation. That seems to me a life-affirming vision: the courage to take the risk of responsibility, becoming co-authors with God of the world that ought to be.

NOTES

1. Robert Kennedy, 'A Tiny Ripple of Hope', speech to the National Union of South African Students' Day of Affirmation, Cape Town, 7 June 1966, in Brian MacArthur (ed.), *The Penguin Book of Twentieth-Century Speeches* (London: Penguin, 1993), pp. 366–73.

2. See Jonathan Sacks, *The Dignity of Difference* (London: Continuum, 2002), and the literature cited there.
3. Christopher Lasch, *The Minimal Self: psychic survival in troubled times* (New York: W. W. Norton, 1985).
4. *Mishneh, Sanhedrin* 4:5.
5. W. B. Yeats, 'The Second Coming', in Norman Jeffares (ed.), *W. B. Yeats: selected poetry* (London: Macmillan, 1984).
6. Albert Camus, *The Rebel* (Harmondsworth: Penguin, 1962), p. 267.
7. Blaise Pascal, *Pensées*, trans. A. J. Krailsheimer (Harmondsworth: Penguin, 1966), pp. 149–55.
8. Robert Kennedy, 'A Tiny Ripple of Hope', in *The Penguin Book of Twentieth-Century Speeches*, p. 371.
9. Theodore Roosevelt, 'Speech at the Sorbonne, Paris, 23 April 1910', in *The Works of Theodore Roosevelt, Memorial Edition* (New York: Charles Scribners, 1923–26), vol. 15, p. 354.
10. Maimonides, *Commentary to the Mishnah, Makkot* 3:17.
11. Iris Murdoch, *Metaphysics as a Guide to Morals* (London: Chatto & Windus, 1992), p. 496.
12. W. B. Yeats, epigraph to *Responsibilities and Other Poems* (London: Macmillan, 1916). The phrase was popularized by Delmore Schwartz, who took it as the title of his first book: *In Dreams Begin Responsibilities* (Norfolk, CT: New Directions, 1938).

Index